IMAGES
of America

TAMPA'S HISTORIC CEMETERIES

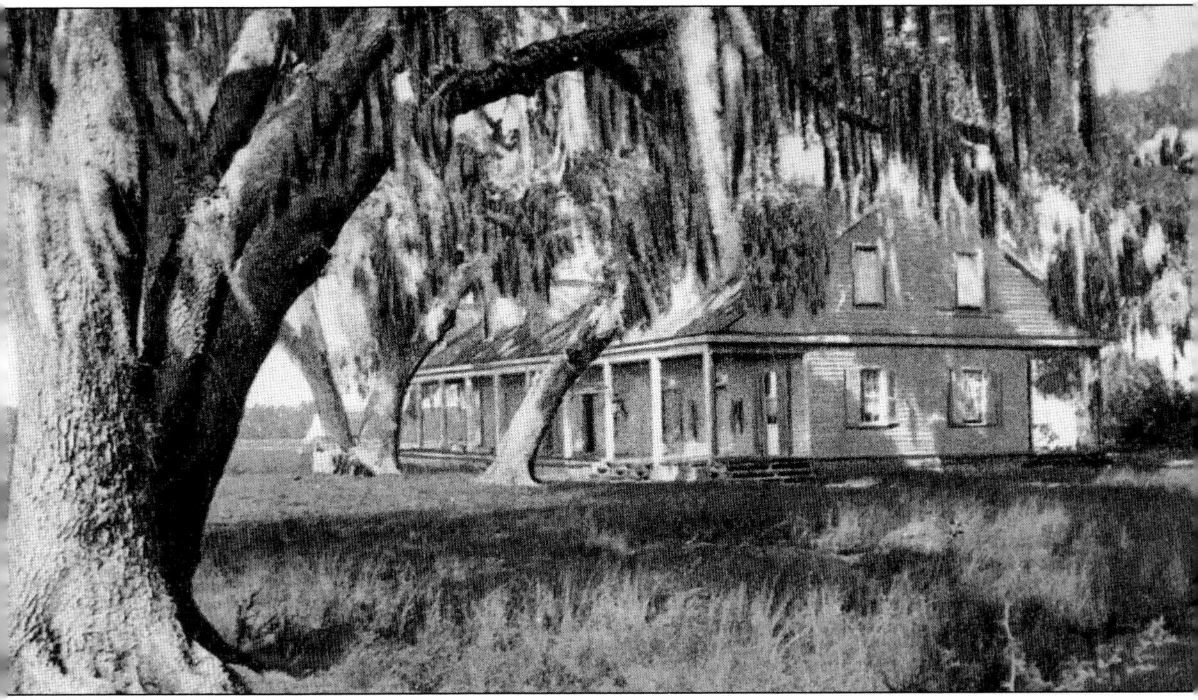

This is an early postcard of the Robert J. Hackley family home and plantation surrounded by massive oak trees draped in Spanish moss. Hackley was an Englishman whose family had purchased large amounts of land from Spain before 1819. The site would be chosen for the location of a 16-square-mile US garrison/cantonment military post. The home and land would become the center of activity for Fort Brooke. When soldiers arrived on January 10, 1824, to establish the military outpost, they found that Hackley had cleared the land and built a fine home and wharf.

ON THE COVER: Oaklawn Cemetery, at the corner of Harrison, Morgan, and Jefferson Streets, opened in 1850 north of Fort Brooke. The cemetery was originally called Old City of Tampa Burying Grounds.

IMAGES
of America

TAMPA'S HISTORIC CEMETERIES

Shelby Jean Roberson Bender and Elizabeth Laramie Dunham

ARCADIA
PUBLISHING

ISBN 978-0-7385-9853-6

Published by Arcadia Publishing
Charleston, South Carolina

Printed in the United States of America

Library of Congress Control Number: 2012946548

For all general information, please contact Arcadia Publishing:
Telephone 843-853-2070
Fax 843-853-0044
E-mail sales@arcadiapublishing.com
For customer service and orders:
Toll-Free 1-888-313-2665

Visit us on the Internet at www.arcadiapublishing.com

Rest in Peace...

Contents

Acknowledgments

We would like to thank the following individuals for their ongoing support and efforts to preserve our local history and for their assistance during our research: Andy Bender, Travis Puterbaugh, Tampa Bay History Center, Andrew Huse, University of South Florida Special Collections Library, Grant Rimbey, Temple Terrace Preservation Society, Susan Carter, Henry B. Plant Museum, Maureen Patrick, Tampa Historical Society, and Bob Baggett Photography. Additionally, we thank the many historians who knew the importance of researching, writing, and sharing their results of our state and local history.

Photo Credits

All photographs were the result of our own efforts, unless otherwise noted:

(HBPMA)	Henry B. Plant Museum Archives, Tampa
(JMMP)	John McEwen and Maureen Patrick
(TBHC)	Hillsborough County Collection, Tampa Bay History Center
(THCPL)	Tampa–Hillsborough County Public Library System
(THS)	Tampa Historical Society
(USFSPC)	University of South Florida Special and Digital Collections

INTRODUCTION

Tampa has a very rich and varied history, beginning over 10,000 years ago. The area was briefly explored in the early 16th century, but no permanent American or European settlements occurred until after the United States acquired Florida from Spain in 1819. *Tampa's Historic Cemeteries* will focus on some of the oldest cemeteries in the city of Tampa, each of which has a history to tell through the people who are buried within its boundaries.

Archaeological evidence indicates that the shores of Tampa Bay have been inhabited for thousands of years. The current location of Tampa was once populated by various indigenous cultures, including the Tocobaga. When the Spanish explorers arrived in the early 16th century, there were no permanent American or European settlements in the area. In 1824, the US Army established a frontier outpost (named Fort Brooke, after Col. George Mercer Brooke) at the site of today's Tampa Convention Center. This story is set in motion with Oaklawn Cemetery, Tampa's first public burial ground, named as the final resting place for "White and Slave, Rich and Poor."

Buried at Oaklawn are many of Tampa's pioneer families, 13 mayors of the city, one Florida governor, two Florida Supreme Court justices, and the framers of five state constitutions. A portion of the cemetery was set aside for slaves and "marginal" persons (such as pirates), and public monies were designated to bury indigents. Two mass graves exist at Oaklawn: one for soldiers from the c. 1824 Fort Brooke and one for victims of the 1887–1888 yellow fever epidemic.

One source states that the "Board of County Commissioners incorporated the land, north of Harrison and east of Morgan Streets." Current history acknowledges that no county commission existed at the time, and its predecessor, the Board of Trade, was not organized until May 7, 1885, "at a meeting of the town's boosters in Branch's Opera House." Those boosters—Dr. John P. Wall, John T. Lesley, Thomas A. Carruth, and others—would one day be laid to rest in Oaklawn Cemetery.

Cemeteries like Oaklawn exemplify the mid-19th-century movement to "domesticate" death. The severe and invariably religious views on death and the afterlife that were held in the country's colonial period softened by the early nineteenth century, stressing heavenly bliss, familial reunion in heaven, and the feelings of the bereaved. Cemeteries, traditionally either family plots or crowded church graveyards, gave way to carefully designed public burying grounds where landscaping, paved pathways, statuary, and grave markers all supported the image of the afterlife as a restful garden. Oaklawn is an early example of this trend, called the "rural cemetery" and in the Southern tradition of fenced family plots.

Some of the grave locations were unknown until recent years, when a collection of historical maps of the burial plots were discovered and placed in the collection of the Tampa Bay History Center.

Julius Jeff Gordon (December 10, 1926–June 11, 2004), a longtime Tampa resident, devoted the last years of his life to genealogical research and caretaking. He replaced headstones and was a tireless supporter of the care and preservation of Oaklawn. He made what is, to date, the most comprehensive genealogical study of the descendants of Oaklawn Cemetery. With the support of many Tampans, one of his last wishes—to be buried there—was granted.

Adjacent to Oaklawn is the St. Louis Cemetery, where many of Tampa's early citizens of the Catholic faith are interred. Vicente Martinez Ybor is buried there. Tampa's historic community, Ybor City, is named for the Spanish immigrant and cigar manufacturer.

Woodlawn Cemetery opened in 1888 and includes Confederate and Union soldiers. Enemies on the battlefields, they came to their final resting place in peace. Adjacent to Woodlawn Cemetery on the east is the Old Centro Asturiano Cemetery, established in 1904 for family and members of El Centro Asturiano de Tampa in Ybor City, and two Jewish cemeteries, Rodeph Sholom Cemetery (established in 1881) and Schaarai Zedek Cemetery (established in 1896). In the northwest corner is the Beth Israel Cemetery and Showmen's Rest Cemetery, established in 1951 for members of the circus and carnivals and for outdoor amusement workers by the Ladies' Auxiliary of the Greater Tampa Showmen's Association.

Also located within the Ybor neighborhood are the adjoining Cementerio del Centro Español and L'Unione Italiana Cemetery. The Centro Asturiano Memorial Park Cemetery, established in 1942, is on the east side of town near Myrtle Hill and Garden of Memories. The Mary Help of Christians School Cemetery is also located in this vicinity.

While it is not possible to include all of the cemeteries within city limits, those selected are within the vicinity of the downtown area or considered to have had a relationship with Tampa's early pioneering families.

Today, Tampa is a part of the metropolitan area most commonly referred to as the Tampa Bay area. For US Census purposes, Tampa is included in the Tampa–St. Petersburg–Clearwater, Florida, Metropolitan Statistical Area. The four-county area is composed of roughly 2.7 million residents, making it the second-largest metropolitan statistical area (MSA) in the state and the fourth largest in the southeastern United States behind Miami, Washington, DC, and Atlanta. The Greater Tampa Bay area has just over four million residents and generally includes the Tampa and Sarasota metro areas. The 2010 US Census reported Hillsborough County's population to be 1,229,226 individuals, with a density of 1,082 people per square mile, and the City of Tampa as the home to 335,709.

Tampa's rich history and heritage continues to grow and indeed has a story to tell, most of it just six feet under! It is our hope that this book, *Tampa's Historic Cemeteries*, will be of interest to many people: those with family connections, genealogists, and new residents who, perhaps like us, approach history from a different perspective.

One

Oaklawn

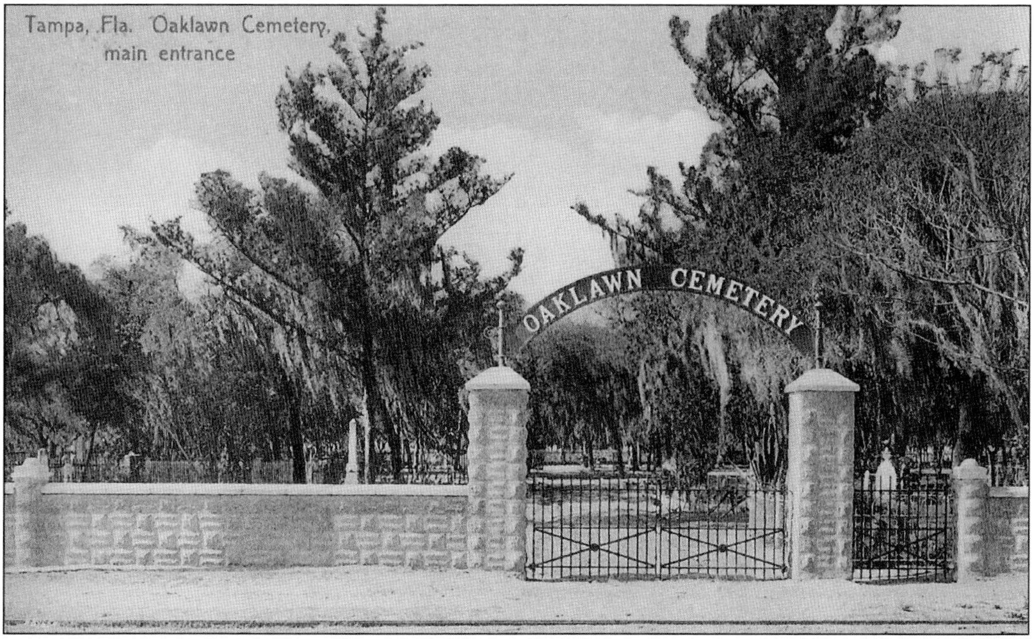

Oaklawn Cemetery, opened in 1850 north of Fort Brooke, was originally called Old City of Tampa Burying Grounds. Early accounts indicate that the first burial was of a slave who lived on the Alafia River plantation of Rev. L.G. Lesley, a Methodist minister, or of Nancy C. Hagler, who died in childbirth at the age of 16. Her husband was the sheriff and revenue collector and may have been motivated to create Oaklawn. The cemetery was dedicated as a historic cemetery in 1976.

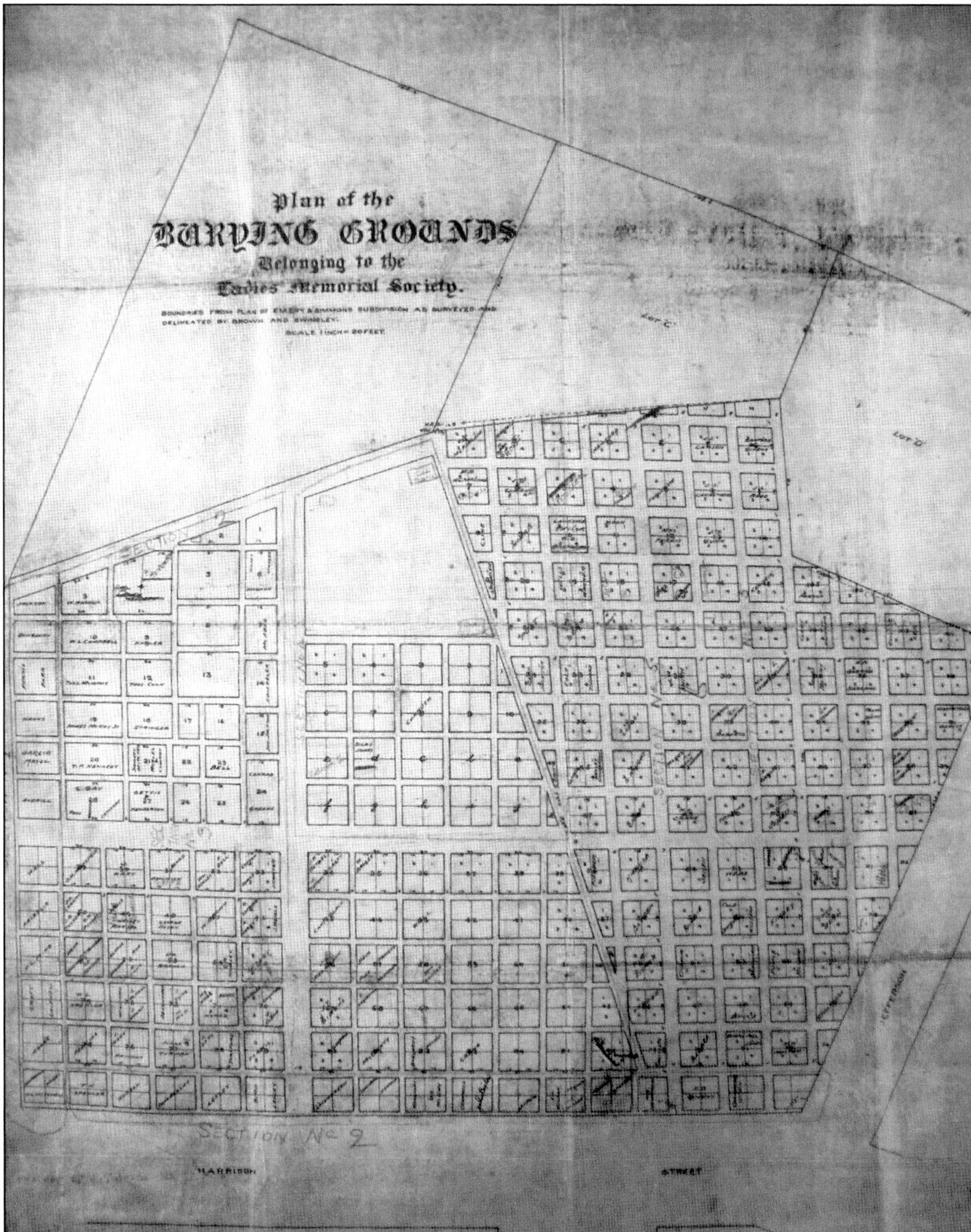

The Oaklawn map was probably drawn within the first 10 or 15 years of the cemetery's 1850 founding. The majority of the plots appear unsold, and fewer than 50 burial sites are shown. Names familiar to visitors of Oaklawn today—Lesley, McKay, Ashley, Hooker, and Magbee to list a few—appear as owners, but not yet occupants, of plots on the map. Both the 1847 Tampa map and the 1860s Oaklawn map are in fair to poor condition and are in need of conservation. The 1853 map of Tampa (also drawn by John Jackson) is in the History Center's Hillsborough County Collection. That map was conserved in 1995 by the History Center and serves as an interesting and important comparison with Jackson's earlier work. (TBHC.)

Joseph Bradford Lancaster was born in Kentucky in 1790 and died on November 25, 1856, in Tampa, Florida. The son of John and Catherine Miles Lancaster, he married Annie Blair in 1815 in Lebanon, Kentucky. He was a Mason, attorney, member of the Legislative Council of the Territory of Florida in 1825, a judge in Alachua County, and was a member of the Methodist Church. On February 16, 1856, he became the first mayor of Tampa.

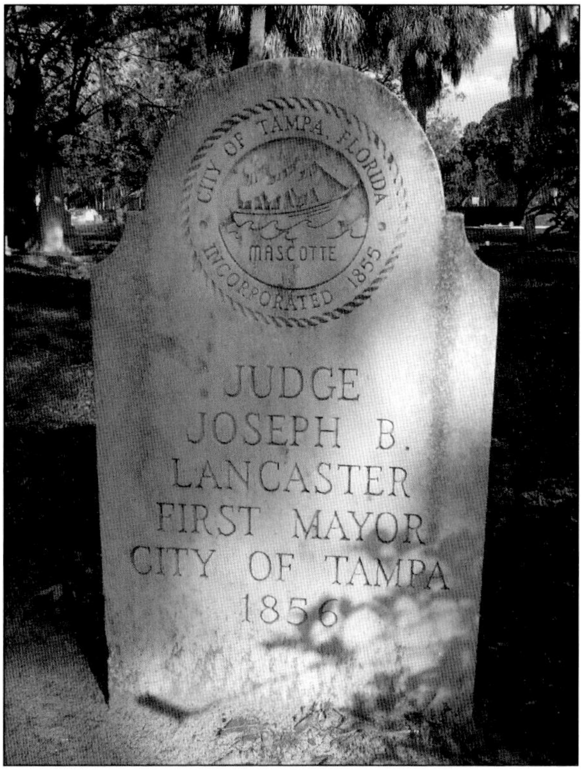

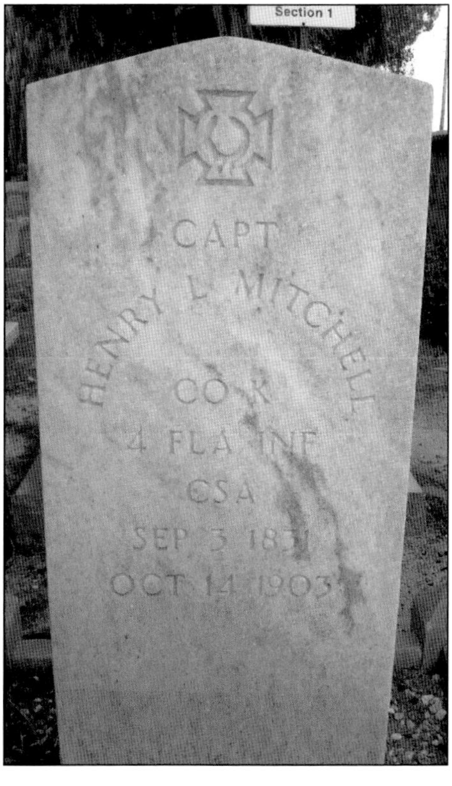

Henry Laurens Mitchell, born in 1831 in Alabama, was one of nine children born to Thomas and Elizabeth Starns Mitchell. He was elected the 16th governor of the state of Florida, serving from January 3, 1893, to January 5, 1896. He was buried in Oaklawn Cemetery on October 14, 1903.

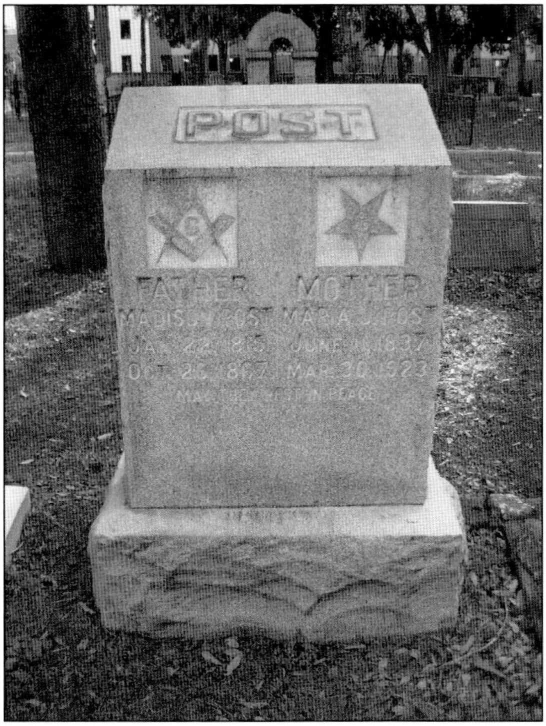

Madison Post (b. January 27, 1815, in New Jersey, d. October 26, 1867) came to Tampa in 1849 and built the Palmer House hotel at Water and Whiting Streets. He was a member of Hillsborough Lodge No. 25 Free and Accepted Masons, the Confederate States Army, and was elected as the third mayor of Tampa in 1858.

Mariah Jane Moore Post, pictured here, was born on June 11, 1837, and died on March 30, 1923. She and her husband, Madison Post, had six children: Dr. Duff Post, Jacob J. Post, Hollie S. Post, Antoinette Post, Linnie Darling Post, and Madison Post Jr. Mariah was a member of the Eastern Star and, along with her father, Joseph Moore, spoke fluent Miccosukee, the Seminole language. Joseph was the founder of the Hillsborough Lodge No. 25 F. and A.M. (THCPL.)

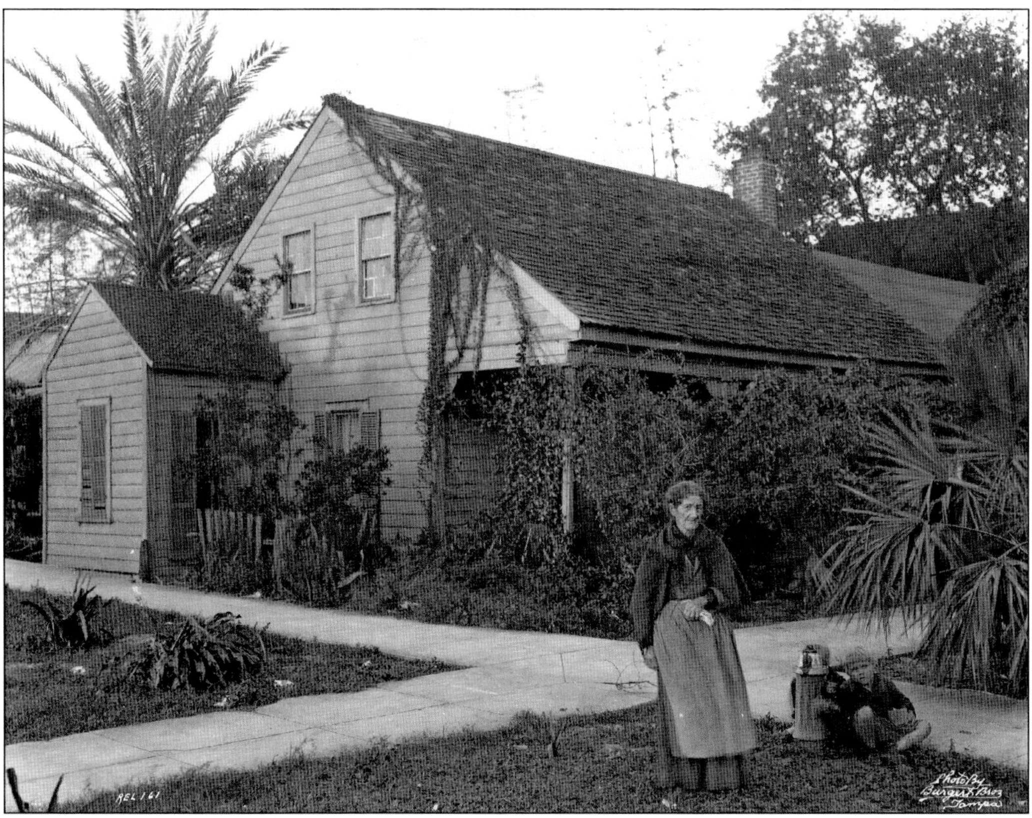

John Henry Krause, born on September 17, 1833, in Prichsnitz, Germany, came to Tampa about 1855 and established a blacksmith shop on the northeast corner of Franklin and Zack Streets. This site later became the location of the first Citizens Bank and Trust. A wheelwright by trade, he owned the Southern Iron Works, which was known to make fine wagons, carts, and buggies used all over South Florida.

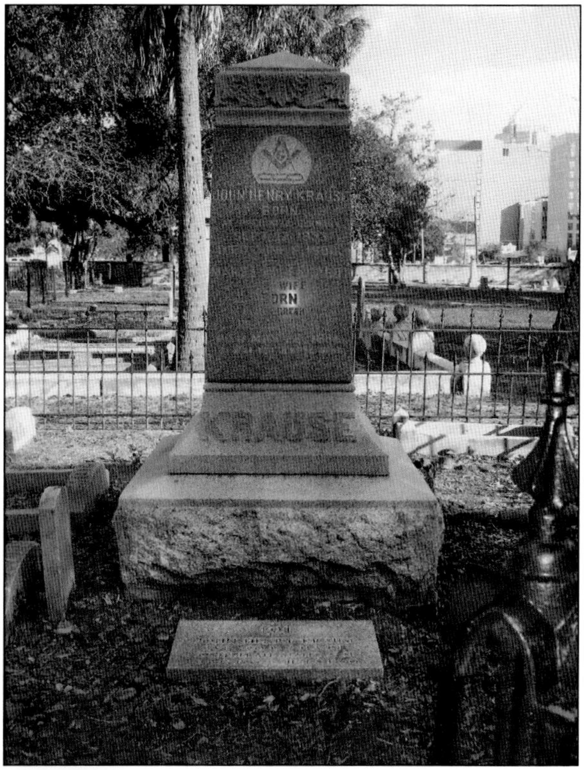

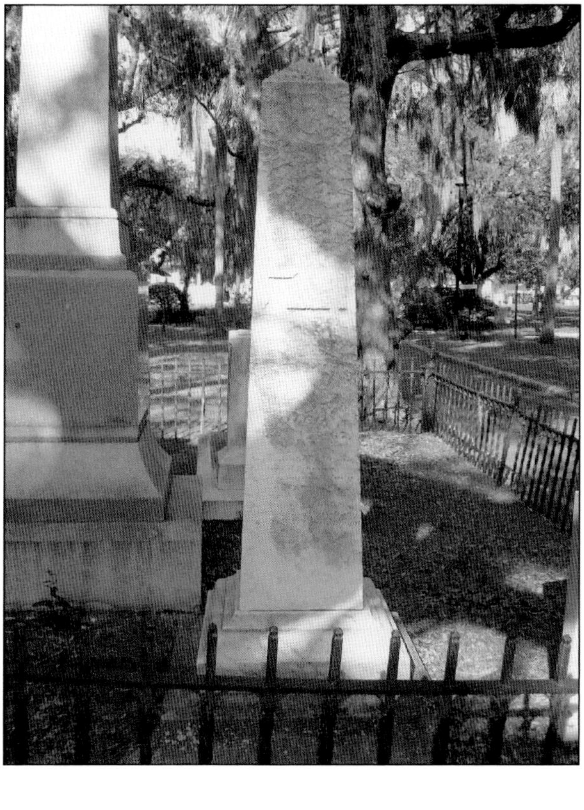

James Gettis (b. May 1, 1816) arrived in Tampa in 1848 from Pennsylvania. An attorney and member of the controversial Know Nothing Party, he was active and vocal in politics. A tireless promoter of Tampa's development, he, along with other influential locals, made several attempts to establish rail service to the city in the years prior to the Civil War. Captain Gettis served in the Confederate States Army, Company B, 7th Florida Infantry. He was a city councilman, state representative, and judge.

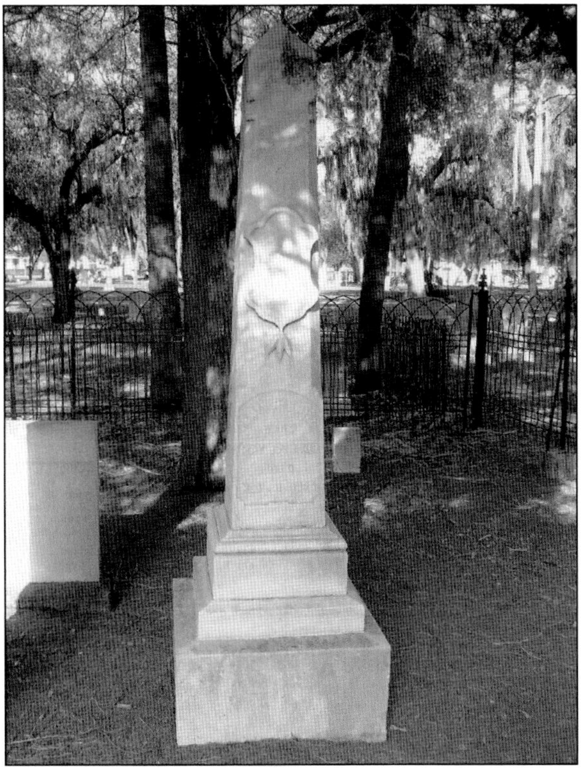

James McKay Sr. was born on May 17, 1808, in Thurson, County Caithness, Northern Island. He married Matilda Alexander Cail in St. Louis, Missouri, in 1837. They moved their family from Alabama to Tampa in 1846, and he was elected Tampa's mayor in 1859. A master seaman by the age of 24, he operated commercial sailing and steam vessels, transporting cattle to Cuba and other southern ports, and was a blockade-runner during the Civil War. He died on November 11, 1876, in Tampa.

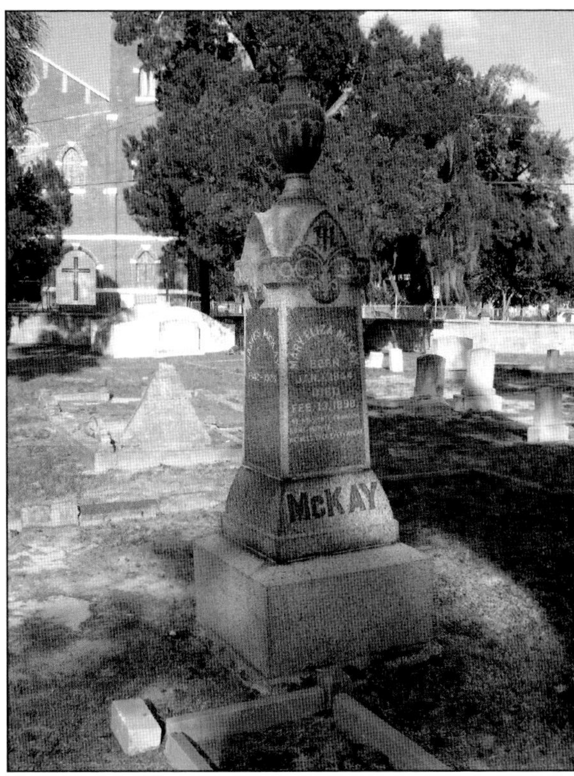

Capt. James McKay Jr. (b. November 27, 1842, in Mobile, Alabama, d. September 5, 1925) was a member of the 4th Florida Infantry, Confederate States Army. He organized the family's maritime activities into the Mallory Line and was the civilian contractor responsible for loading troops and materials onto ships during the Spanish-American War. Like his father, James was a mayor of the city of Tampa, serving in 1902. He was a two-term Florida state senator and postmaster of Tampa in 1914.

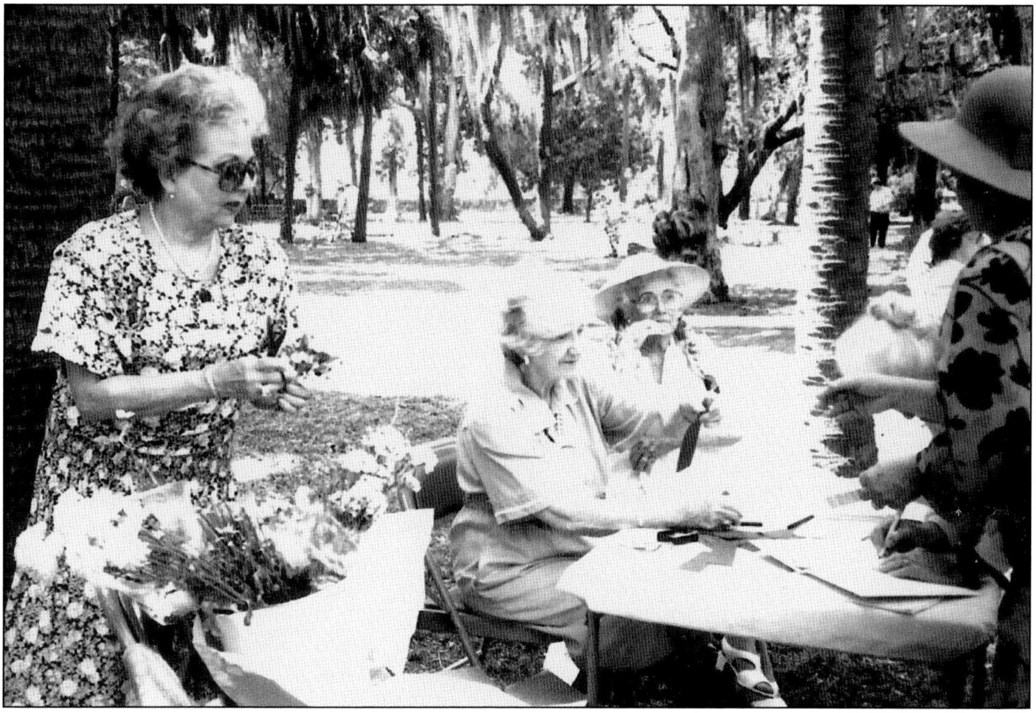

The Tampa Historical Society sponsors an Annual Oaklawn Cemetery Ramble. Volunteer members of the society conduct guided tours and continue to gather information on the families that are buried there. Society members are shown greeting guests at the registration table. (JMMP.)

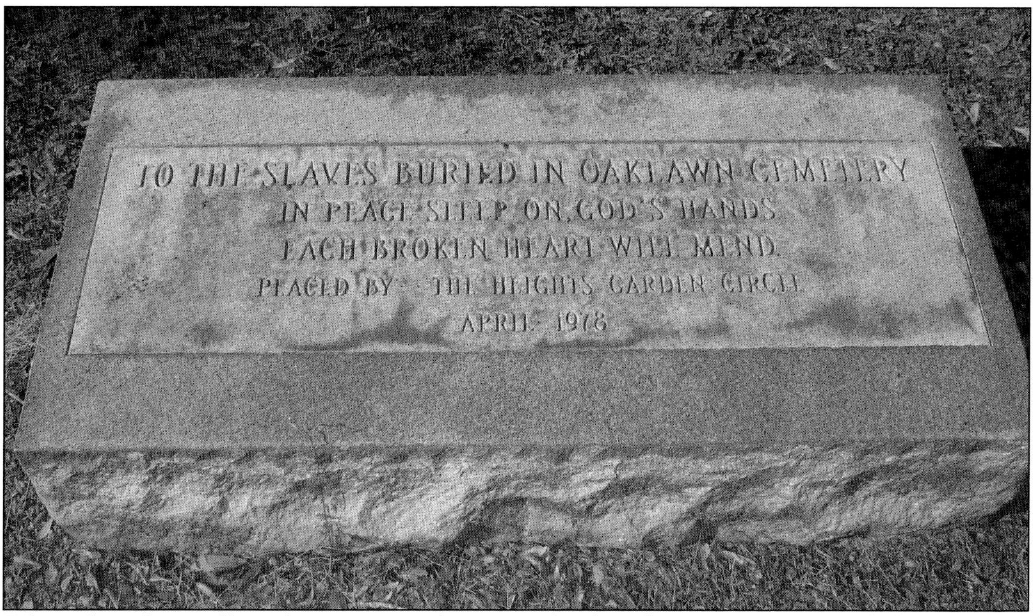

When platted, a small northeast section that joins what later became St. Louis Catholic Cemetery was reserved for the burial of slaves. In 1978, the Heights Garden Circle placed this memorial stone dedicated to the slaves buried in Oaklawn Cemetery. It reads in part, "In peace sleep on God's hands each broken heart."

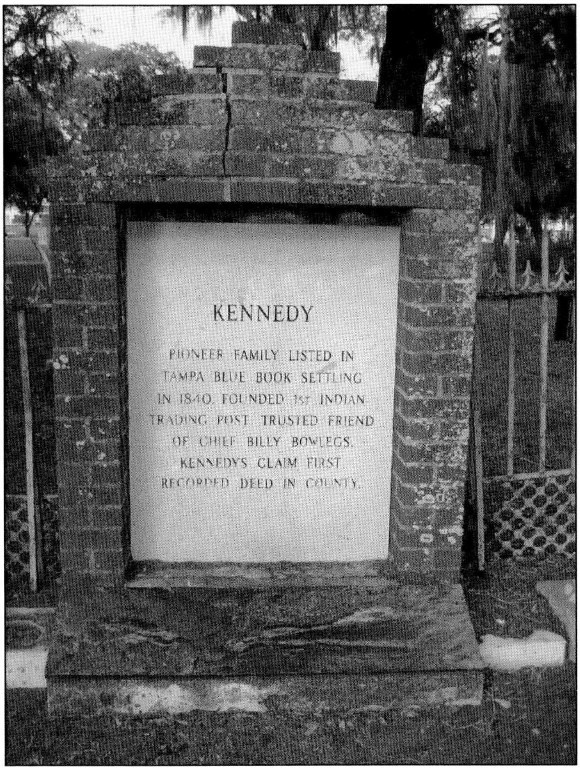

According to family Bible records, the Kennedy family is of English descent. Thomas Pugh Kennedy, born on December 31, 1812, in Philadelphia, Pennsylvania, was the son of Thomas Kennedy Pugh and Jane Penrose Pugh. Fluent in Spanish, Thomas went to Brazil in 1833 for six months. He was imprisoned in Texas in 1837 by the Mexican government at Matamoras. Later that year, he came to Florida, where he was employed by the Quartermaster Department of the US Army. On December 31, 1843, he married Adelaide P. Cristy, niece of Fort Brooke commander Maj. Donald Fraser. Kennedy's left leg was amputated due to rheumatic fever in 1853. He died on August 25, 1858, and his funeral service was conducted by the Odd Fellows. The willow is a symbol for sorrow, grief, and sadness.

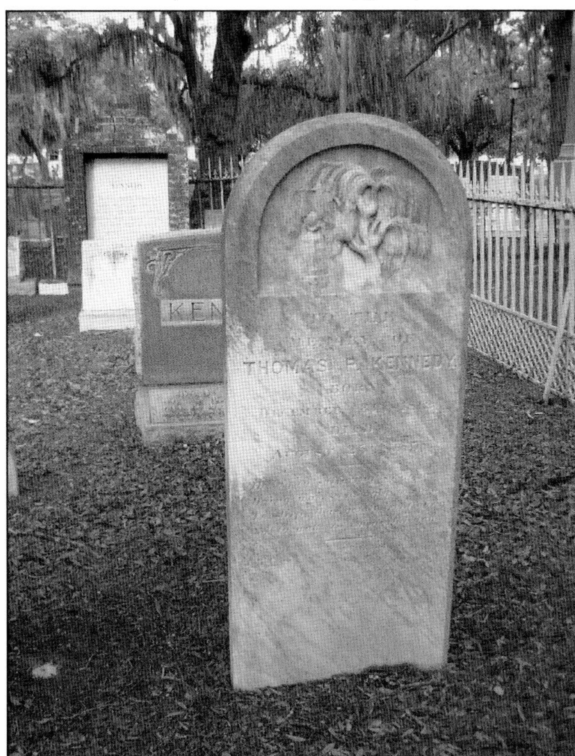

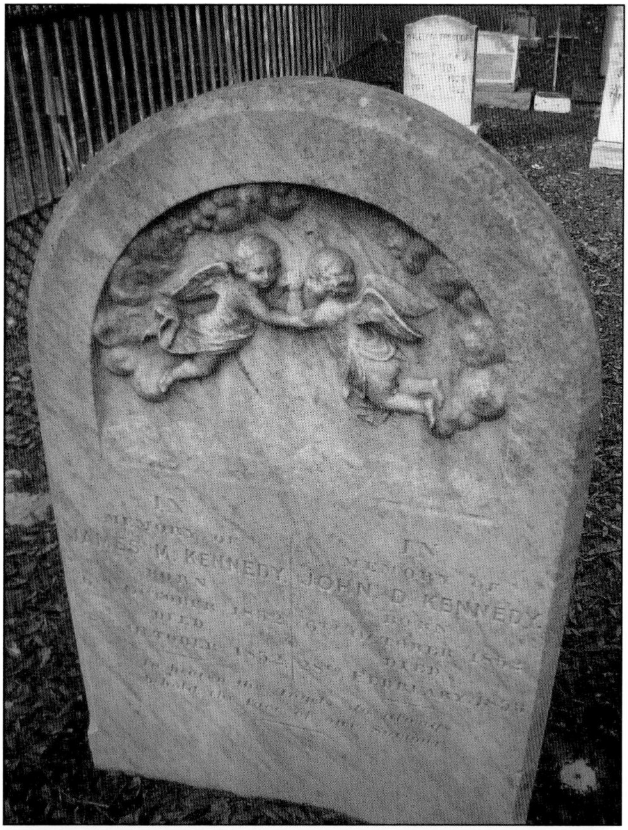

This tombstone is dedicated to twin sons James M. and John D. Kennedy, born to Thomas Pugh Kennedy and his wife, Adelaide P. Cristy. James lived only two days, while John D.'s short life ended when he was just four months, 22 days old. The angelic cherubs are holding hands, reunited in heaven.

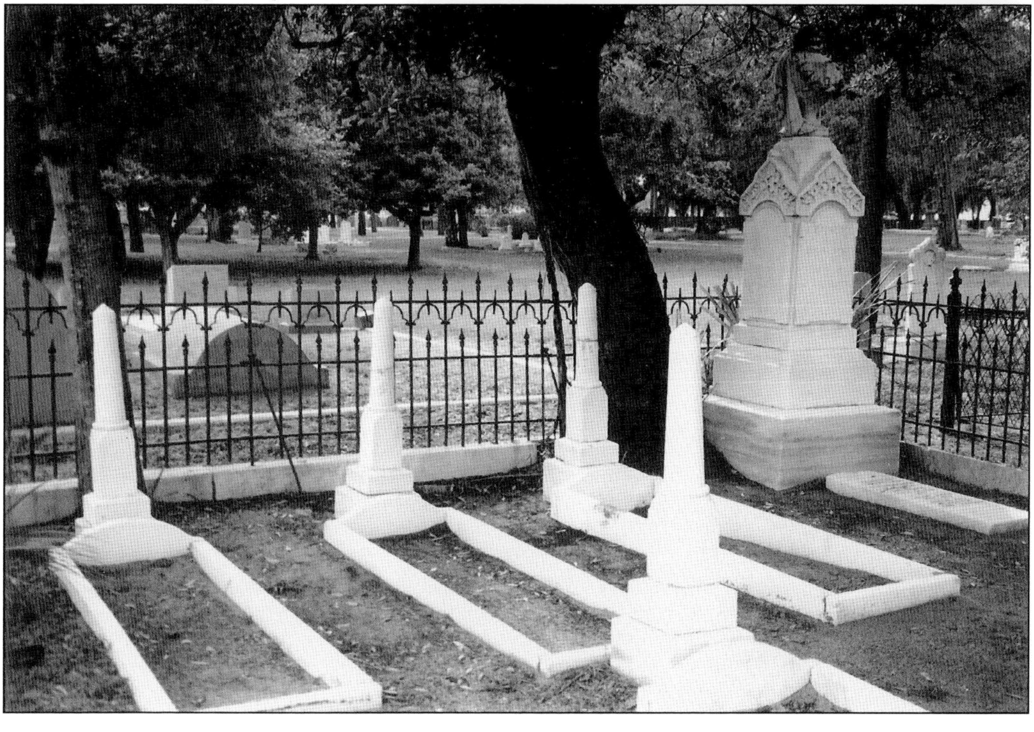

James T. Magbee was born in 1820 in Heard County, Georgia. Married multiple times, he was a practicing attorney, Mason, judge of the Sixth Circuit Court (often referred to as "The Scalawag Judge"), Florida state senator, publisher of the *Tampa Guardian* newspaper, and a framer of the Florida Constitution in 1865. He died on December 12, 1885. Other family members buried in this plot on land donated by him are his second wife, Julia Ann, his sister Rachel Magbee, and his mother, Susan Magbee. (JMMP.)

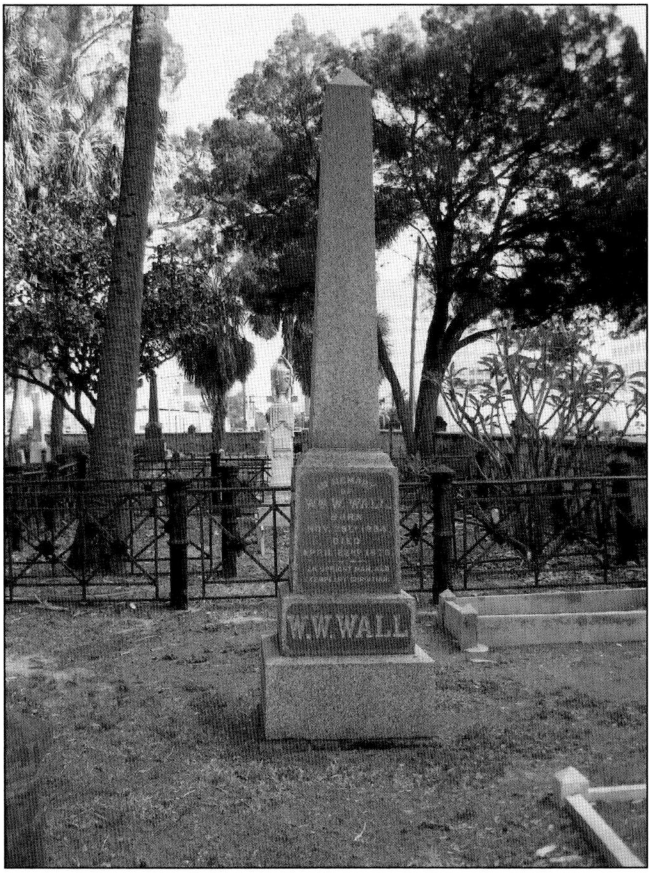

William W. Wall was born on November 29, 1834, in Hamilton County, Florida. The oldest son of Perry G. Wall and Nancy Hunter Wall, he moved to Tampa about 1860 and operated a general store located at the northeast corner of Washington and Marion Streets. He married Minnie May of Greensboro, Alabama, on March 7, 1861. Their children included sons James Edgar, Perry G. II, and Charley L. and daughters Willie, Lillie, Daisy, and May. Perry II served as Tampa's mayor from 1924 to 1928 and was cofounder of Knight & Wall Company. The Tampa Hardware Store (below), located at the corner of Lafayette and Tampa Streets, carried farm supplies, tools, sporting goods, mill supplies, and building materials. (THCPL.)

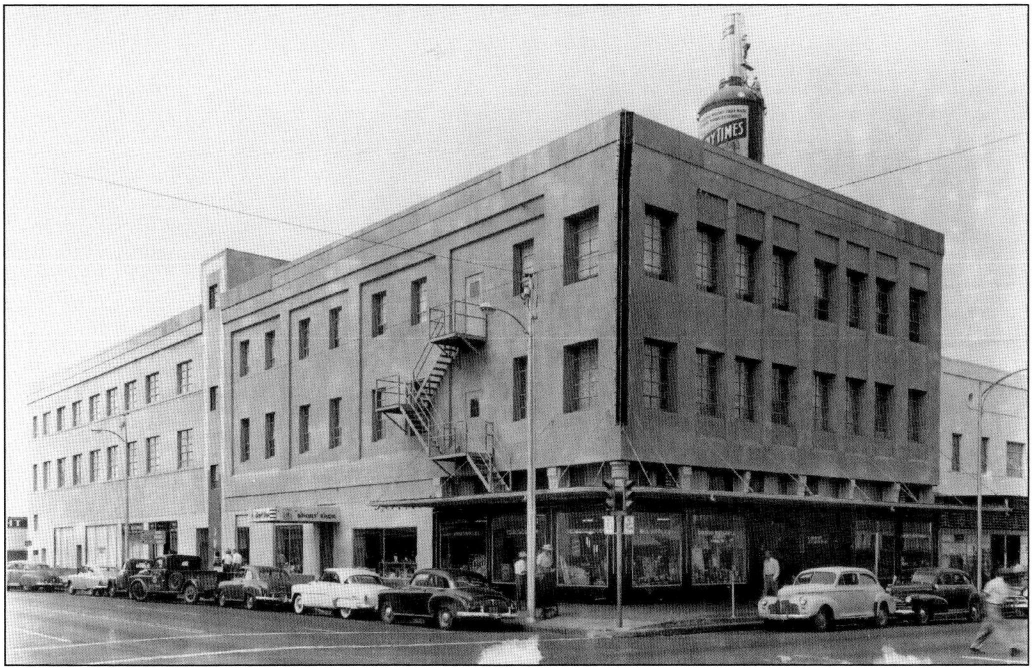

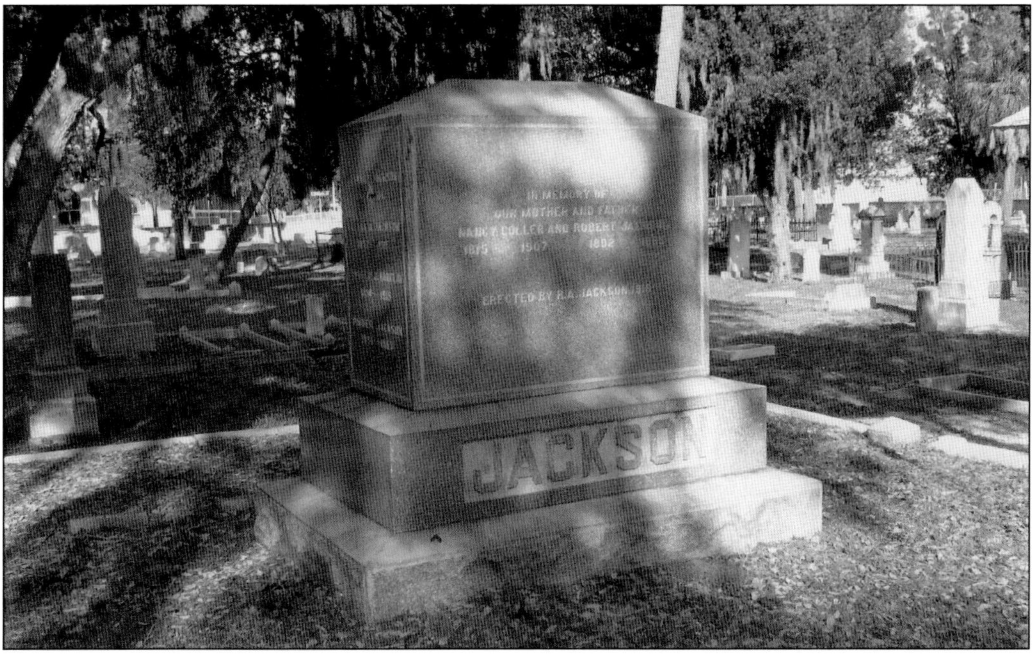

Nancy Coller (b. January 22, 1814) married Dr. Robert Andrew Jackson, a Philadelphia-born surgeon stationed at Fort Brooke, on September 14, 1836. Andrew had become the first bridegroom of Tampa and received a permit under the Armed Occupation Act for 160 acres of land on the Alafia River. Dr. Jackson (1802–1865) also served as a probate judge of Hillsborough County. Robert and Nancy were the parents of William Parker, Robert Andrew, Cordelia, Mary Josephine, Levi Oscar, Maria Theresa, and John Brown Jackson. Nancy was one of 11 children born to Levi Coller of Massachusetts and his wife, Nancy Dixon of St. Augustine. It is believed that some members of the early Coller family were buried at the Fort Brooke Civilian Cemetery, located in the southwest section of the military post. Their remains were later removed and relocated to Oaklawn. Coller's home at Six Mile Creek was destroyed by Native Americans in 1838. Dr. Levi Oscar (below) married Estelle Bruton and moved to Bainbridge, Georgia. He served as a private in the Confederate States Army, Company G, 1st Regiment, Georgia Volunteer Infantry.

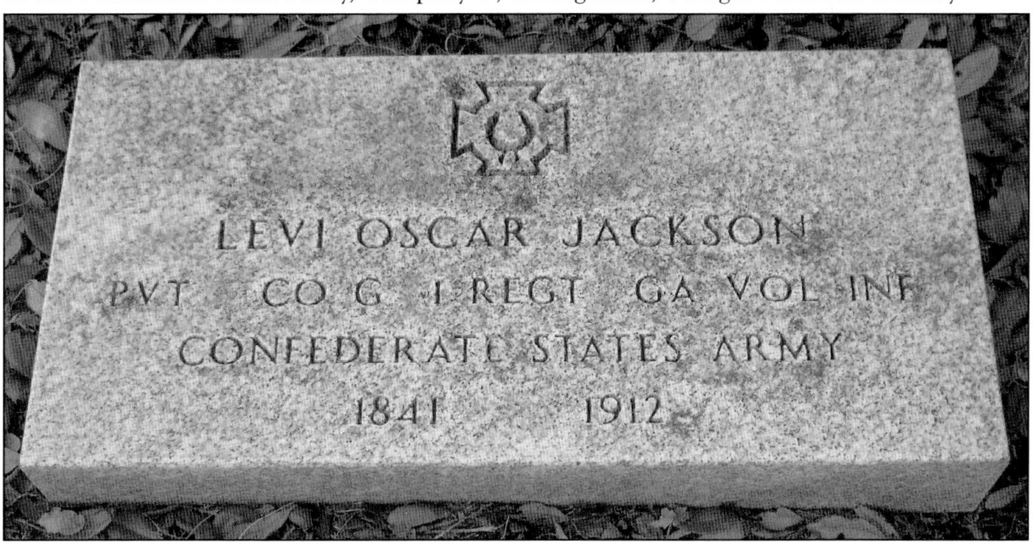

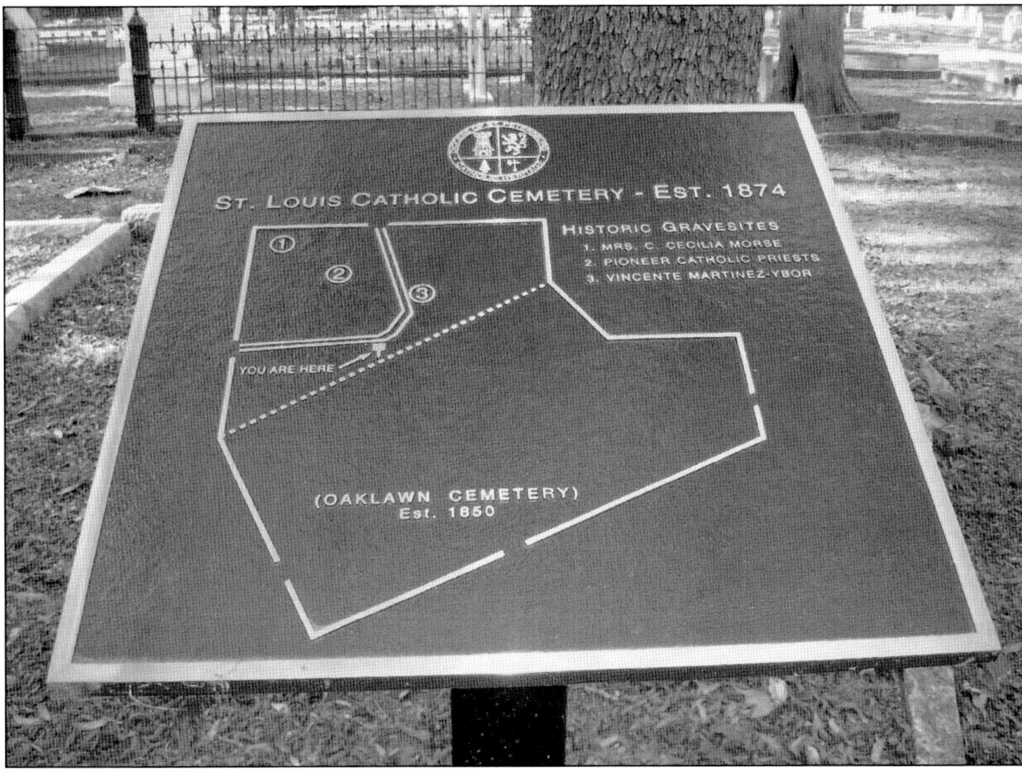

The St. Louis section was established in 1874 for burial of Catholics, including five Tampa pioneer priests: Fathers Bayard, Stenzel, Peterson, Swemberg, and O'Sullivan. Three of them succumbed to yellow fever in the late 1880s. These are the oldest known priests' graves on the west coast of Florida. C. Cecilia Morse, born June 3, 1838, and a true pioneer of Catholic parochial education in the Diocese of St. Augustine (now St. Petersburg), was buried in this section. She died on June 13, 1926.

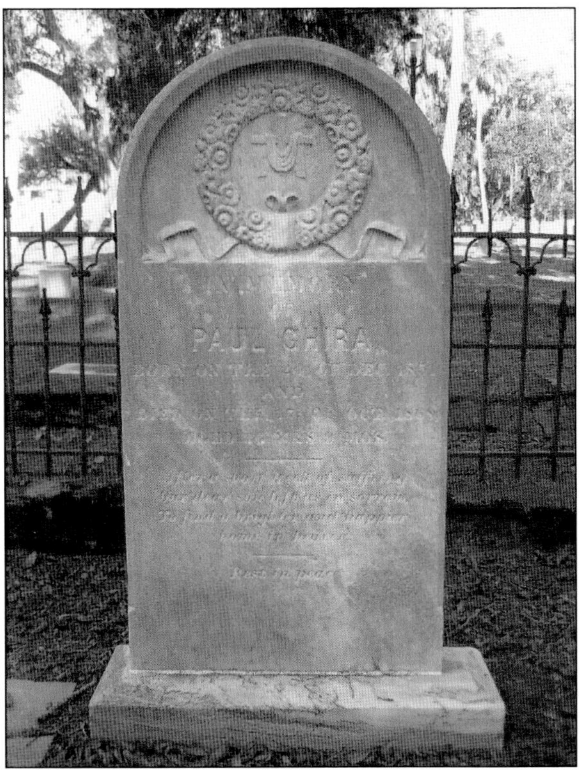

Paul Ghira, born on December 24, 1851, was the oldest son of Italian-born Domenico Ghira and Domenica Masters of St. Augustine. He died on October 17, 1868. His father, a very prosperous businessman with interests in shipping and mercantile trade, became the owner of some of Tampa's most valuable land.

Domenico Ghira was born on March 19, 1816, in Italy. His family lived in the Trieste region of Italy before moving to Boston, Massachusetts, in 1840. Finally settling in Tampa in 1849, Domenico married Domenica Masters on March 24, 1851. She bore him six children: Paul, Mary, Francis J., Euphemia, Josephine, and Flora. Flora married John B. Mahoney at St. Louis Church on Saturday, June 28, 1885. Domenico died in Tampa on May 22, 1897.

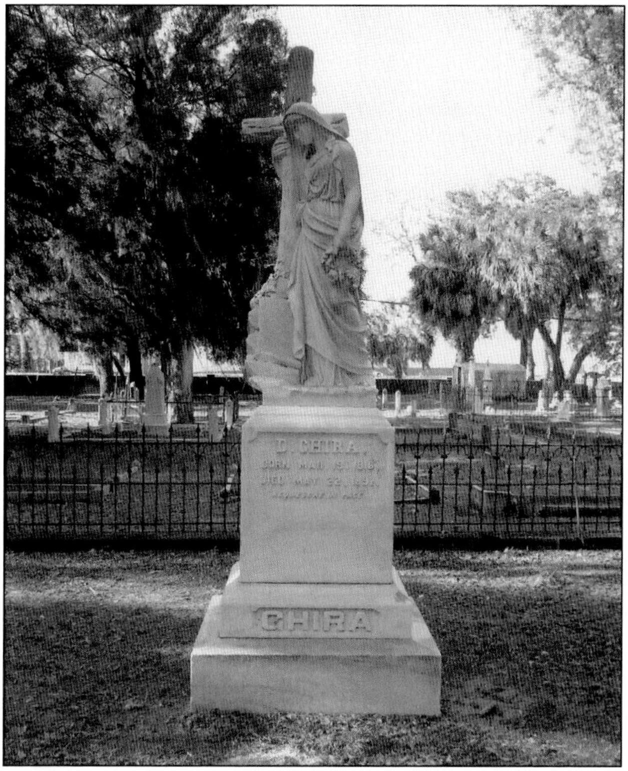

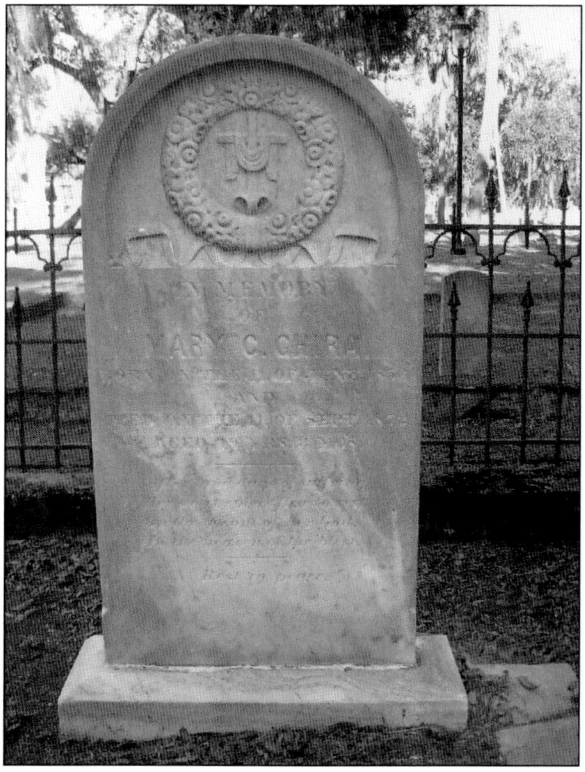

Mary Ghira was born on June 11, 1853, and died on September 10, 1872. A memoriam to her printed in New York on October 4, 1872, reads, "And must thy merry laugh be heard no more? Are thy black ringlets mingling with the dust? Why so soon did'st thou loose thy grasp on life's frail oar? God's ways are oft mysterious, but always just."

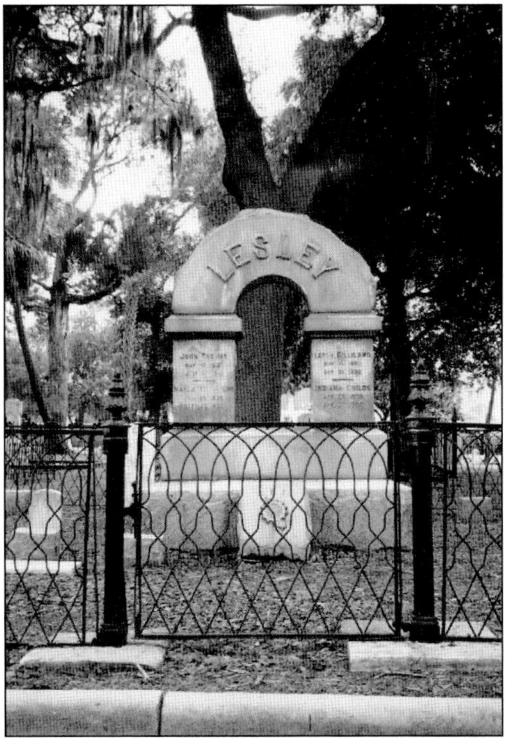

Born on May 12, 1835, in Madison County, Florida, John Thomas Lesley died on July 13, 1913. The son of Leroy Gilliland Lesley and Indiana Childs Livingston, he married widow Margaret Adeline Brown Tucker. Lesley served as a captain in the Florida Mounted Volunteers in the Seminole Indian Wars and a lieutenant in the Billy Bowlegs War of 1856–1858. In 1863, he organized a "Cow Cavalry" company, which became known as the Tampa Home Guard. He amassed a fortune, becoming one of the cattle barons of Florida as well as the largest property owner in Hillsborough County. He served as sheriff, tax collector, and mayor of Tampa (1869). In addition, Lesley was a state legislator, state senator (1879), member of the Constitutional Convention of 1885, clerk of the circuit court (1892), and the collector of customs at the Port of Tampa. His son Theodore Lesley was county historian and an ardent preservationist of local records. Another son, William Taliaffero Lesley (below), married Sarah R. Yancey on December 7, 1898, and died on December 7, 1904. (JMMP.)

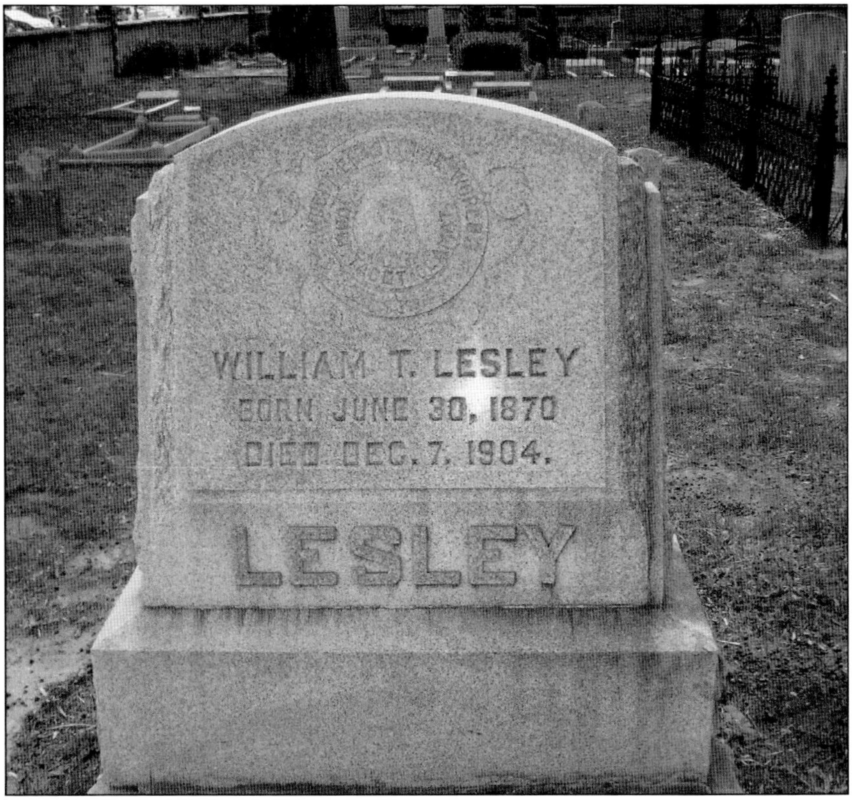

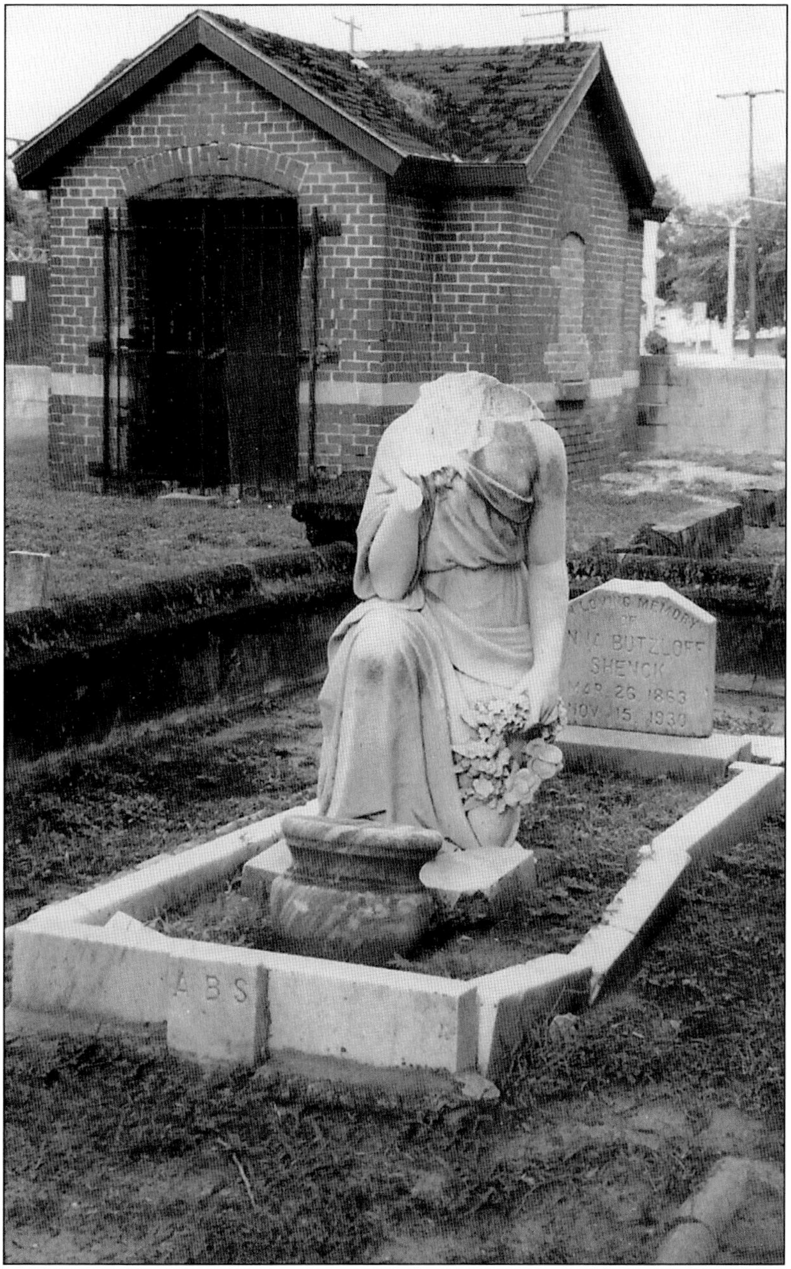

The statue of a woman on Anna Bingenheimer Butzloff Shenck's grave was horribly vandalized in the 1970s when someone broke off the statue's head and one hand. She and her husband, Paul, were German immigrants and members of Sacred Heart Church. Anna was born on March 26, 1863, in Oppenheim, Germany. Paul co-owned the Tampa Steamway Bakery, was a member of the Woodmen of the World, and died on February 2, 1918. Their daughter Valeria Butzloff was born in Chicago on April 29, 1886, and died on October 12, 1907, in Denver of tuberculosis at the age of 21. Devastated by her death, the Butzloffs brought their daughter home for burial in Oaklawn. A picture of Valeria adorns her tomb. Son Joseph was born in Georgia in 1896. He resided at 305 South Edison Avenue. Joseph's daughter Elizabeth Ann was born on July 9, 1928.

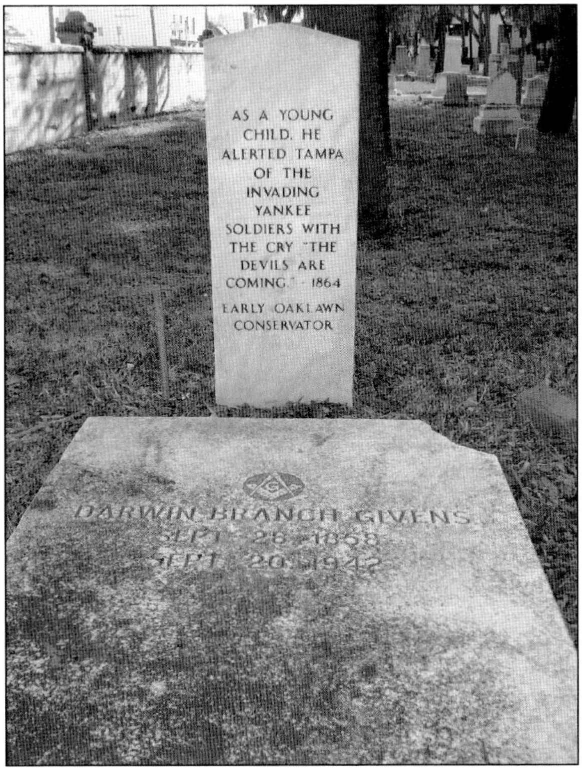

Darwin Branch Givens was born in 1832 and died in 1858. As a young child, he alerted everyone that the Yankee soldiers were coming to Tampa, saying, "The Devils are coming!" He too is credited with the early conservation of this cemetery. He married Anna Morris of Tampa's pioneer Morris family. To this union were born three children: Morris M., who attended Washington & Lee University, attaining a law degree and practicing law in Tampa; Darwin Creyon, who married Claribel Pugh of Charlottesville, Virginia; and Fay, who married Lt. Henry N. Sumner. Dr. Franklin Branch (1802–1882) was an early druggist at the corner of Florida and Washington Streets. He served the Confederate States Army as a surgeon in Addison's Company 1 Detachment of the Florida Mounted Volunteers.

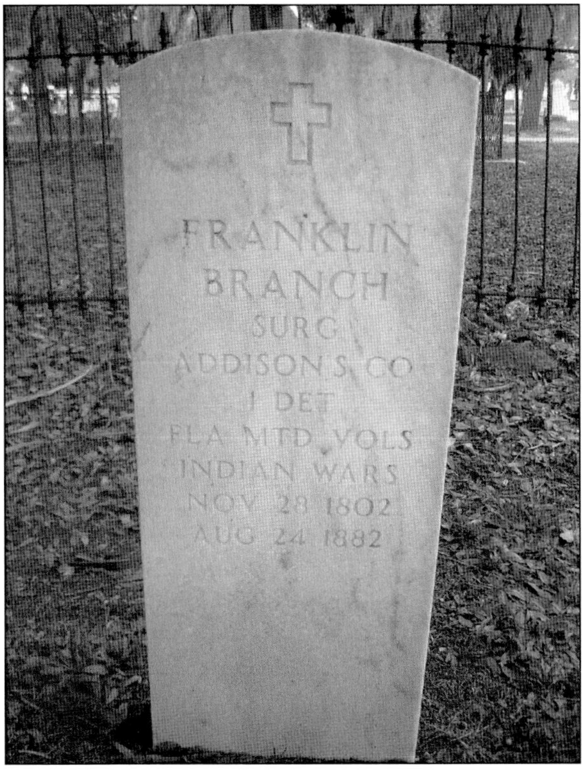

James Edgar Wall was born in Tampa on March 10, 1872. He married Florrie Bell Bowman at the First Methodist Church of Plano, Texas, on January 10, 1894. While living in Texas, he operated the ranch of his father-in-law, Jack Bowman. Returning to Tampa, he was later appointed postmaster, serving from 1933 to 1948. He was a member of the board of trustees of Florida Southern College, a member of First United Methodist Church, a 32nd degree Mason, and was instrumental in the formation of the Florida State Fair. He died in Tampa on December 18, 1954.

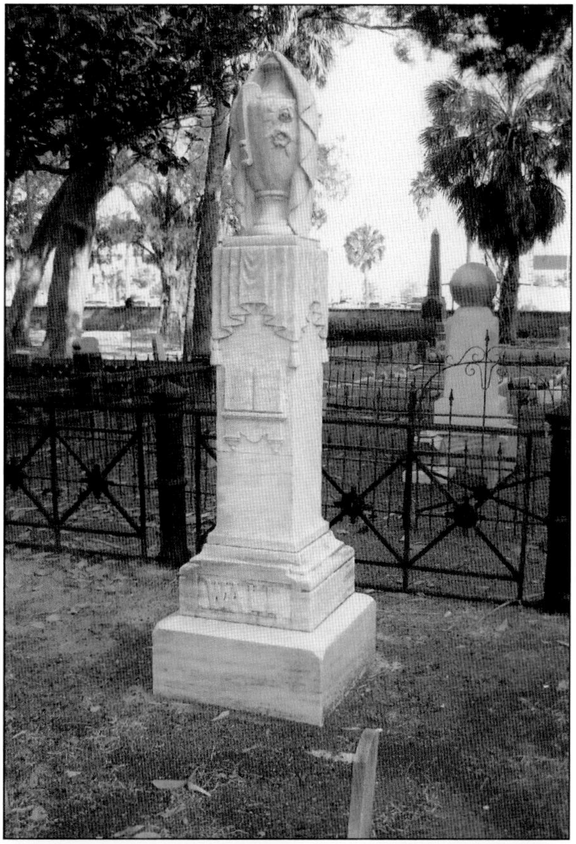

Perry G. Wall II (far right), the brother of James Edgar Wall, and Elizabeth Barnhard (third from right), postmistress, are part of the mail handler's caravan inspecting a recent arrival of a Florida Airways plane carrying mailbags intended for the good citizens of Tampa. Wall's family had a longtime association with providing the citizenry with the delivery of their mail. Wall was mayor from 1923 to 1928. (THCPL.)

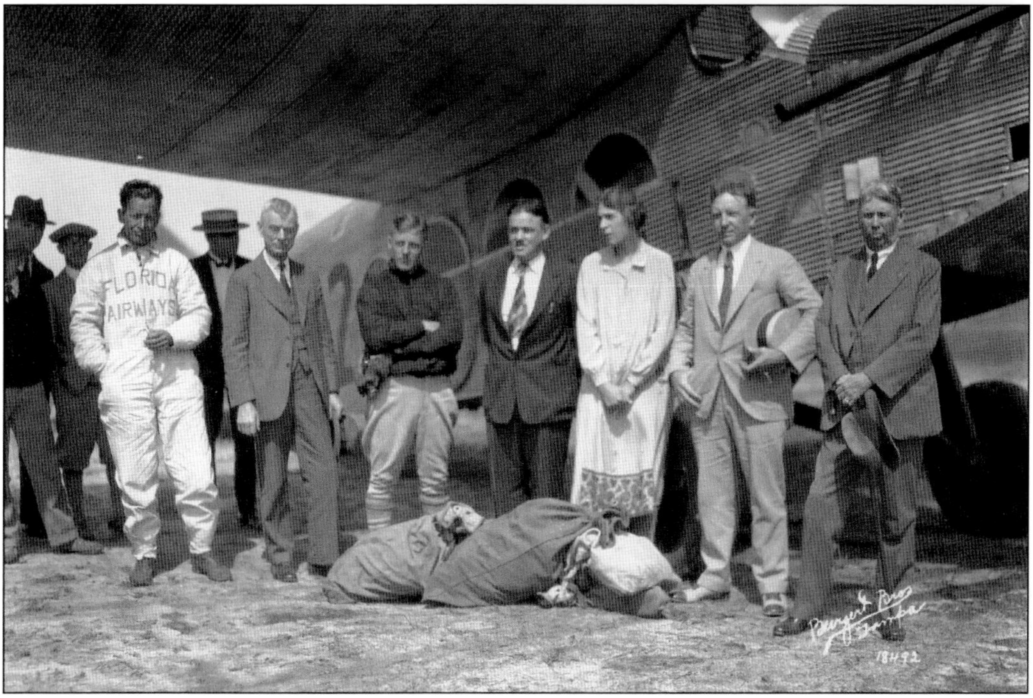

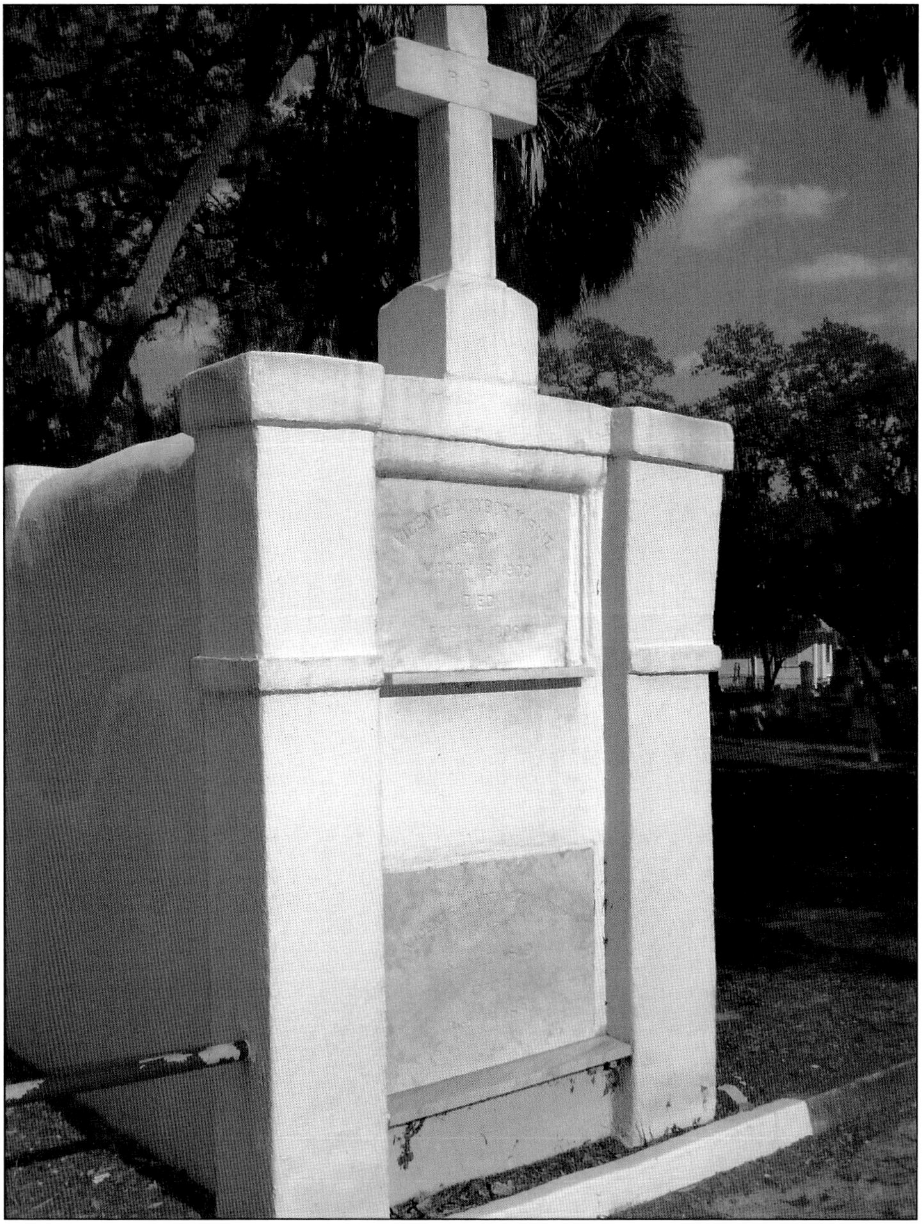

Vicente Martinez Ybor, born in Valencia, Spain, on September 7, 1818, is considered the founder of Ybor City. At 14 years of age, he left Spain for Havana, Cuba, to work as a grocery clerk. By 1853, he had started his own cigar factory. In 1885, he entered into an agreement with the Tampa Board of Trade that led to his purchase of 40 acres of land and the establishment of the cigar business. In 1896, two years before the sinking of the *Maine*, Spanish general Valeriano Weyler declared an embargo on tobacco exports from Cuba to the United States, hoping to shut down cigar factories. Ybor and other leading manufacturers persuaded H.B. Plant to send his ships, the *Olivette* and *Mascotte,* to Havana before the embargo deadline. The ships returned with their staterooms filled with Havana leaf. Vicente Martinez Ybor is buried in the Catholic section of Oaklawn Cemetery (St. Louis Catholic Cemetery). Today, Ybor City recognizes this great businessman with his name and prominent statuary.

Tampa Historical Society members host an Annual Oaklawn Ramble, inviting guests to come out and learn about the history of Oaklawn Cemetery and the people buried there. Tour guide and Tampa Historical Society member Larry Rayburn (right) is seen describing Ybor's grandson Vicente Ybor Y Ruiz, who was not quite three years old when he died in 1906. He is buried with his grandfather, who preceded his death in 1896. (THS.)

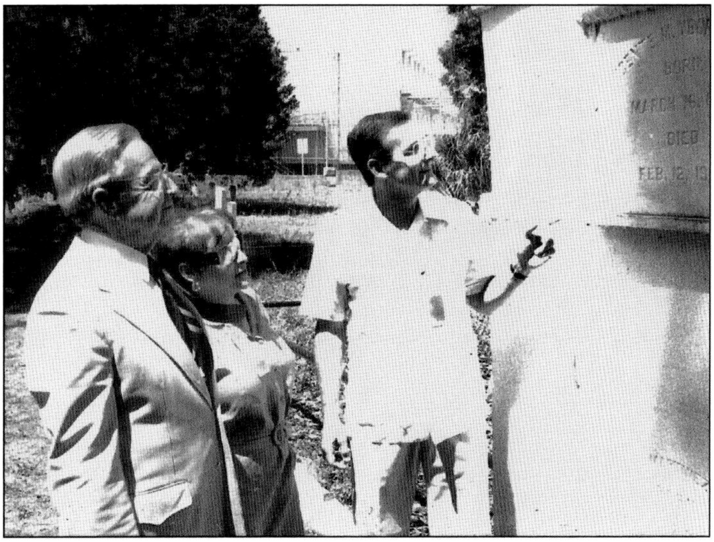

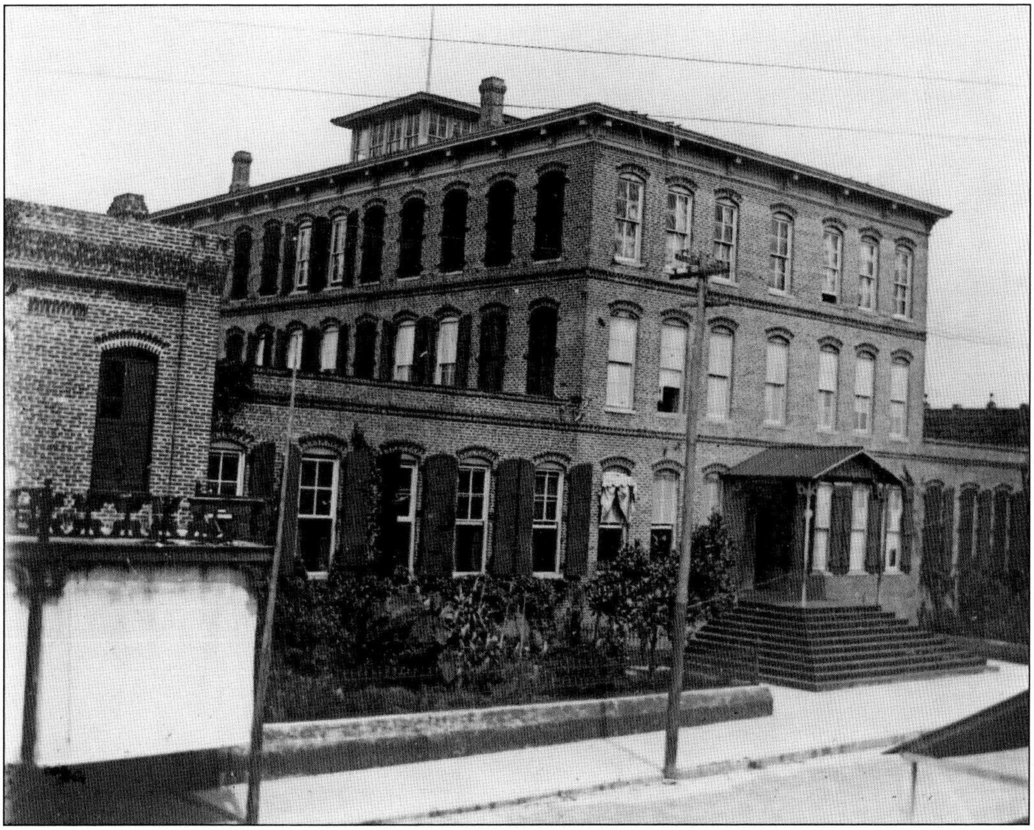

The establishment of the cigar industry in Tampa during post–Civil War times gave the area hopes for survival. Vicente Martinez Ybor had contemplated moving his cigar operation to Galveston, Texas; however, his friend Gavino Gutierrez told him that Tampa had a suitable climate and plenty of land to support the manufacturing and sales of his cigars. Enticed by tax incentives, Ybor moved his operation to Tampa and built the V.M. Ybor Cigar Factory. (THCPL.)

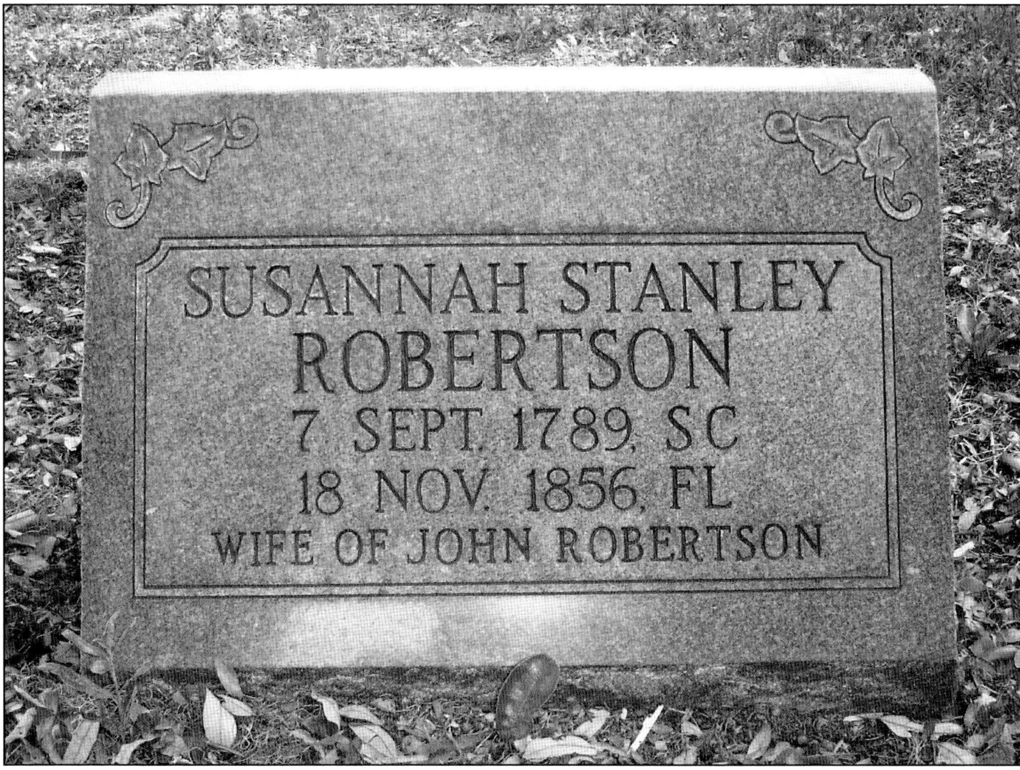

Susannah Stanley Robertson's grave location was not identified until the discovery of early maps of the *Plan of the Burying Grounds* belonging to the Ladies Memorial Society. These maps have been placed in the collections of the Tampa Bay History Center. Robertson's descendents held a memorial dedication for this marker in the spring of 1994.

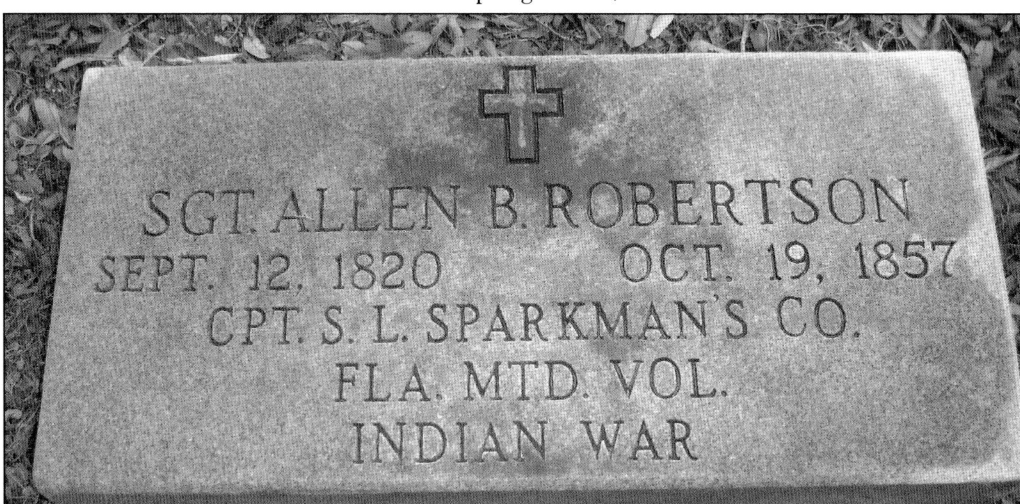

Sgt. Allen B. Robertson's grave was also identified from the *Plan of the Burying Grounds*. He had proudly served the Confederate States Army in Capt. S.L. Sparkman's company of the Florida Mounted Volunteers in the Indian Wars. His descendants secured a veteran marker for placement on his gravesite.

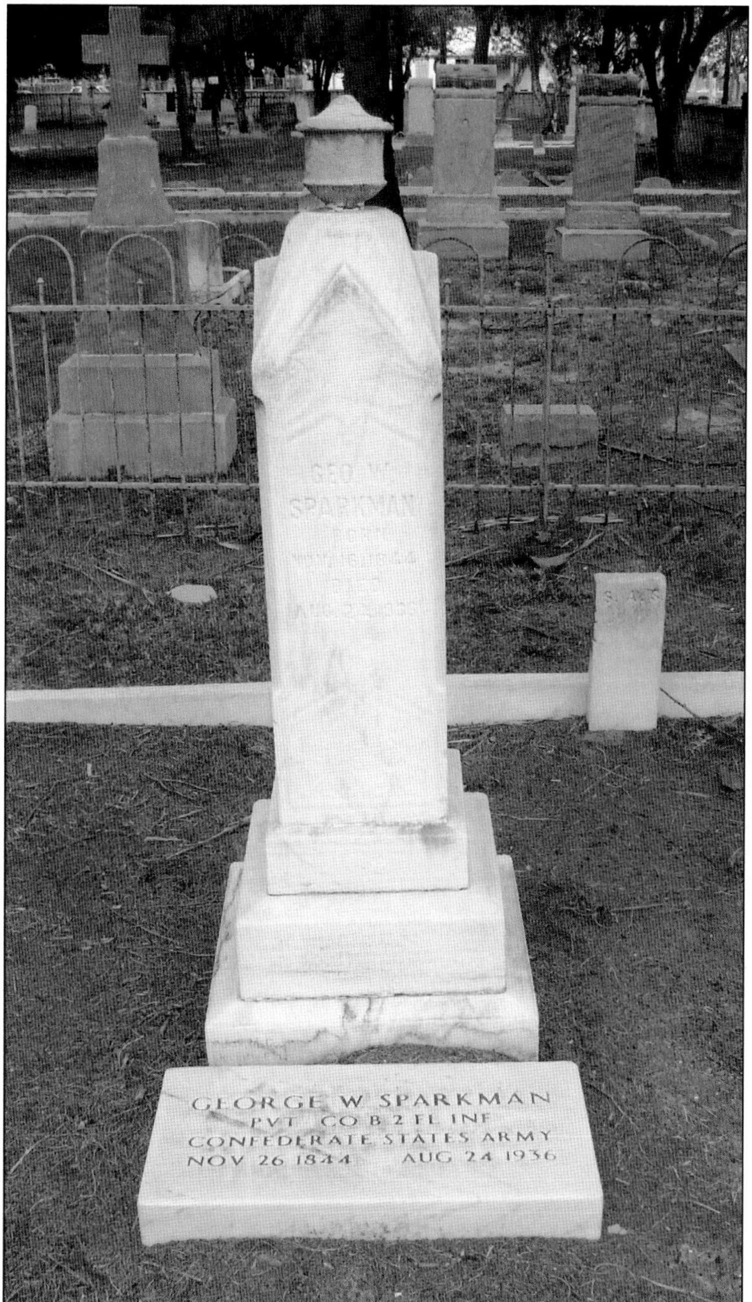

George W. Sparkman's monument was made by the Jacksonville Monument Company. Sparkman (November 16, 1844–August 24, 1936) is buried within the burial plot of one of Tampa's funeral directors, Martin Lovengreen. Sparkman was a bookkeeper for Gunn and Seckinger Company, a wholesale grocery company owned by John T. Gunn and J.B. Seckinger, and an agent for the Benner's Schooner Line. He served as a private in Company B, Second Florida Cavalry, during the Civil War. He was married twice: first to Susan A. Matthews (September 30, 1849–May 6, 1894) and then to Ada Sparkman.

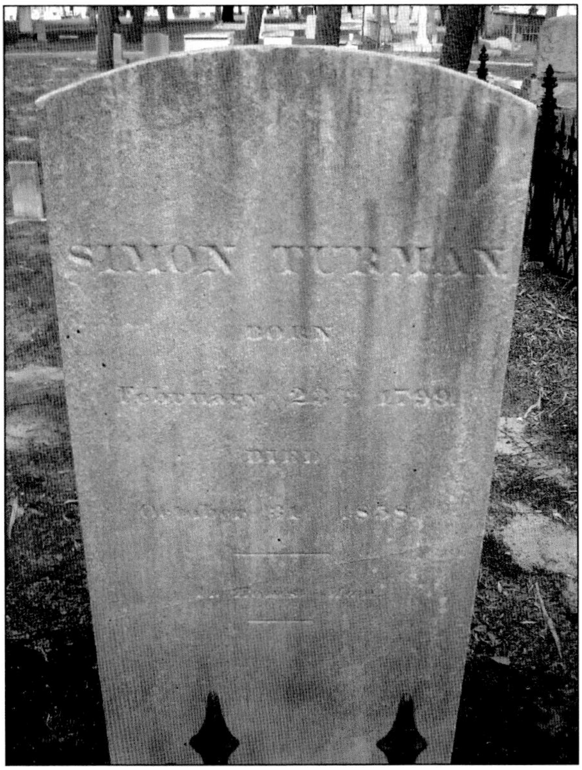

Simon Turman (b. 1799) was editor of the *Florida Peninsular* newspaper in Tampa. He served as a member of the board of county commissioners, was the first superintendent of public schools, the judge of probate court, and clerk of the circuit court. He moved to Hillsborough County in 1843, two years prior to Florida's statehood, with his wife, Abija, whom he had married in Indiana about 1824. Abija, born in New York on April 22, 1799, was the daughter of Nancy Rundel and Seth Cushman. A nearby memorial marker remembers their son Simon Turman Jr. (1829–1861), who had served the Confederacy at Resaca, Georgia, the site of his burial.

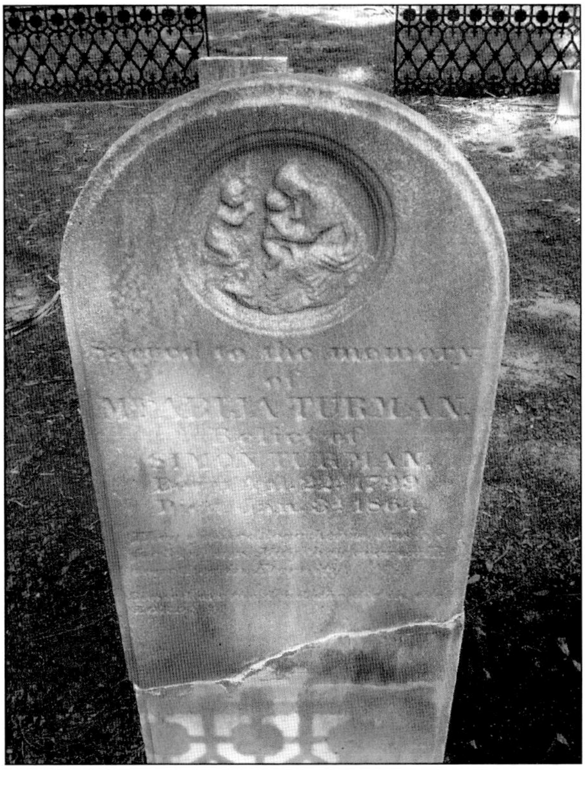

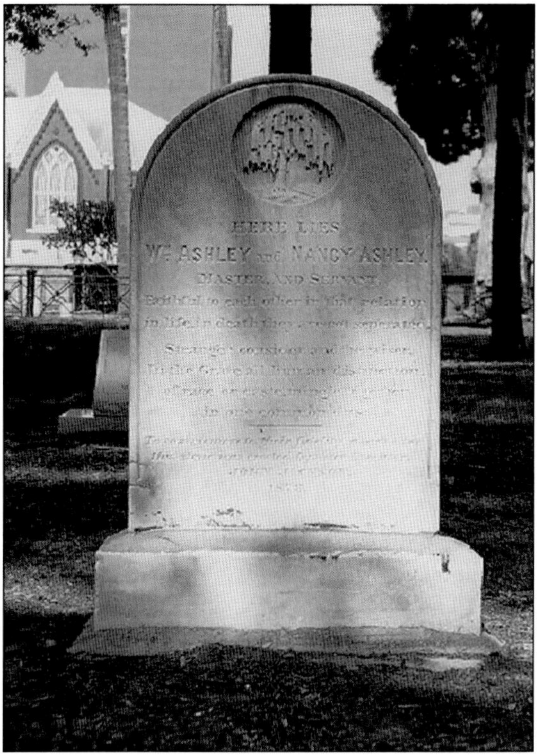

William T. Ashley's famous gravestone is perhaps the most talked about in Oaklawn Cemetery. Ashley was a prominent white civic leader, serving as city clerk. Nancy, the African American servant who bore his surname, was his longtime companion and, it was presumed, his wife outside the law. Following instructions left to William's executor, John Jackson, the Ashley grave was opened to receive Nancy upon her death and, "to commemorate their fidelity in each other," a headstone was erected telling the story of the forbidden love between master and servant. Ashley Drive (below), one of Tampa's most prominent streets along the Hillsborough River, is one of the main gateways into the city. (Right, GravRdr; below, THCPL.)

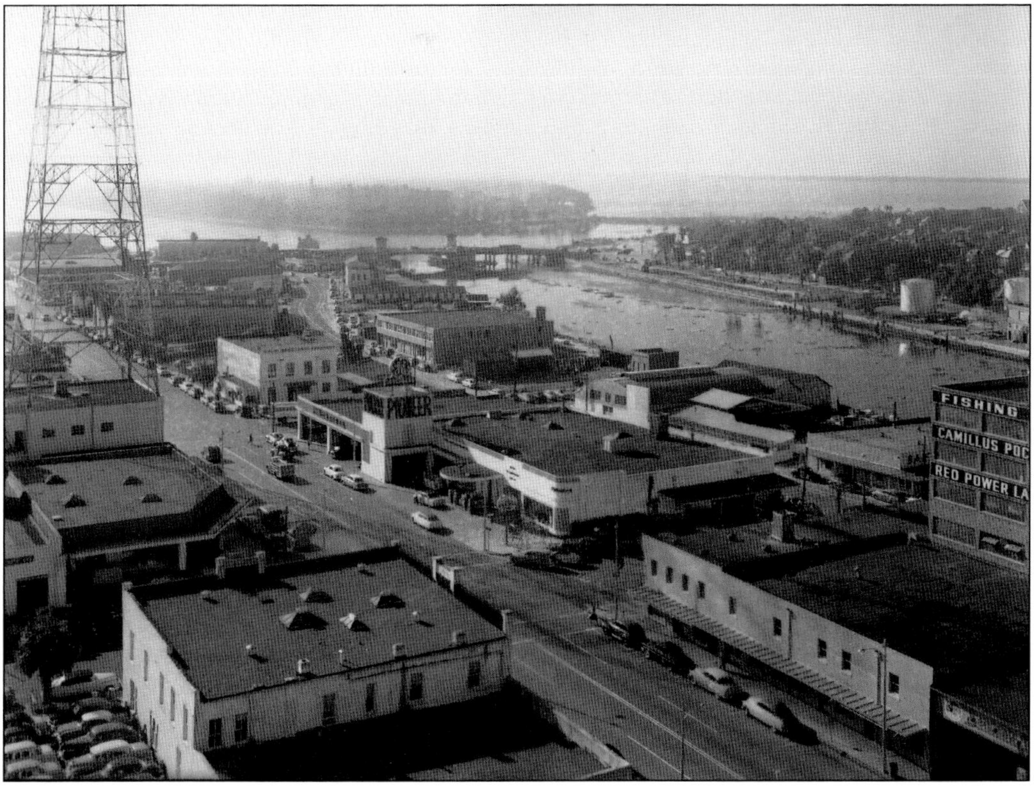

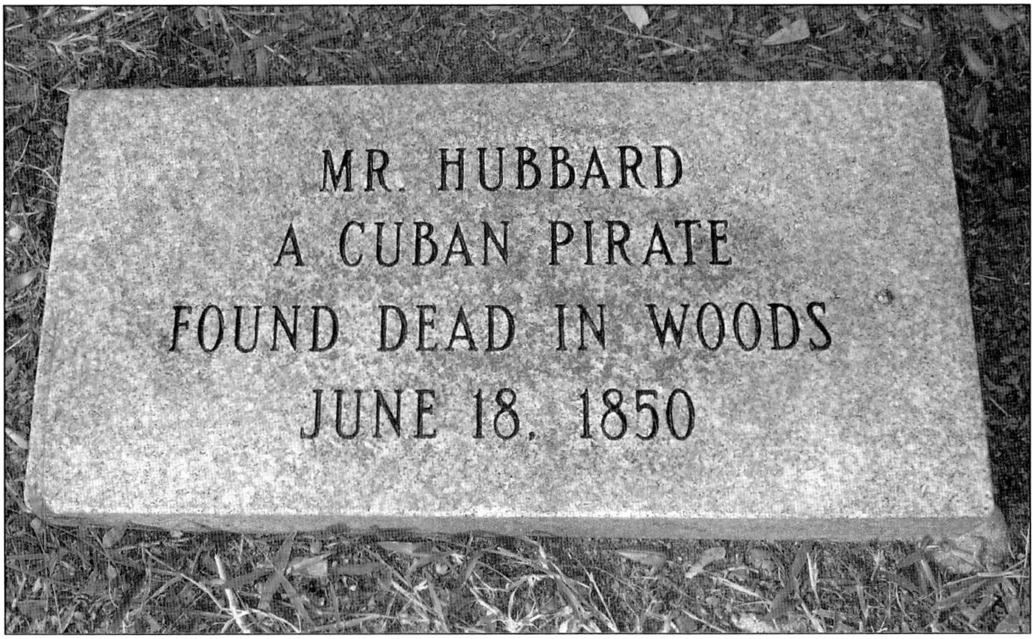

Memorial markers have been placed in Oaklawn Cemetery to remember some of the early graves that went unmarked for years. Mr. Hubbard, a Cuban pirate, was found dead in the woods on June 18, 1850 (above). Drowning victim Toney Davis died at Bell's Wharf on March 20, 1868 (below). A total of 88 victims of the yellow fever epidemics of 1853, 1858, 1868, 1871, and 1887 are memorialized by a marker placed by the Tampa Historical Society in 1997. The Fort Brooke mass grave contains the remains of 102 settlers and soldiers who were originally interred at the fort. During the 1987 construction of the Tampa Convention Center, the remains of American Indians who perished over 200 years ago were discovered and removed to Oaklawn. A marker honors the memory of these and all American Indians who have lived and cherished the land called Florida. The cemetery includes a strangers' section, children's lot, yellow fever alley, and an African American section.

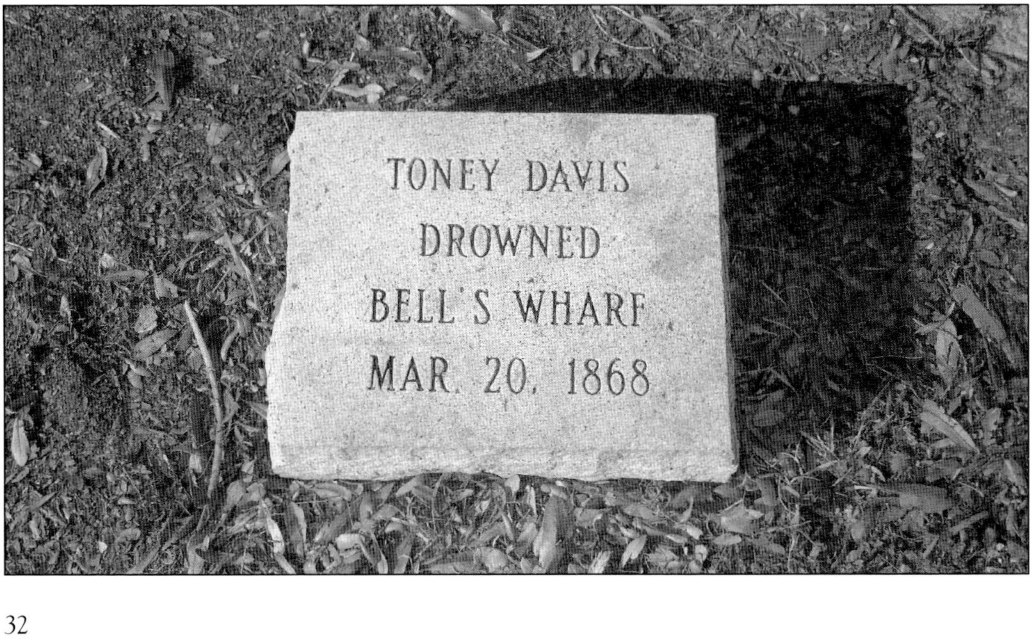

Two

Myrtle Hill and the Garden of Memories

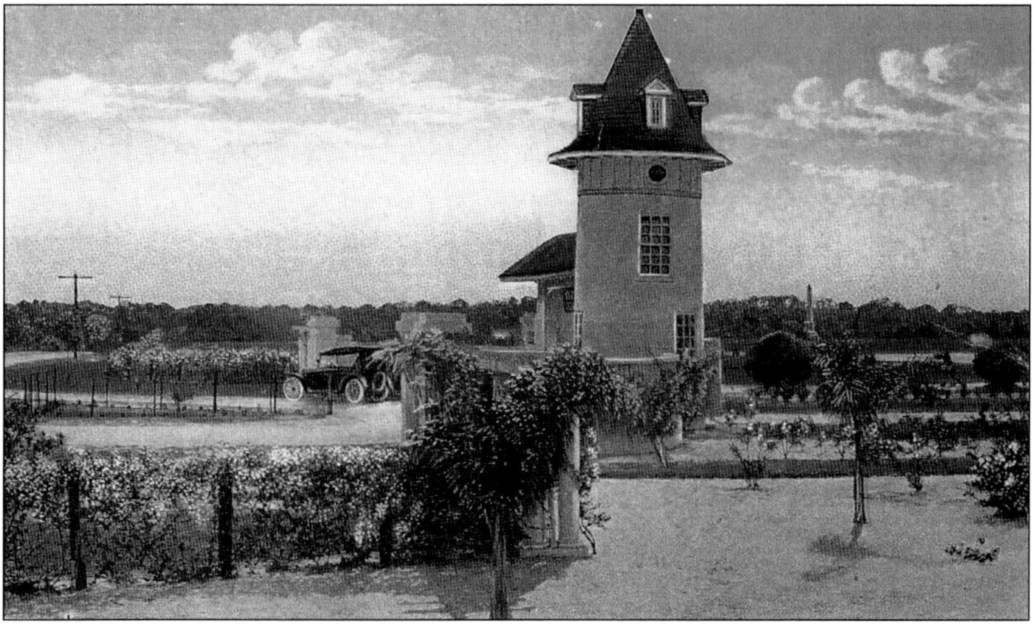

The third city cemetery was founded in 1917 by Daniel S. Wells, T.O. Wilson, and Clifton Benson. It is situated on a 105-acre tract of land north of Martin Luther King Jr. Boulevard. An early postcard of the gated entrance to Myrtle Hill Cemetery shows a tower house that was perhaps used as the sexton's facility. (TBHC.)

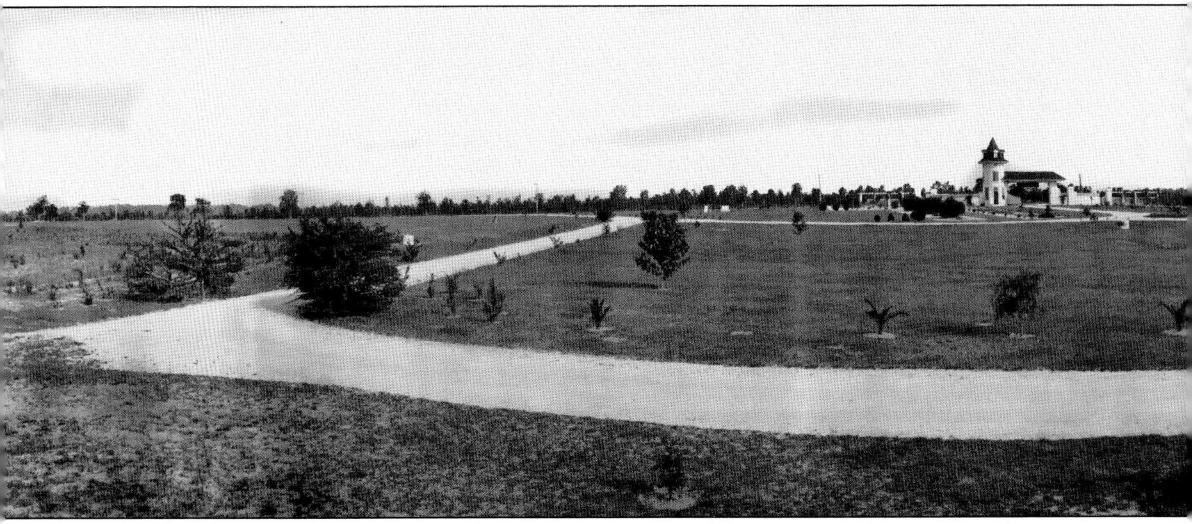

This Burgert Brothers Cirkut photograph of Myrtle Hill Cemetery, taken on April 13, 1921, shows its early covered roof entryway with the circular drive layout. The lush and well-landscaped trellis wall entry greeted mourners and visitors. Many of the massive and stately oaks and palms shading the graves today were planted during these early years. Also within the cemetery is a Catholic section begun in 1926 when the nearby Catholic church closed its cemetery in Tampa

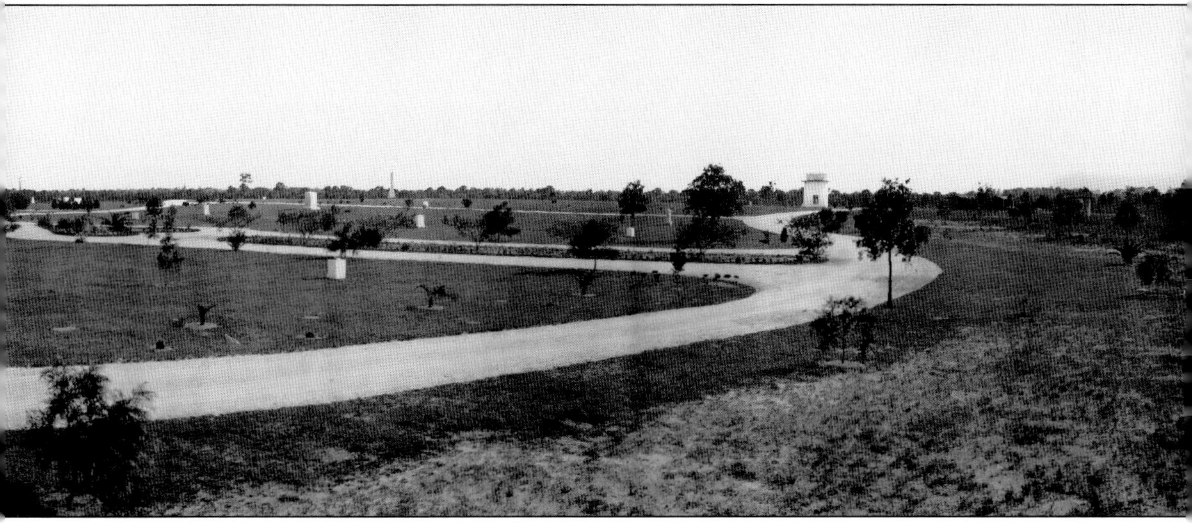

and transferred approximately 100 burials to Myrtle Hill. In 1932, the cemetery featured a garden mausoleum. A chapel area was later constructed in the early 1960s. Today, Myrtle Hill includes the burial sites of many of Tampa's prominent citizens. At one time, Tampa businessmen A.C. Clewis and George B. Howell owned Myrtle Hill Cemetery. It is said that Clewis was dissatisfied with the unkempt condition of the cemetery and purchased it at a sheriff's tax sale. (THCPL.)

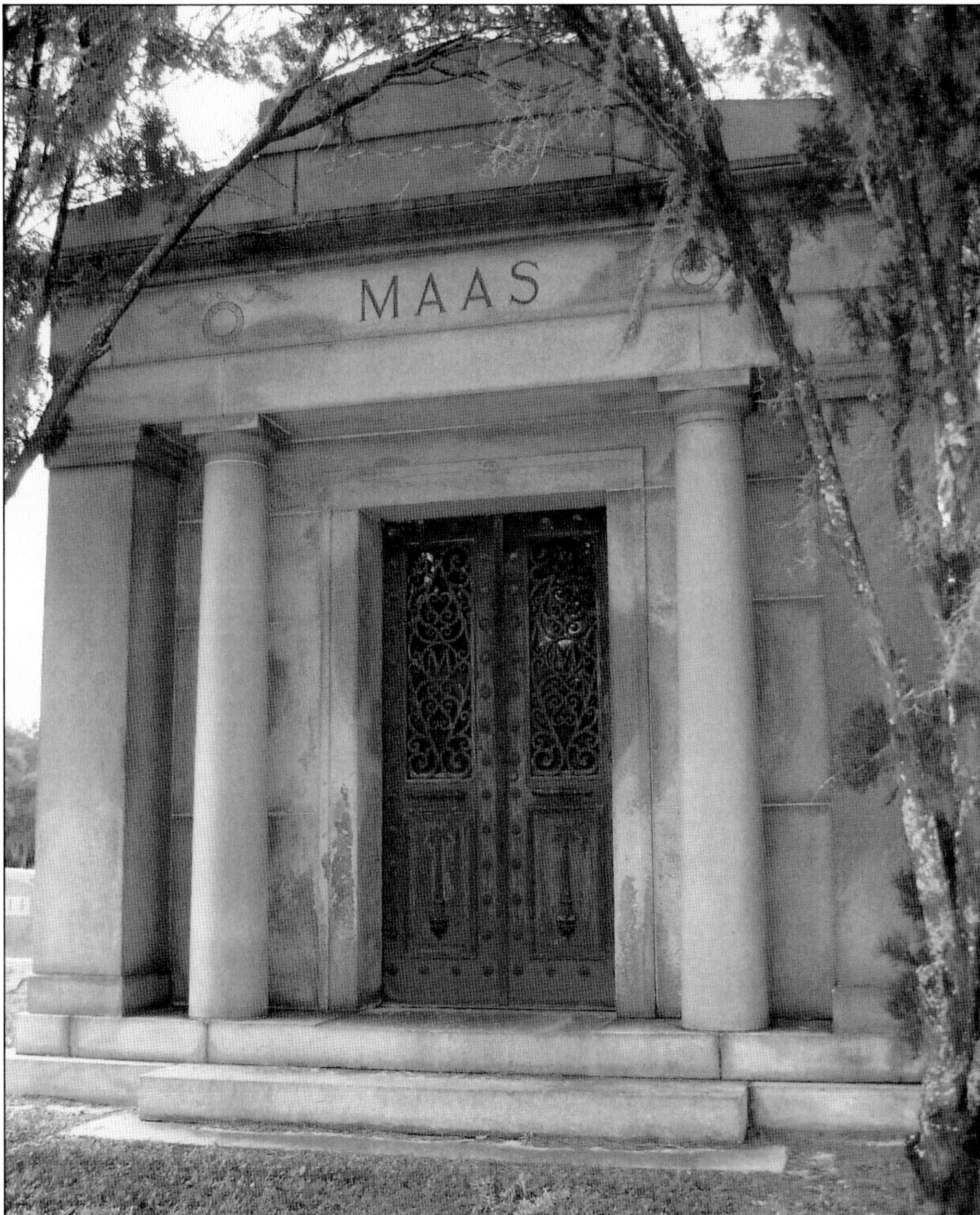

Ten years after arriving in the United States in 1875, Abe Maas set out to find a new location for a store. After visiting several towns in Florida, he decided to start his business in Tampa. Returning to Tampa on December 1, 1886, he opened, The Dry Goods Palace on the ground floor of the J.C. Field Building. The store officially opened on December 10, 1886. His brother Isaac, who had been running a millinery store in Ocala, joined Abe on September 15, 1887, and the store became known as Maas Brothers. The small store was successful and by 1898 had outgrown its space. It moved into the Krause Building, occupying the first floor. In 1907, Maas Brothers was incorporated and Abe was named president. He held this position until 1935, when he was elevated to chairman after the death of Isaac.

Abe Maas (right) was born on May 28, 1855, in Dolgesheim, Germany, and immigrated in 1875 to Georgia, where he ran a store in Dublin for his brother Sol. While in Dublin, he traveled to Cincinnati to marry his childhood sweetheart, Bena Wolf, on September 19, 1883. They had one child, Sol Maas. A tireless community worker, Bena Wolf Maas served 25 years as president of The Children's Home. Throughout the 20th century, The Children's Home was Tampa's most popular charity. Abe was president of Maas Brothers and Maas Realty Company and director of Morris Plan Bank of Tampa, Thompson Cigar Company, and Old People's Home. He was a member of the Board of Trade, Elk's Lodge, Hillsborough Masonic Lodge, Knights of Pythias, and Kiwanis and was past president of the Jewish congregation Schaarai Zedek. After leaving the store on Friday evening, June 6, 1941, feeling fine, he attended the high school graduation of his grandson. Later at home, Maas became very ill, and as the evening progressed his condition worsened. His death came at two o'clock, Saturday morning, June 7, 1941. The c. 1906 photograph of the Maas Brothers store (below) shows men and women dressed in their finest attire. (THCPL.)

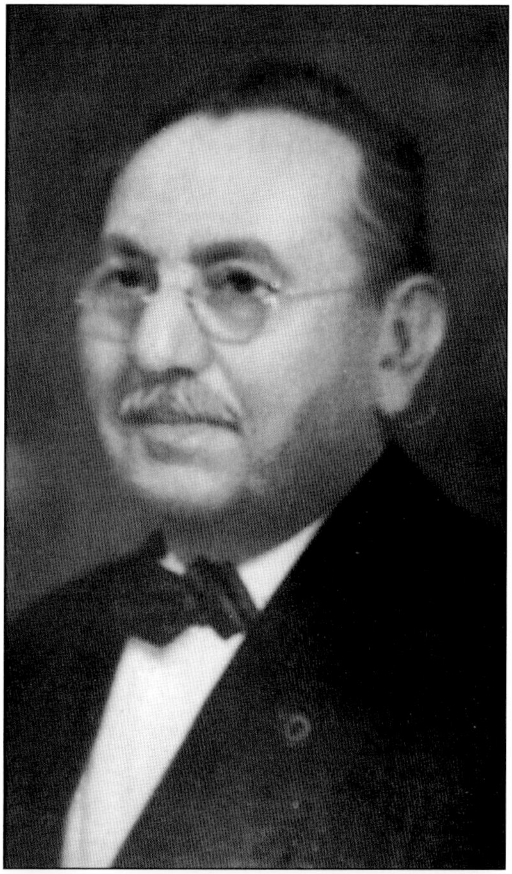

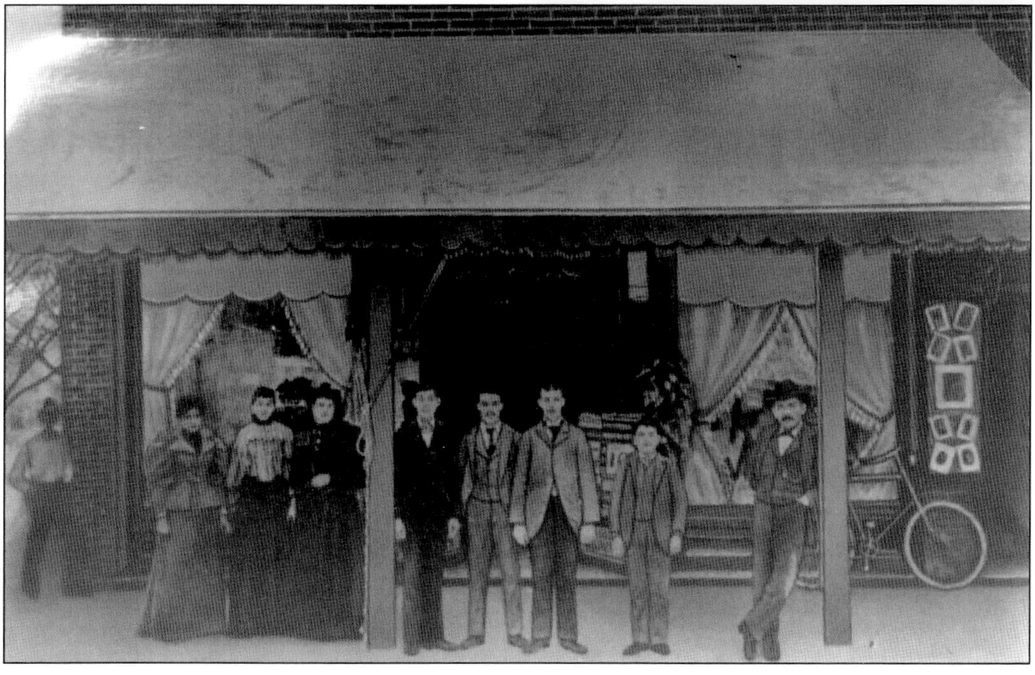

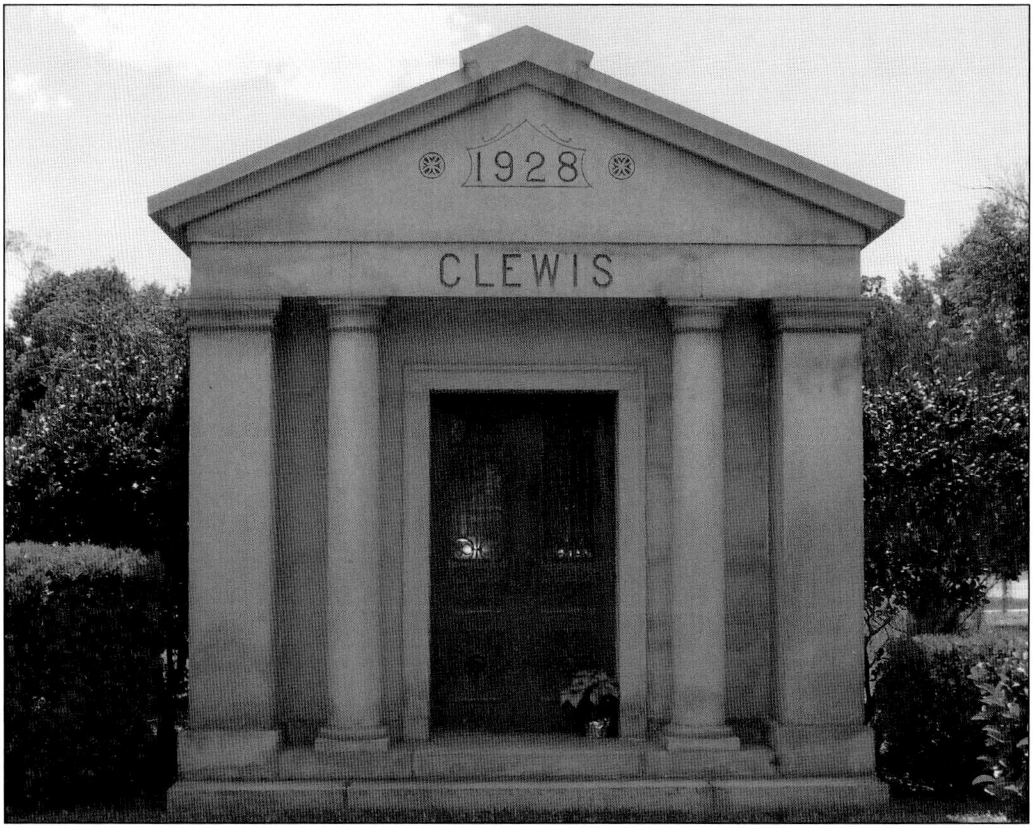

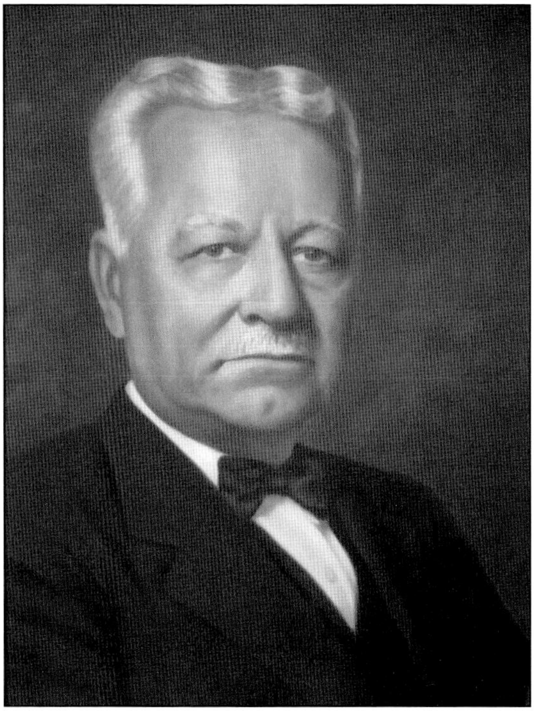

Alonzo Charles Clewis (left) was born on Christmas Day 1864 in Dooley County, Georgia. After the death of his parents, Richard Clewis and Jane Roberts, in 1876 and 1874 respectively, Clewis was raised by an older brother on the family farm and received his meager education in local schools. In 1885, at age 21, he started his business career in nearby Snow Springs, where he opened a modest dry-goods store. Quickly growing restless, he sold the store and made his first venture into Florida that same year. Moving to Tallahassee, he opened a general store. Clewis spent 1888 in Tampa employed by the Hillsborough Loan & Abstract Company. The year closed with a wedding to Amelia Munro, daughter of Robert and Rachel Munro, in Tallahassee. The Clewises had six children, but only Mary Trice and her brother Alonzo Charles Clewis Jr. survived past childhood. (Left, TBHC.)

Mary Trice Clewis (right) was born on February 23, 1898. Called "Princess" by her father, she attended local schools and the Fairmont Finishing School in Virginia. In 1921, she was selected as Queen of Gasparilla and met a gentleman lawyer from New York named George Blaine Howell. They exchanged wedding vows on February 2, 1922. The Clewis family's beautiful Bayshore Boulevard home (below) was completed in 1921. Mary's mother, Amelia Munro Clewis, died on March 15, 1933, and her father, Alonzo Charles Clewis, died at his home on February 16, 1944. He was a member of the Episcopal Church, Tampa Yacht and Country Club, and the Knights of Pythias, and was a Royal Arch Mason and an Odd Fellow. (Right, HBPMA; below, TBHC.)

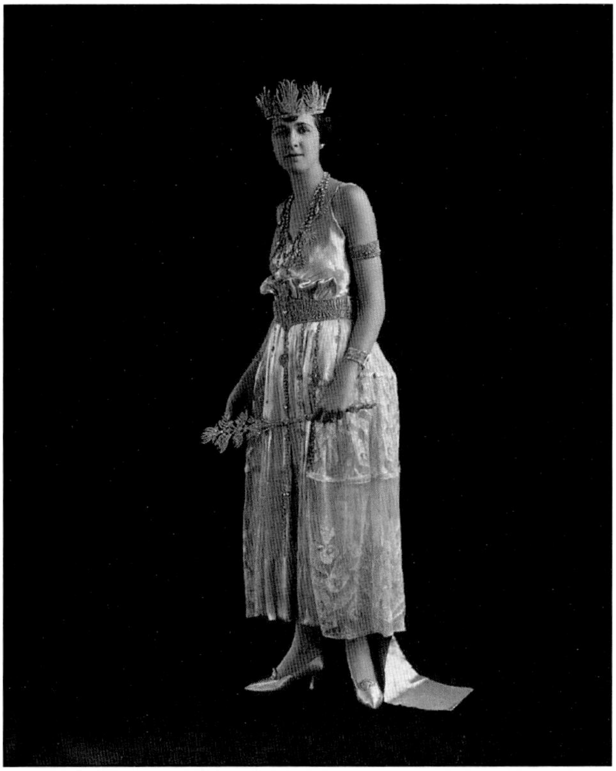

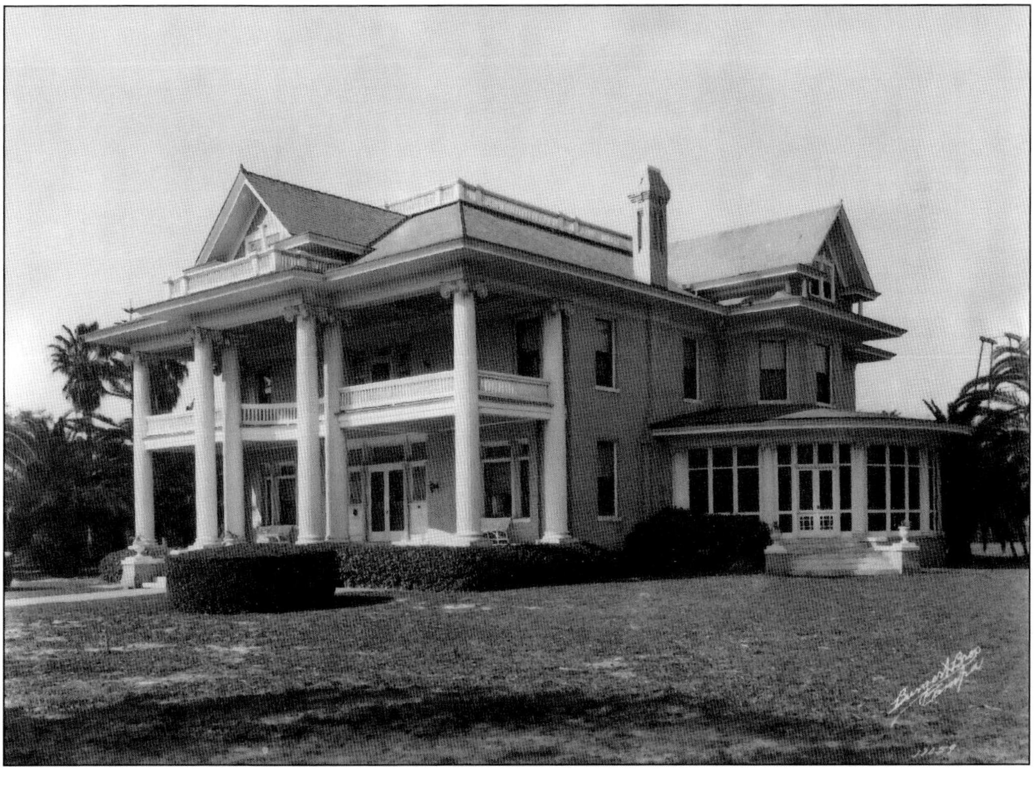

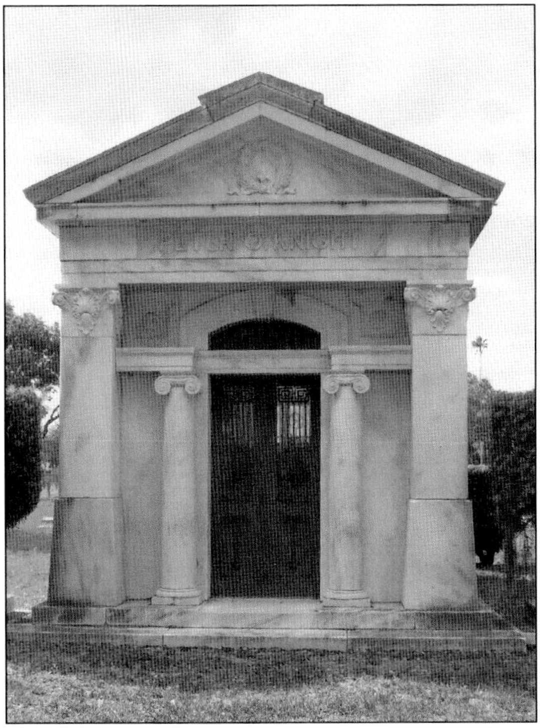

Peter Oliphant Knight was born in Freeburg, Pennsylvania, on December 16, 1865, to James W. and Sarah Elizabeth Kantz. He graduated from Valparaiso University in 1884 with an LLB degree. Moving to Fort Myers, Florida, he took a leading part in the creation of Lee County and was elected Fort Myers's mayor before he was 21. In 1888, he was elected to the state legislature and later moving to Tampa, he served as solicitor of Hillsborough County, as state attorney, and president of Tampa Electric Company. He was married to Lillie Frierson, of Sumter, South Carolina, who died in 1941. Peter O. Knight Airport's administration building was a Works Progress Administration (WPA) project in the Depression years. The aviation facility offered passenger service near downtown Tampa. It is now a privately owned executive airport. The photograph below offers an aerial view of Peter O. Knight Airport and Sheddon Channel. (THCPL.)

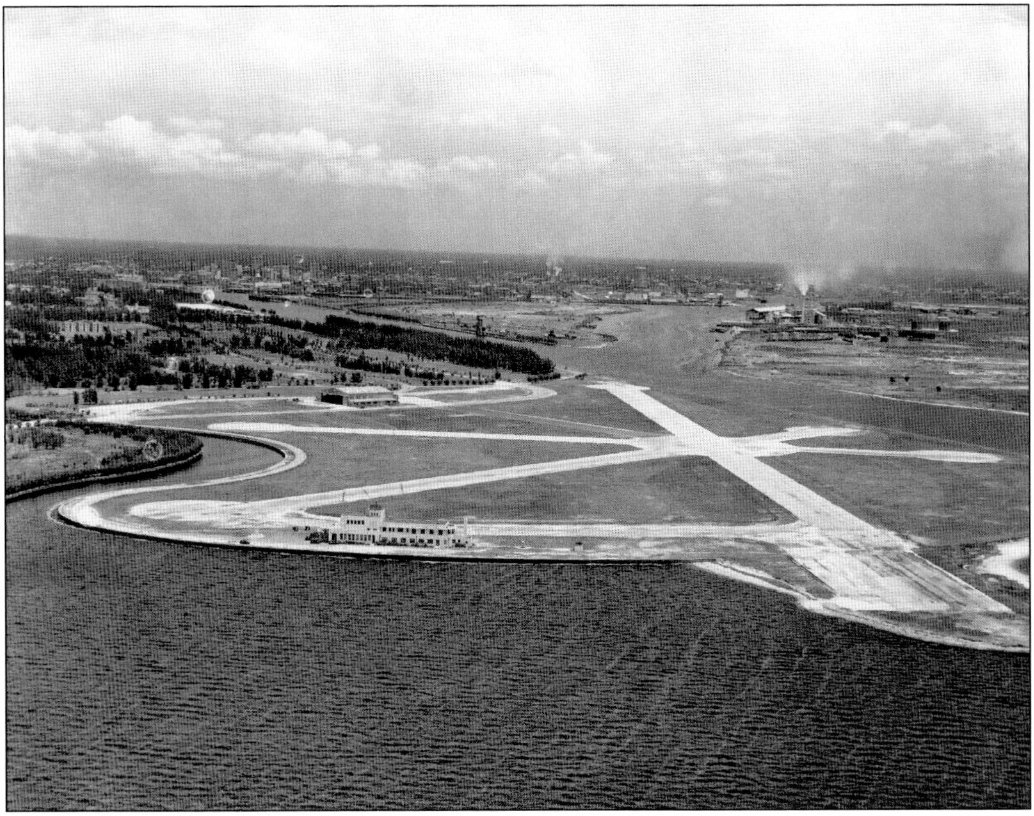

Peter O. (Oliphant) Knight's father, James, was also a prominent lawyer. Two of Peter's paternal ancestors took part in the Revolutionary War. His great-grandfather, John Conrad Knight, of Snyder County, Pennsylvania, volunteered for service in the Continental Army during the early years of the conflict. As a nine-year-old, Richard, Peter's grandfather, went with his father, later becoming a drummer boy. They spent the winter at Valley Forge with General Washington. In the War of 1812, Richard Knight was captain of Knight's Company, First Regiment, Pennsylvania Militia, with Col. Maxwell Kennedy commanding. Peter, at right, followed in his ancestor's footsteps, providing many years of public service. He was a member of the Sons of the American Revolution, serving as the first president of the Tampa chapter, the Military Order of Foreign Wars, and the Patriotic Order of the Sons of America. Below is one of the stained-glass windows from the Peter O. Knight Mausoleum.

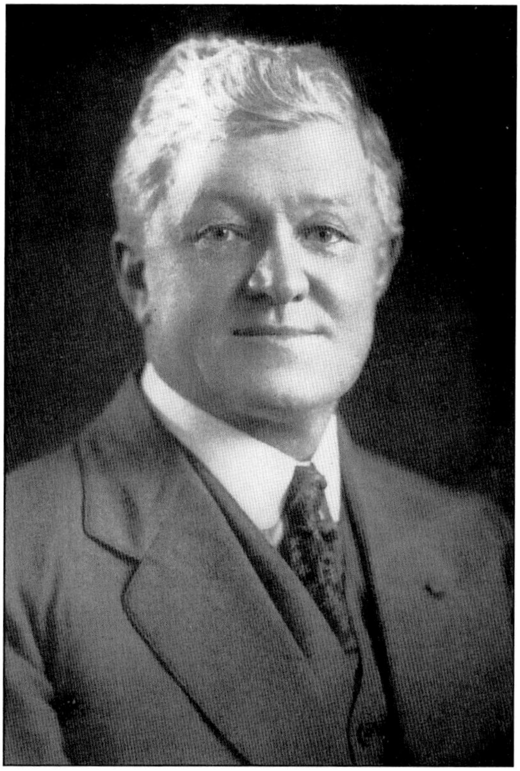

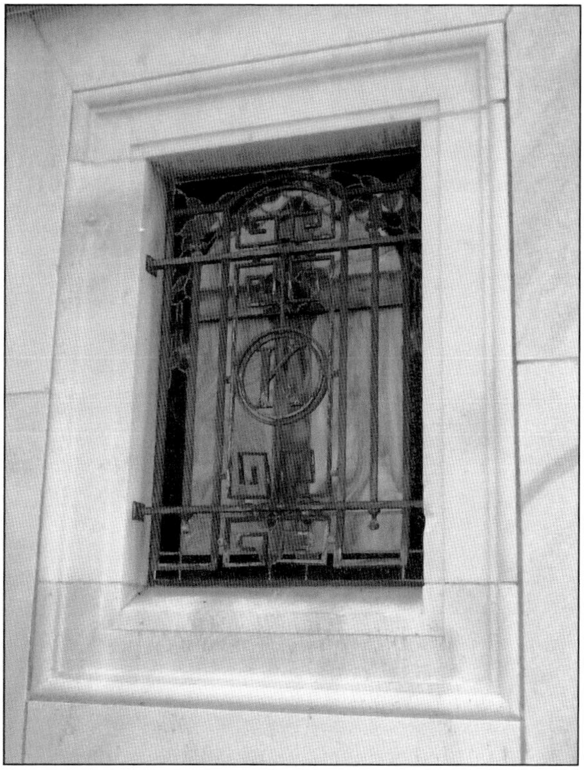

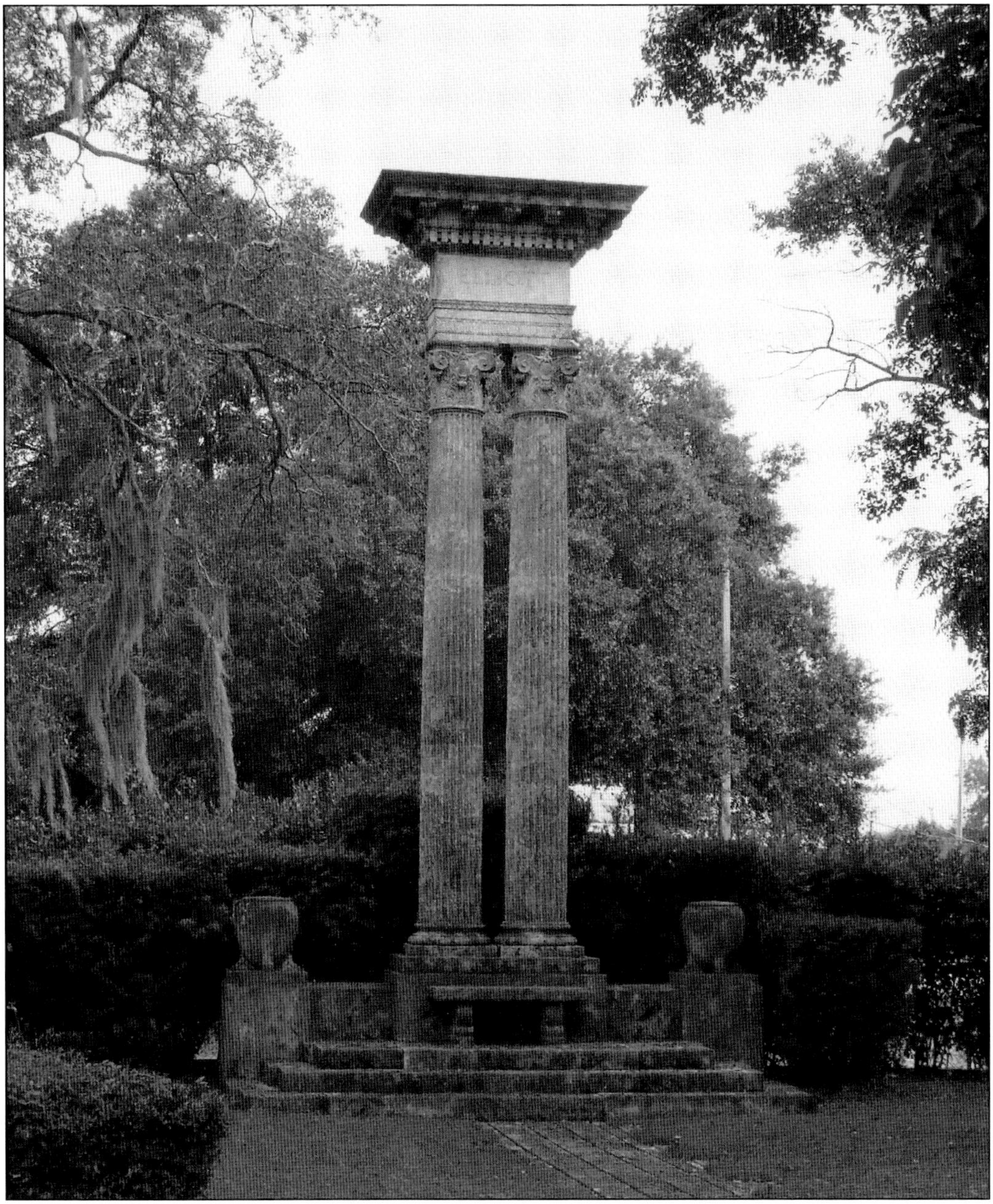

The large Corinthian columns at the M. Leo Elliott family plot are a testament to his lifelong devotion to the built environment. The Corinthian order is one of three principal classical orders of ancient Greek and Roman architecture. Within the Elliott family plot are the gravesites of M. Leo Elliott Sr., M. Leo Elliott Jr., Shelia Elliott Cummins, and Beth Thompson Elliott. Elliott was the dean of architects in Florida and was active in having the Architects' License Law passed by the state legislature in 1915. He held Architect's Registration Certificate No. 5 and was a member of the American Institute of Architects. His buildings, examples of Gothic Revival and mid-century modern architecture, include Tampa's City Hall, the Masonic Lodge, the entrance gates to the City of Temple Terrace, and Temple Terrace Golf and Country Club. Florida's state capitol building expansion during the WPA era benefited from his architectural plans.

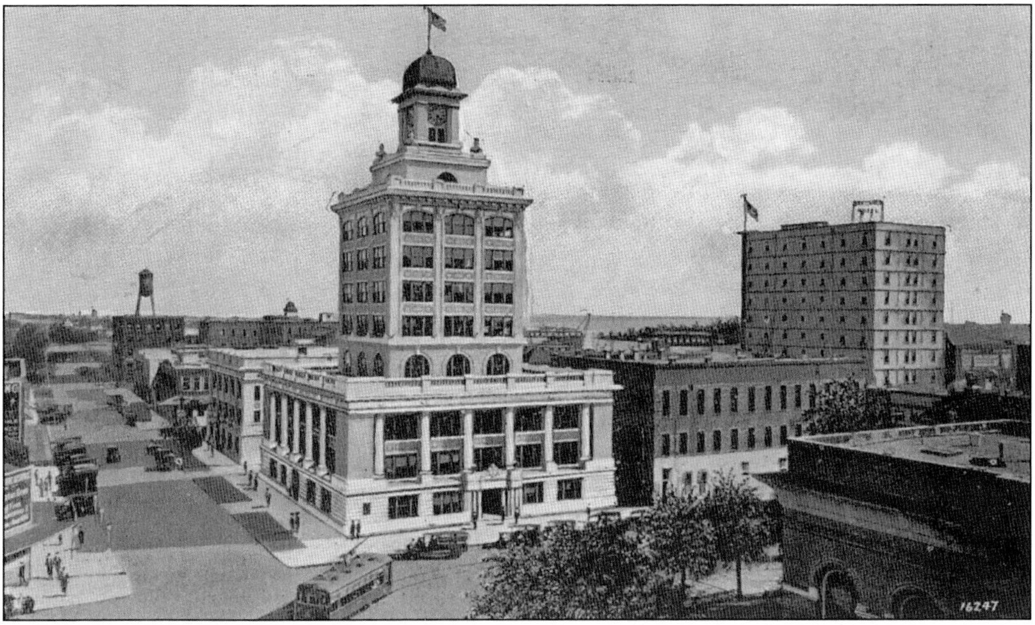

A 1951 family reunion photograph (below) was taken in the front parlor of the home of James W. Elliott at 2607 Fifty-ninth Street. M. Leo Elliott came to Tampa from Woodstock, New York. On October 26, 1910, he married Beth Thompson, daughter of N.O. and Mary Coe Thompson, and they later had two children: Shelia and M. Leo Jr. Elliott's first work in Tampa was the preparation of competitive designs for the Centro Asturiano Club and YMCA buildings. Both designs won first place, and on September 2, 1907, the partnership of Bonfoey & Elliott, Architects was formed. One of its first important commissions was the Tampa City Hall (above). Their partnership was dissolved at the start of World War I. Elliott was one of Tampa's premier architects. (Below, THCPLS.)

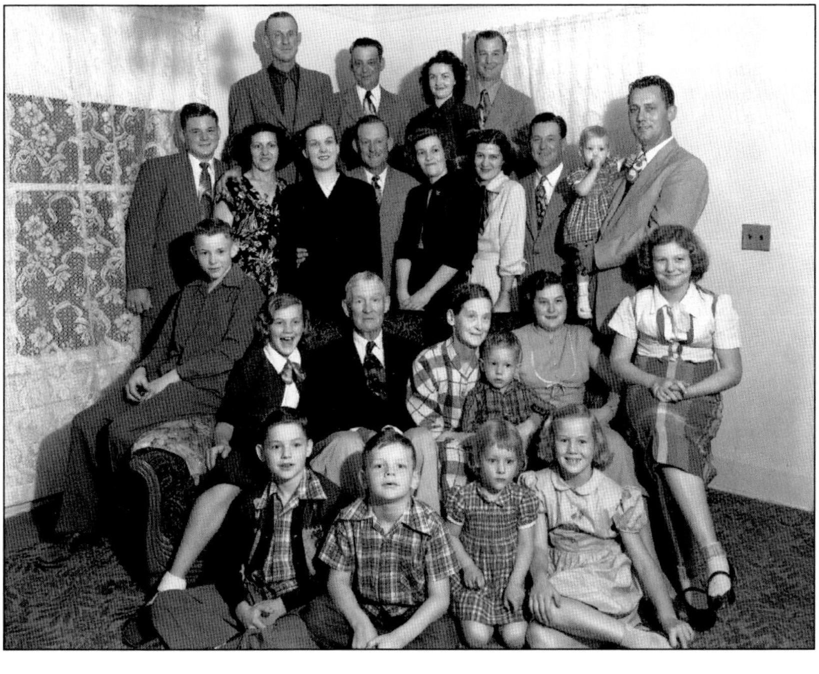

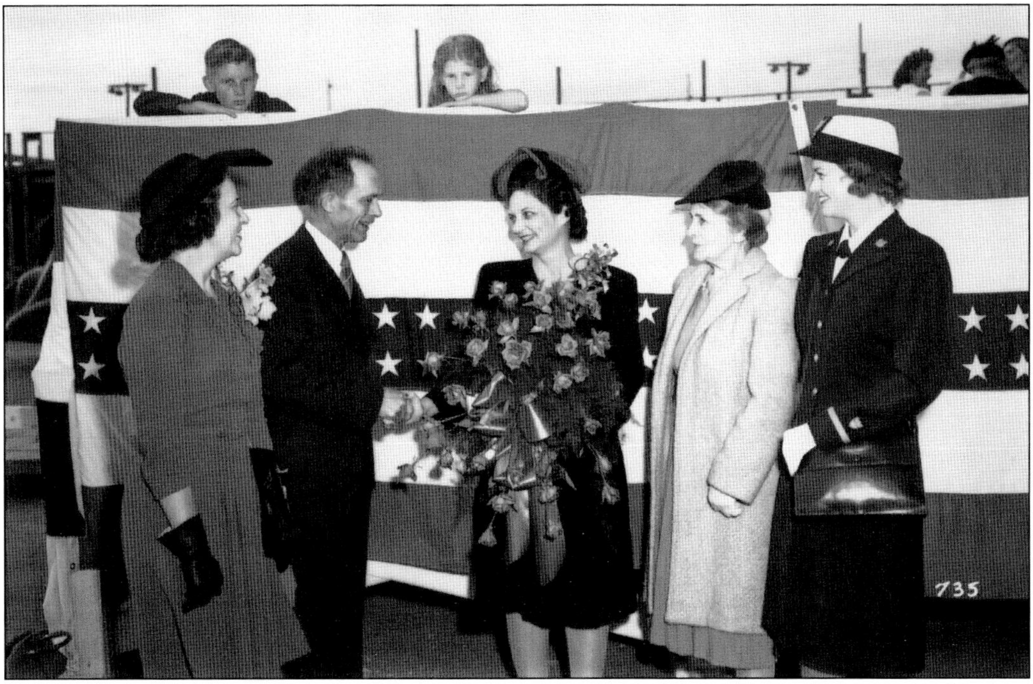

Mayor and Mrs. Curtis Hixon (left) greet dignitaries at a ship launching. Curtis Samuel Hixon was born in Louisville, Alabama, on November 23, 1891. He came to Tampa in 1911, joining his brother Marvin in operating pharmacies. He married Lila Yantis in 1926. He was elected as an alderman in 1929 and 1933 and to the Hillsborough County Commission in 1939 and served three terms as Tampa's 41st mayor from 1943 to 1956. Hixon took an active role in drafting the street plans for the Sulphur Springs area. Drew Field (Tampa International Airport) was deactivated as an army airfield and transferred to the city on October 15, 1947. On May 11, 1956, Mayor Hixon was hospitalized for pneumonia and, 10 days later, passed away of heart failure. In recognition of his dedication, an auditorium and convention center were named in his honor. Lila Yantis Hixon died on May 25, 1991. (Above, THCPLS; below, Cheryl Behrend.)

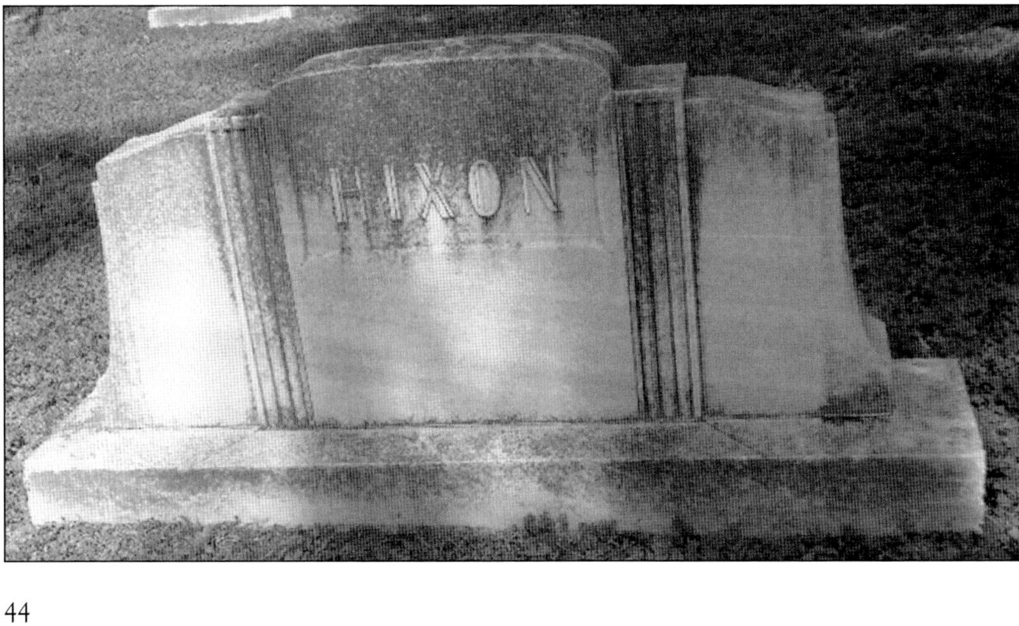

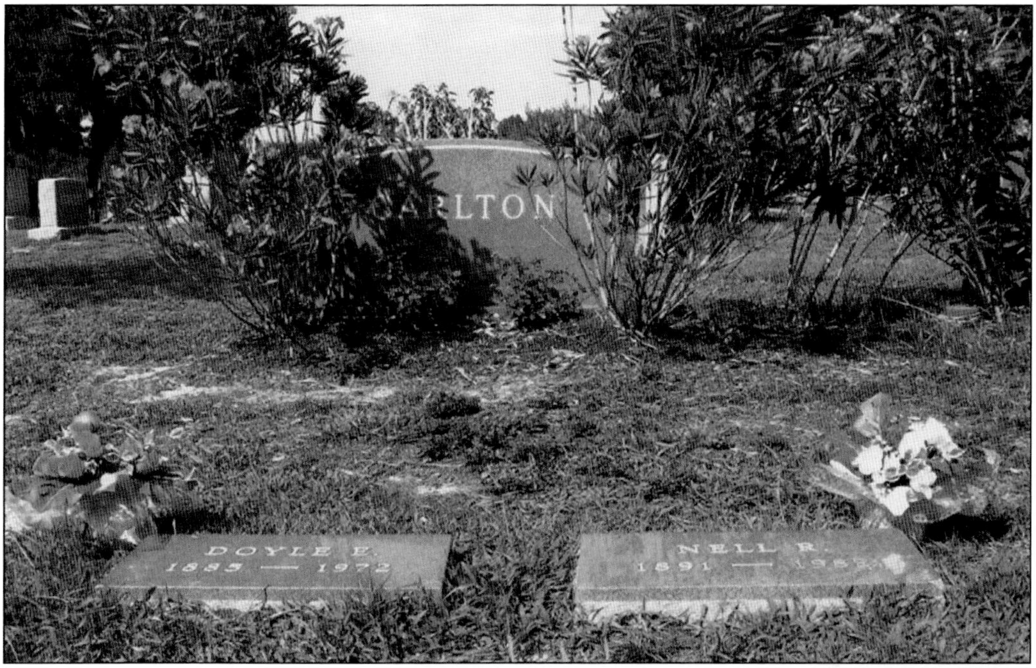

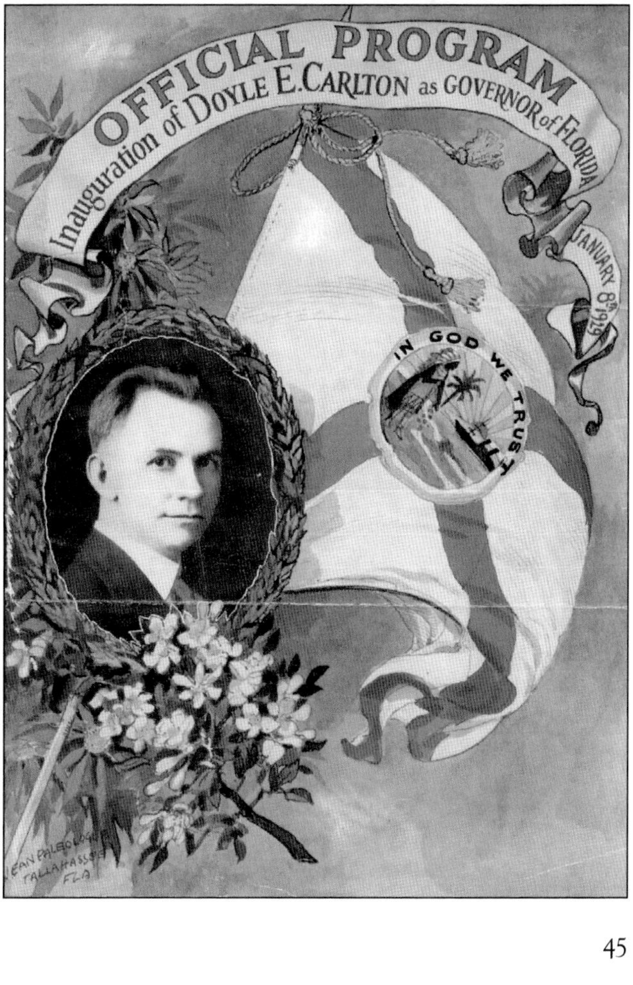

Gov. Doyle Elam Carlton (right) was born to true Florida pioneers, Martha W. McEwen and Albert Carlton, in a rural area west of Wauchula, which is now located in Hardee County. His grandfather, Lt. Alderman Carlton, was a Florida hero, having been killed while fighting in the Second Seminole War. Carlton graduated from Columbia University in the early part of 1912 and married Mississippi belle Nell Ray on July 30, 1912. Elected as Florida's governor in 1928, he served until 1933. When his term ended, he resumed his practice with the Tampa firm of Mabry, Reaves & Carlton. Carlton died on October 25, 1972. (Above, Donna Maines; right, TBHC.)

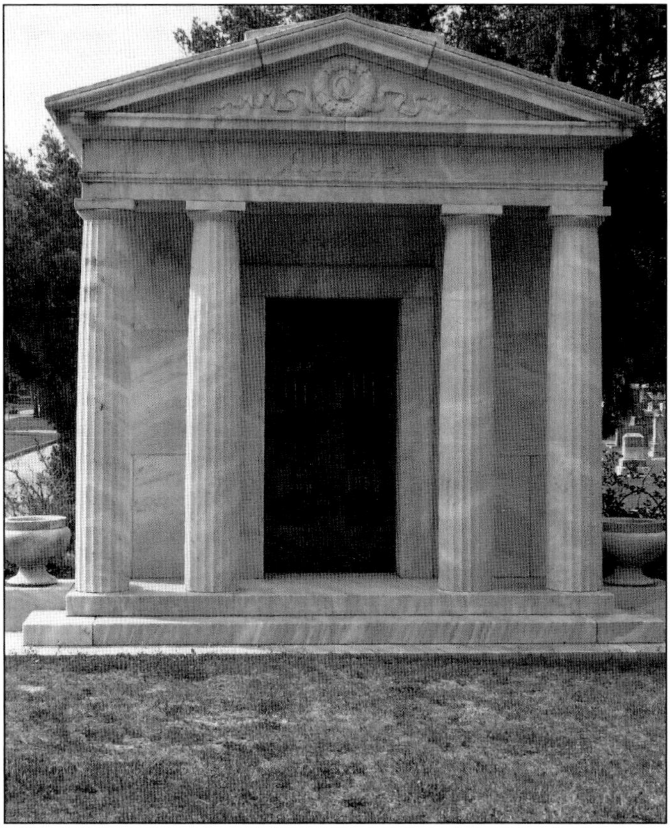

Angel LaMadrid Cuesta was born in Asturias, Spain, on December 21, 1858. After arriving in Tampa in 1893, he established a small cigar-making plant at Port Tampa. In 1896, he and Peregrino Rey organized Cuesta-Rey & Company and located their plant in West Tampa. Cuesta-Rey (originally La flor de Cuesta-Rey, which is still printed on the box) is a brand of handmade cigar. Cuesta had apprenticed in cigar-making in Cuba before he met Rey. An active Rotarian, Cuesta helped organize clubs in Havana and in cities in Spain.

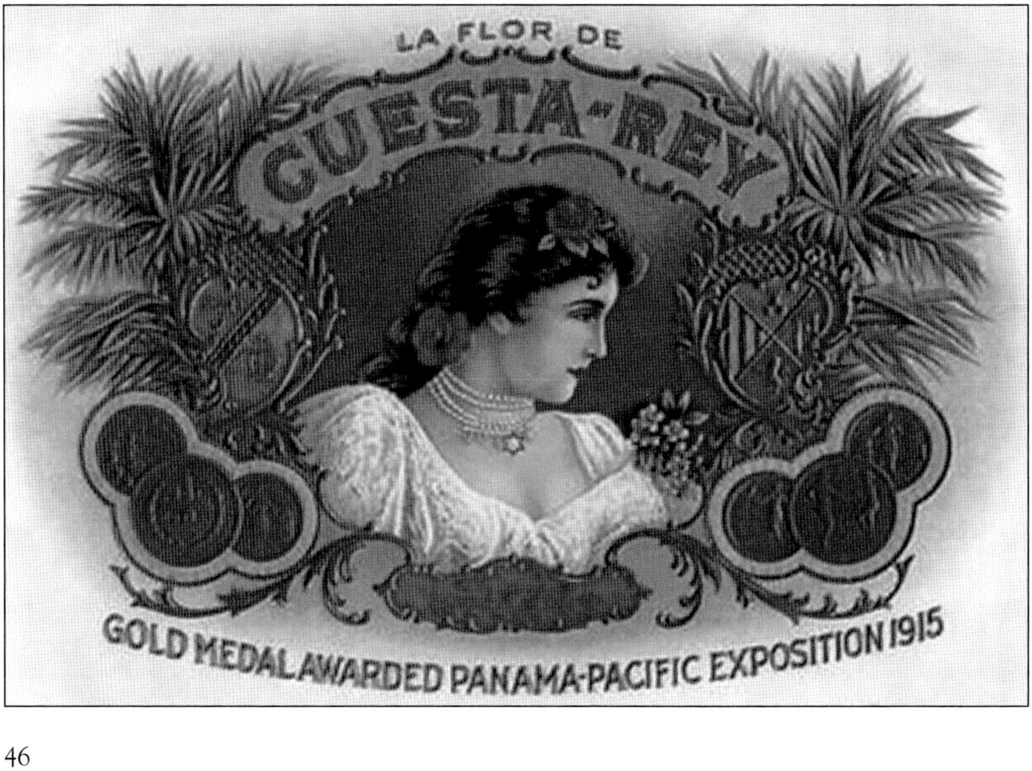

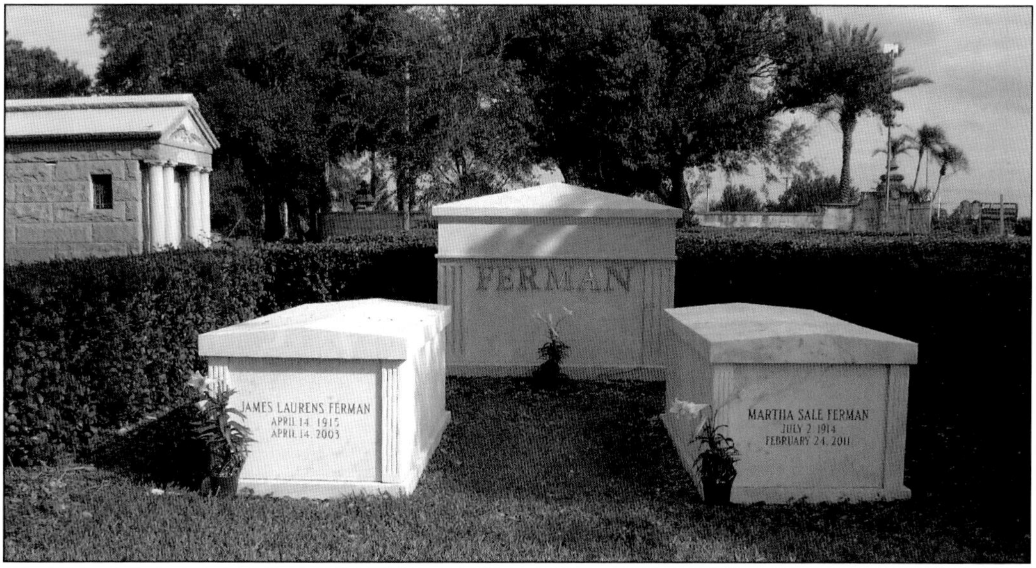

The Ferman family name is one that is widely recognized in the Tampa community. Their Ferman car dealerships have sold almost every model, make, and brand of automobile. James Laurens Ferman attended Tampa public schools and continued his higher education at Emory University. He married Martha Sale of Shellman, Georgia. To their union was born one son, James L. Ferman Jr.

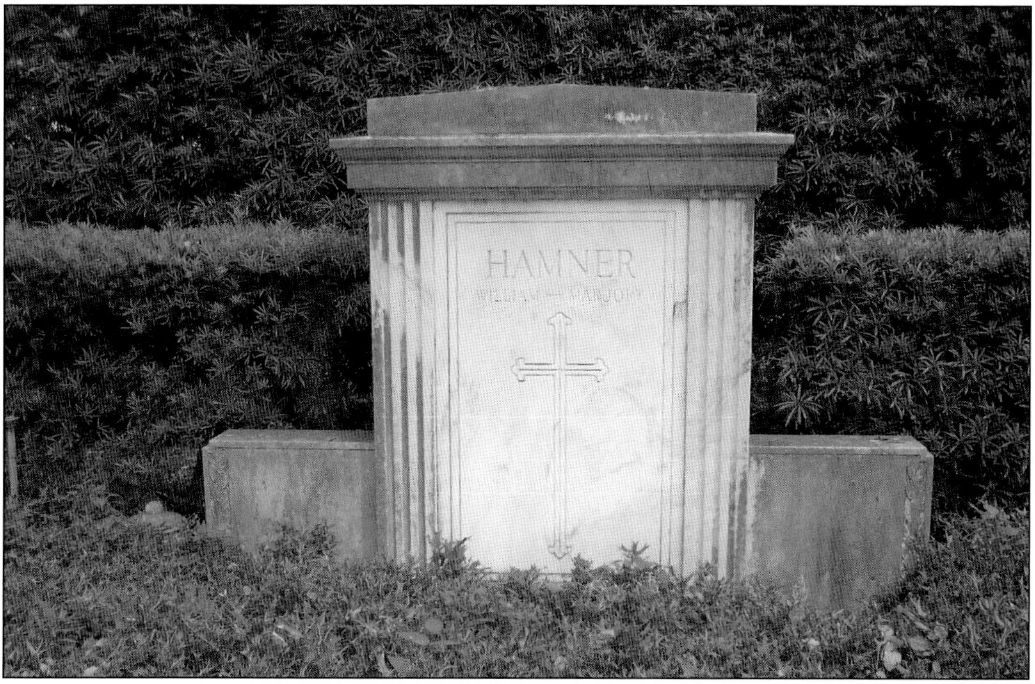

The Hamner family is closely related with the development of Temple Terrace. Having moved to the Hillsborough County area from Kansas City, Missouri, the Hamner family located to the then rural area of Valrico and were engaged in citrus growing, farming, and real estate sales, focusing primarily on rural lands. William Edward Hamner married Marjory Beckwith, daughter of William H. and Lutie Reynolds, on November 17, 1920.

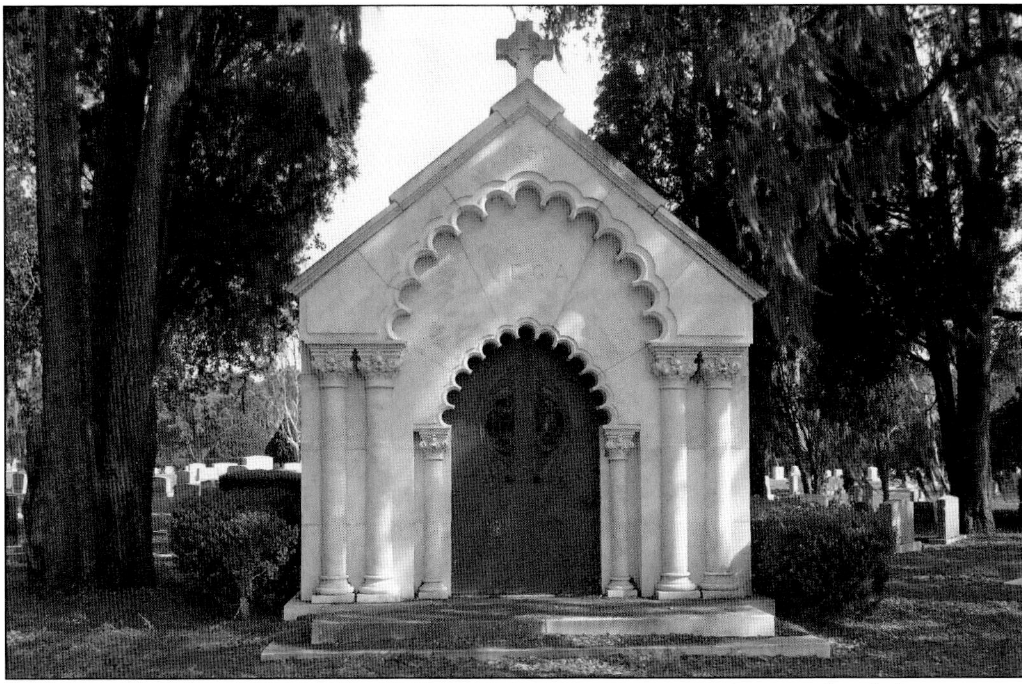

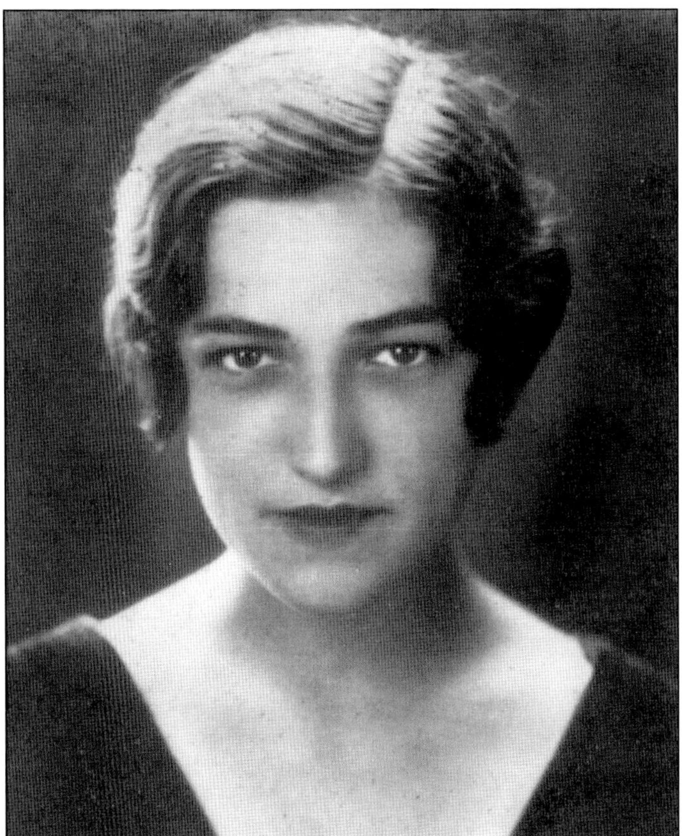

The Vega family has an outstanding record of commitment to the Tampa area, with service to many organizations, including the University of Tampa and The Children's Home. The family was one of the founders of El Centro Español de Tampa. Celestino Camilo (Milo) Vega Jr. was born in Chicago on January 22, 1905, the son of Celestino and Carolina Sanchez Vega. He received his law degree from the University of Florida in 1930. On November 18, 1933, he married Sylvia Corral (left), who was selected as Queen of Gasparilla in 1932. (HBPMA.)

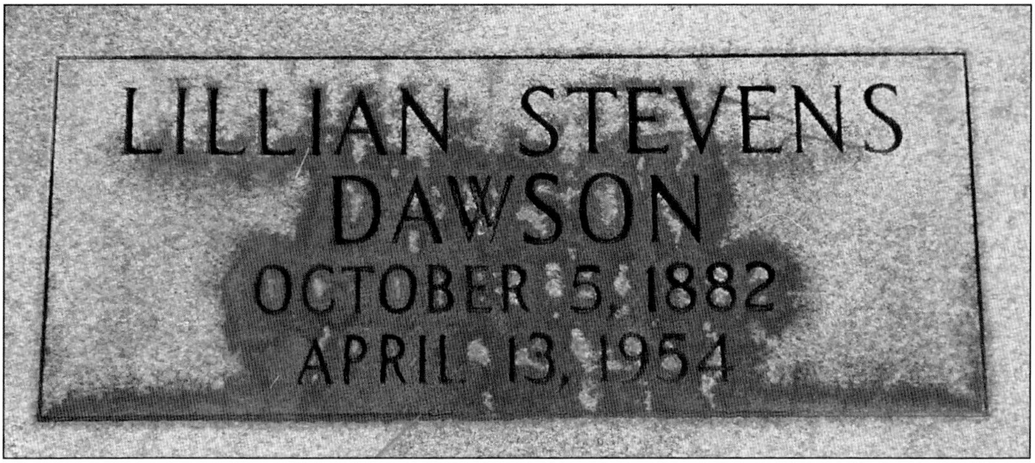

Among Tampa's greatest social affairs, the Gasparilla Debutante and Coronation Balls began in 1904 when Louise Francis Dodge, society editor of the *Tampa Tribune*, and George W. Hardee, then with the federal government in Tampa, conspired to promote the city of Tampa and its May Day celebration. Secret meetings gave birth to the first Ye Mystic Krewe of Gasparilla, whose 40 members planned to surprise the populace with a mock pirate attack on Tampa. With costumes rented from New Orleans, the first Krewe arrived on horseback and "captured the city" during the Festival Parade on May 4, 1904. Tampa has upheld this tradition by celebrating Gasparilla every year, with only 10 exceptions, since that infamous first "invasion." The 1904 Queen of Gasparilla, Mary Lee Douglas Ligat, and Maid Lillian Stevens Dawson, are buried at Myrtle Hill. (Below, THCPL.)

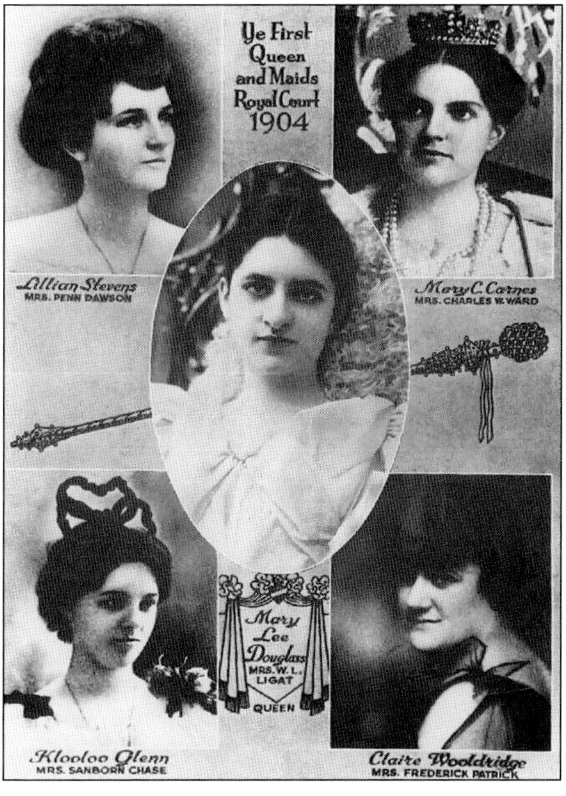

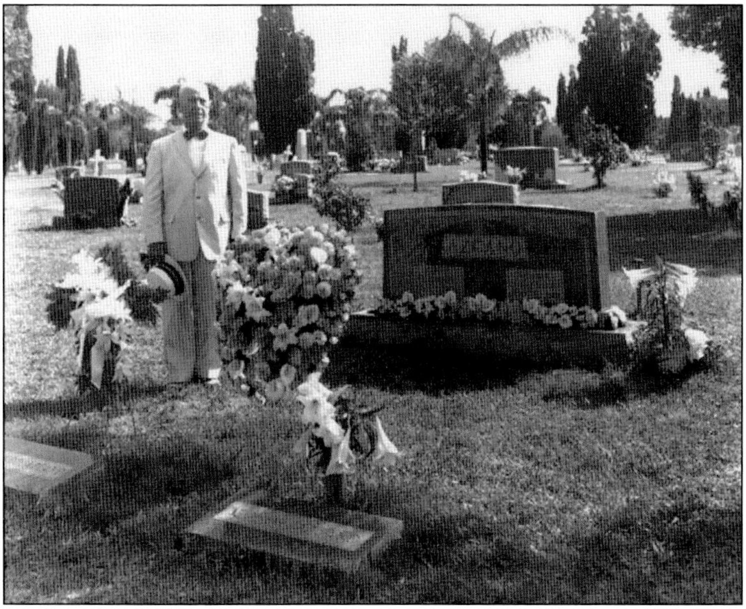

This photograph, taken on April 18, 1960, by the Burgert Brother Photography Company, shows a gentleman dressed in his finest linen suit with hat in hand. The gravestones are those of the Azcano family. Leonor died on April 3, 1959, but her husband, Servanndo, did not pass away until June 27, 1960, so perhaps this is a photograph of him visiting her grave, on Easter Sunday, just months before his passing. (THCPL.)

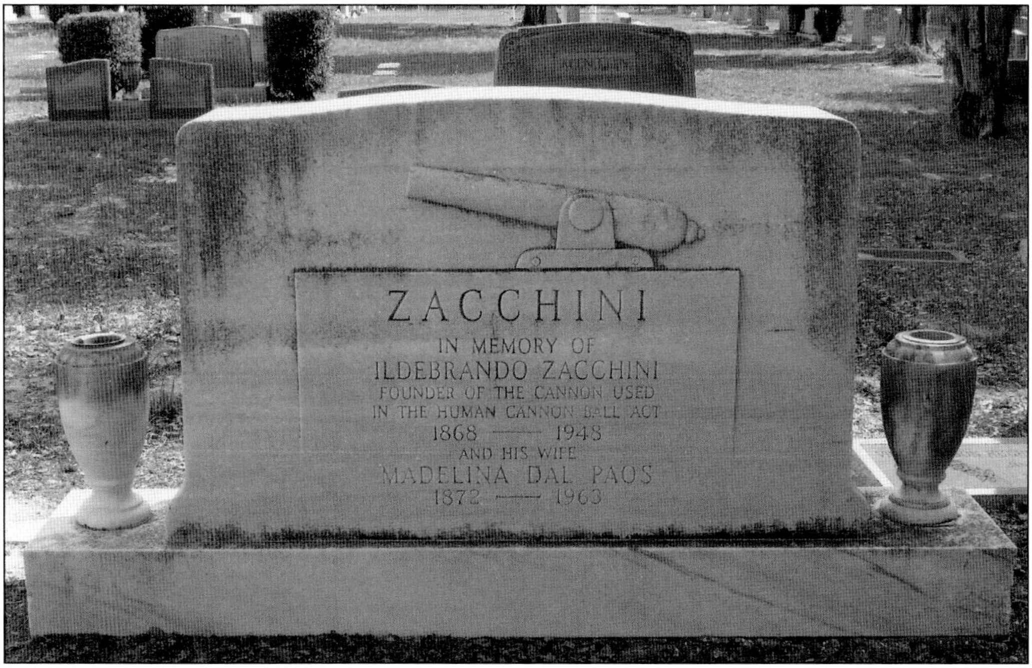

The great Ildebrando Zacchini was the inventor of the human cannonball act. He invented a cannon that used compressed air instead of explosives and shot his son Hugo out of it. Members of the Zacchini family were later inducted into the Ringling Brothers Circus Hall of Fame. Ildebrando died in 1948, and his wife, Madelina Dal Paos, passed away in 1963.

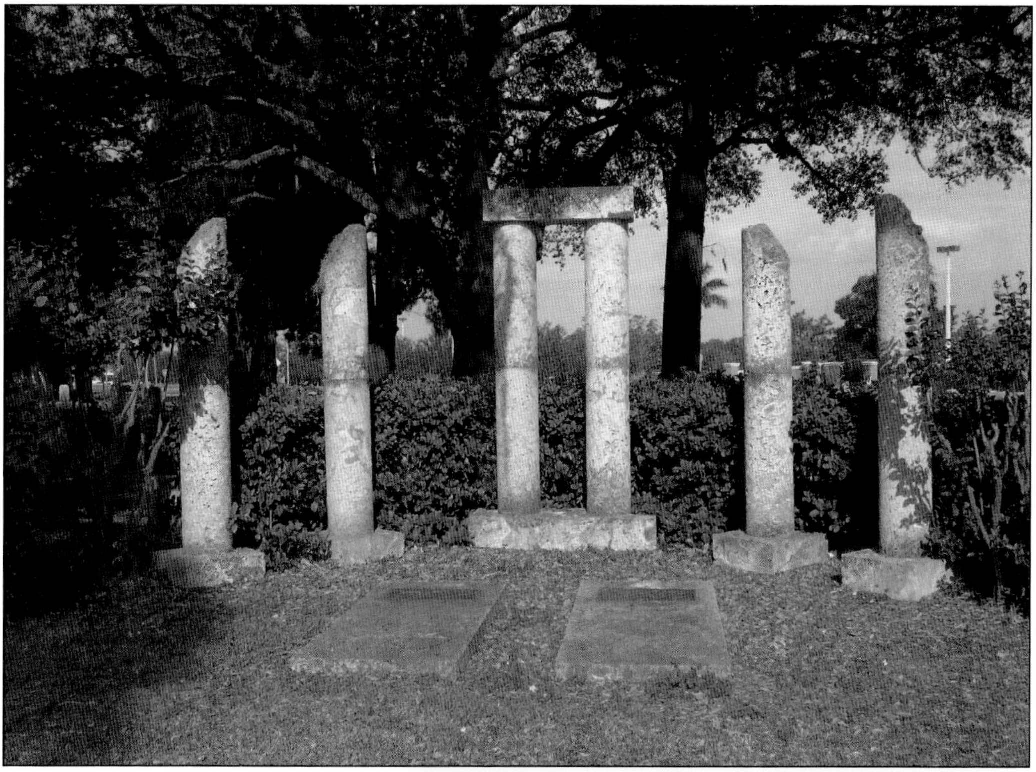

Close to the entry gates of Myrtle Hill are these tall, massive stone columns symbolizing heavenly entrance. Only the middle two columns have caps, while the others are broken, symbolizing how lives have been damaged or ended. Dr. Richard Harrod Blank and his wife, Carol Florez, were remembered as loving husband, father, wife, mother, and friend.

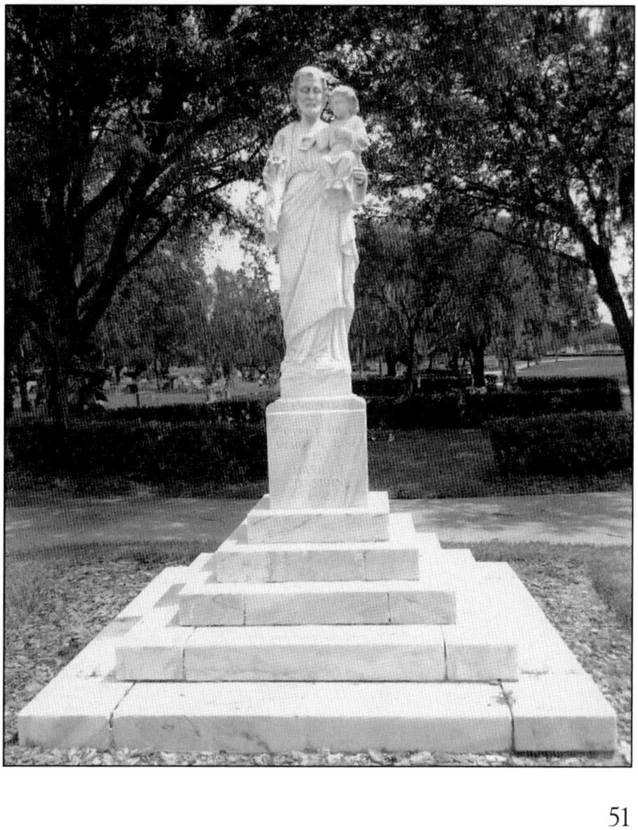

This June 17, 1957, photograph of the south entryway marked by a large memorial stone of Jesus with a child symbolizes the faith of Christians whose children had died at an early age. These parents' only comfort was in knowing that their babies were safely in the arms of Jesus in heaven as they had held them safely in their arms here on earth. (THCPL.)

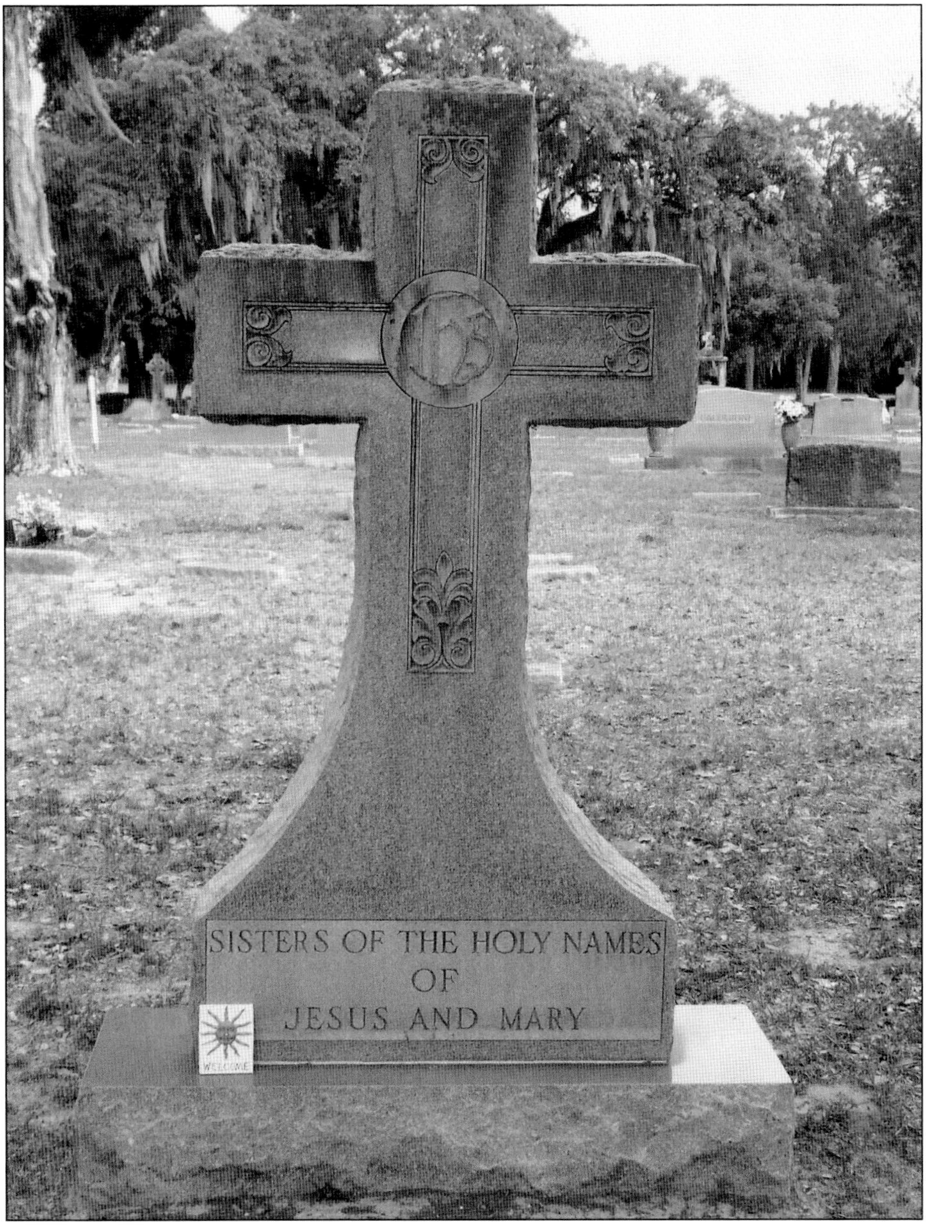

On July 17, 1881, two Sisters of the Holy Names of Jesus and Mary arrived from Key West to open a two-room schoolhouse in a blacksmith shop on Zack Street in Tampa. Initially, 35 pupils were enrolled, but by the end of the first academic year the numbers had increased to 70 day scholars and two resident students. The neighborhood of West Tampa is a treasure trove of vintage architecture, including the Academy of the Holy Names. The marker reads: "On September 14, 1896, Sisters of the Holy Names established the Academy of the Holy Names by order of Bishop John Moore. Sisters Mary Emiline and Mary Hubert were the first teachers in this brick school. By April 1889, the site of the school was moved to a two-story building at the corner of Franklin and Harrison Streets. In 1891, the late Bishop John Moore, second bishop of St. Augustine, purchased property on Twiggs Street, where a larger school, which served the community for 34 years, was built."

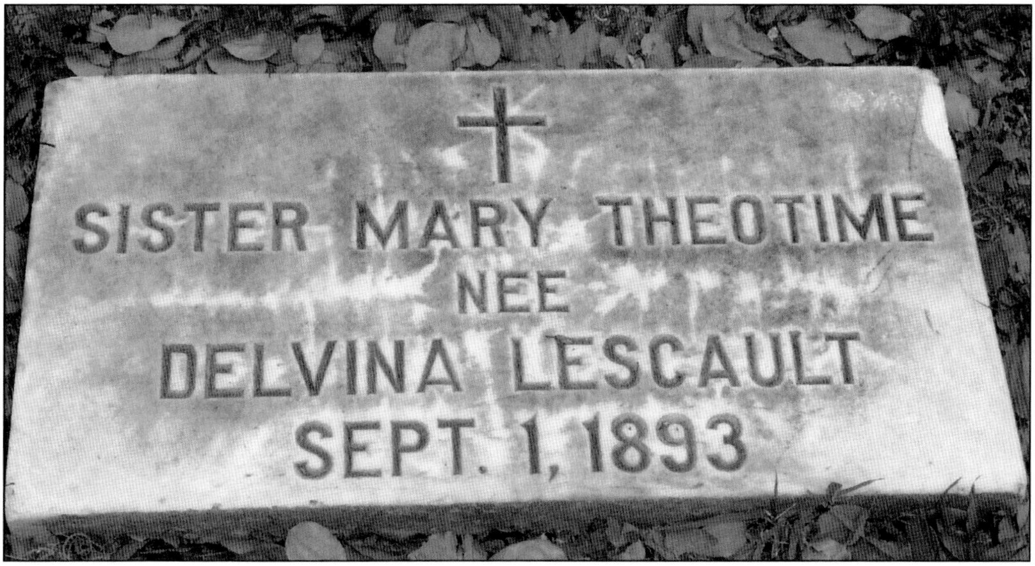

Founded in 1881 by the Sisters of the Holy Names of Jesus and Mary, the mission of the Academy of the Holy Names is to prepare its students to become intellectual, moral, spiritual, and cultural leaders. It is the oldest Catholic school in the Roman Catholic Diocese of Saint Petersburg; however, the school operates independent of the diocese. The school's motto is "Esse Quam Videri" ("to be rather than to seem"). The academy is the oldest school in Tampa and the second-oldest high school in Florida. All burial markers are identical to these of Sisters Mary Theotime and Mary Emile (above) and Sister Mary Fabius (page 55).

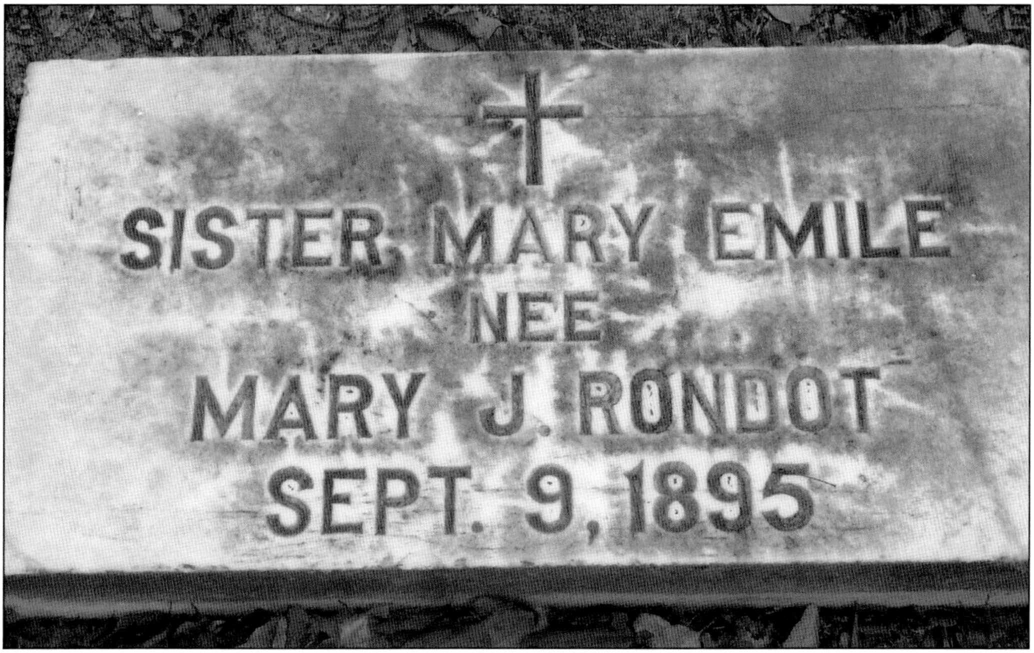

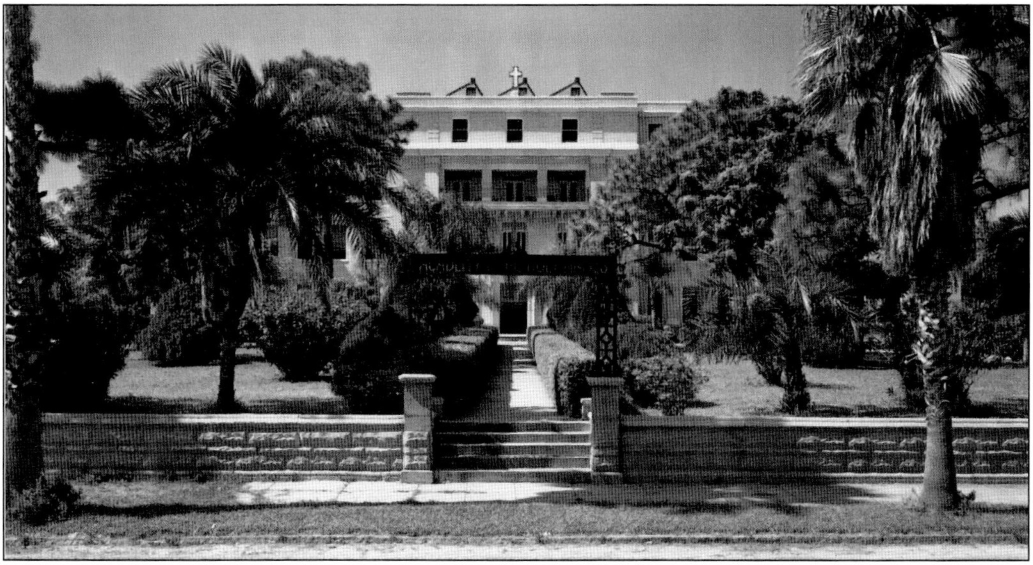

By 1926, further growth necessitated larger accommodations, and the Academy of the Holy Names was moved to temporary quarters on Central Avenue while the present building on Bayshore Boulevard was under construction. Bishop Barry, bishop of St. Augustine, laid the cornerstone in 1928, and Florida's governor-elect Carlton spoke at the ceremony. The school's centenary was celebrated during the 1980–1981 school year. At that time, a historical marker was unveiled in front of the school on Bayshore Boulevard to commemorate 100 years of service of the Sisters of the Holy Names on Florida's West Coast. (THCPL.)

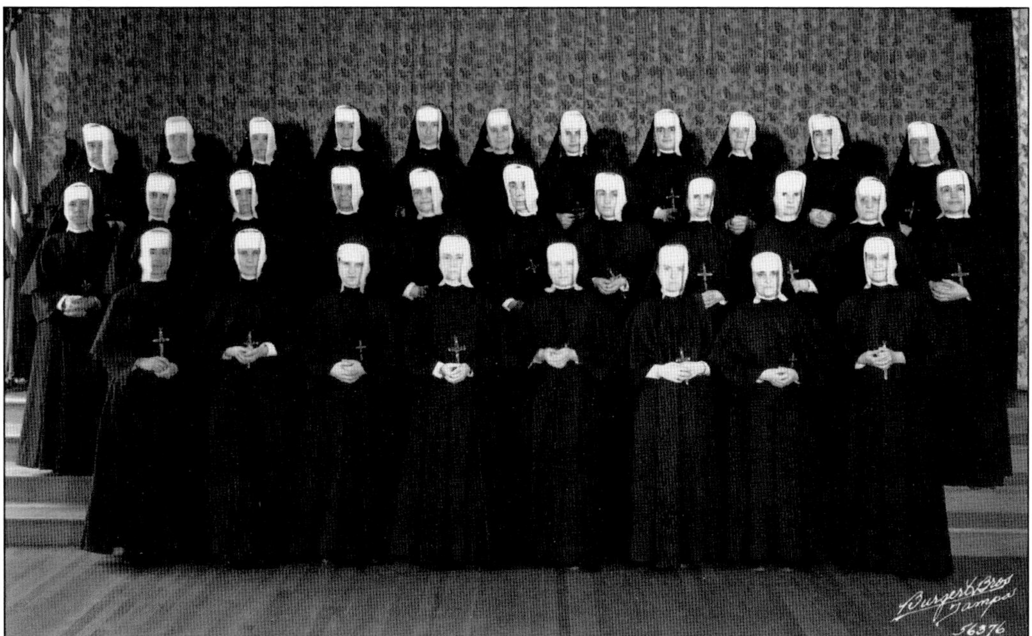

On November 29, 1896, Friar William Tyrrell, SJ, offered the first Catholic mass in West Tampa in the second-floor chapel. It is here that the history of St. Joseph Parish begins. In 1930, when the academy was moved to Bayshore, the Salesian Sisters took charge of the West Tampa school, renaming it St. Joseph School. In 1955, the school moved to Cherry Street and MacDill Avenue.

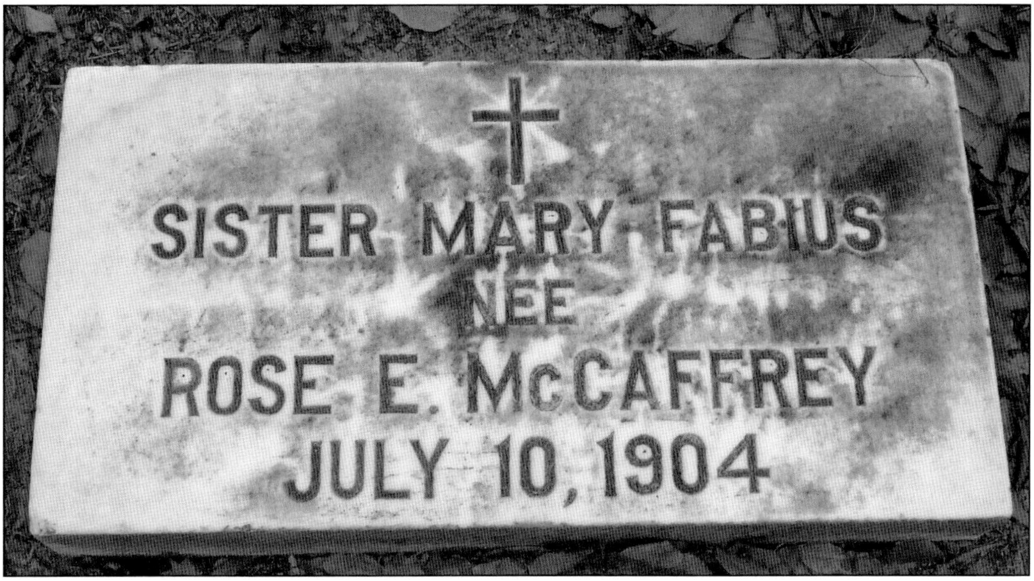

The synoptic gospels, first Mark and then Matthew and Luke, depict Jesus as presiding over the Last Supper. References to Jesus's body and blood foreshadow his crucifixion, and he identifies them as a new covenant. In the gospel of John, the account of the Last Supper (below) has no mention of Jesus taking bread and wine and speaking of them as his body and blood; instead, it recounts his humble act of washing the disciples' feet, the prophecy of the betrayal (which set in motion the events that would lead to the cross), and his long discourse in response to some questions posed by his followers, in which he went on to speak of the importance of the unity of the disciples with him and among each other.

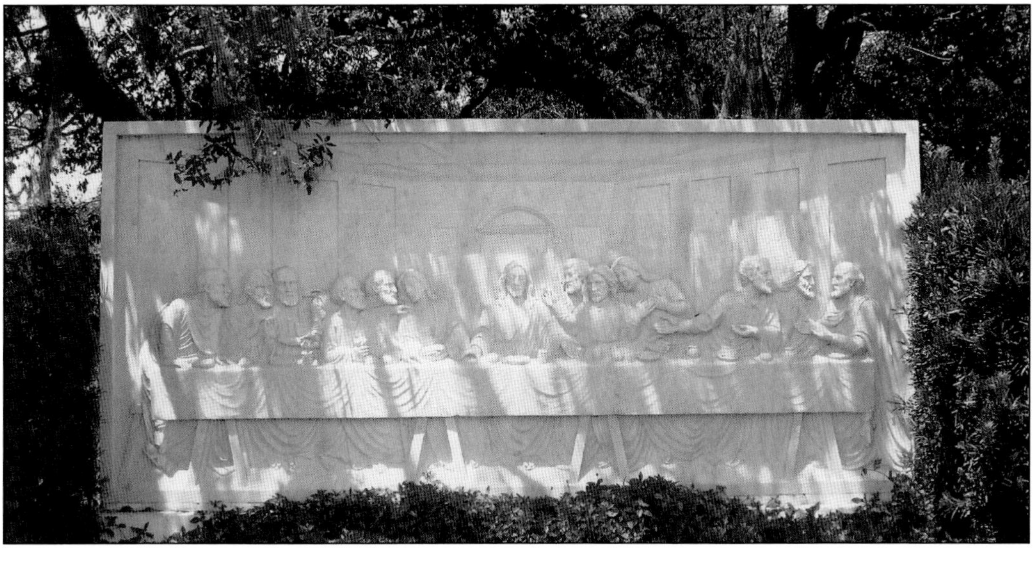

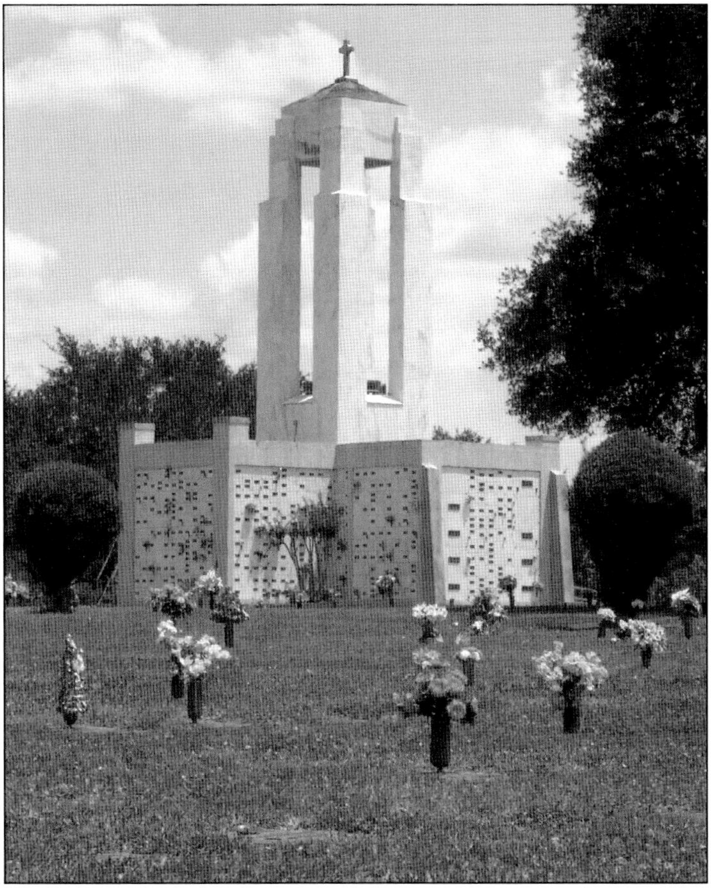

Bordering Myrtle Hill Memorial Cemetery is the Garden of Memories Cemetery. Founded in 1937 by Sen. Ray C. Knopke and Roy Timble, Garden of Memories was the first memorial park in Hillsborough County. Consisting of 100 acres, the cemetery is located at 4002 North Fiftieth Street in northeastern Hillsborough County. Its focal point is the Chimes Tower, which exceeds five stories and was the first columbarium ever built by a cemetery for cremated remains.

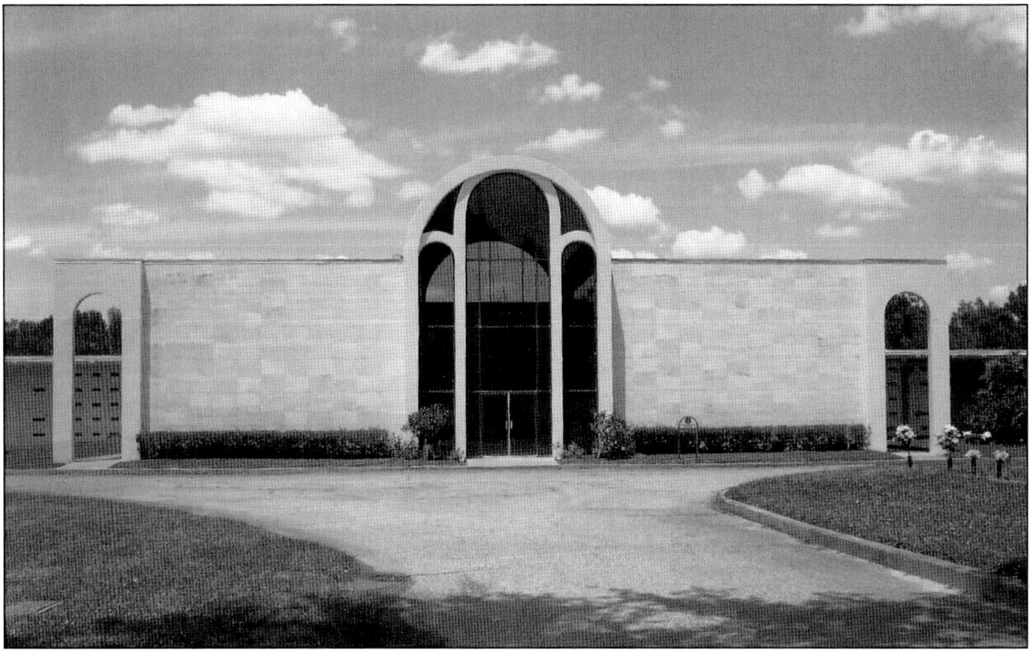

Three

WOODLAWN

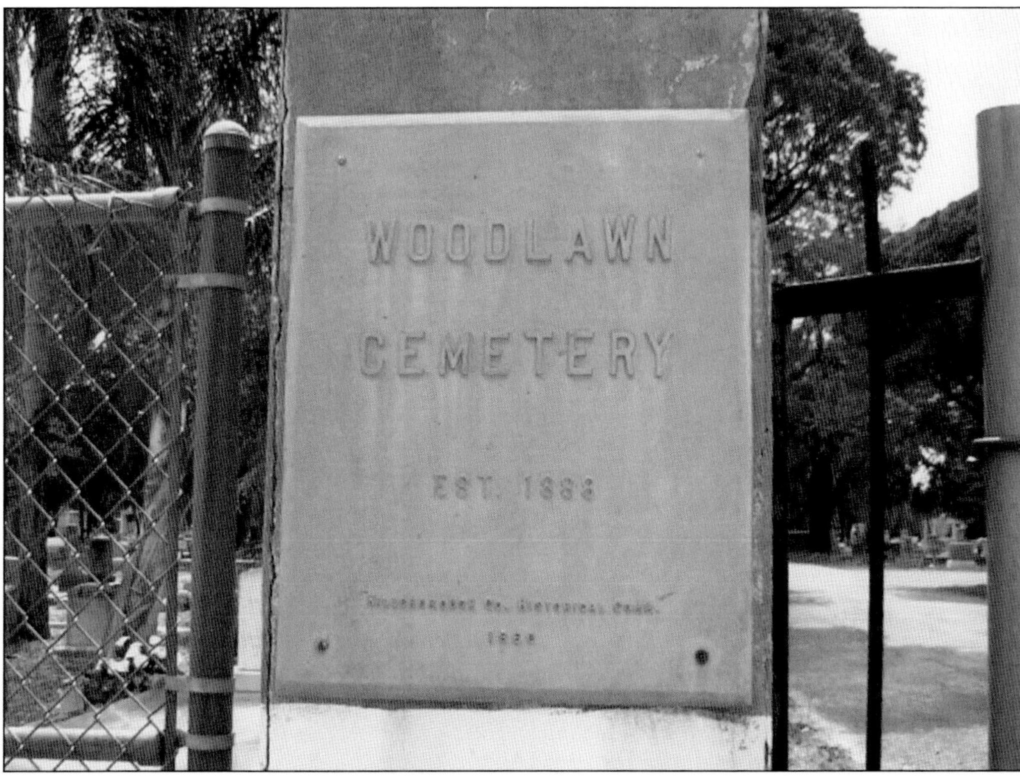

The City of Tampa opened Woodlawn Cemetery in 1888. The final resting place for some of Tampa's most prominent citizens, the 28-acre cemetery is just north of downtown at 3412 North Ola Avenue. Gravesite records burned in a 1986 fire, and city officials assume there were no spaces remaining. Woodlawn is actually an assemblage of cemeteries. On the edges of Woodlawn are the Beth Israel, Old Centro Asturiano, Rodeph Sholom, and Schaarai Zedek and Showmen's Rest Cemeteries.

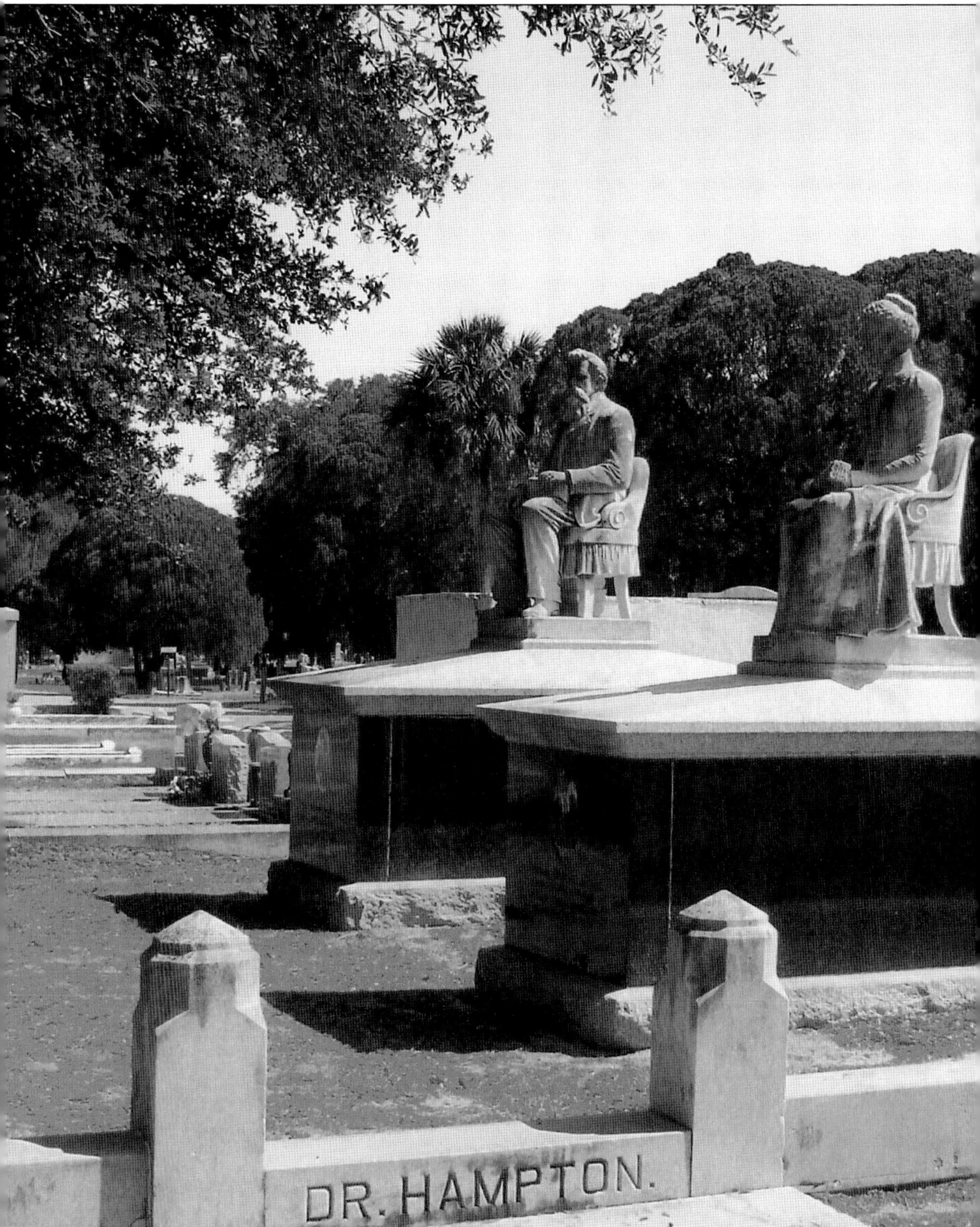
DR. HAMPTON.

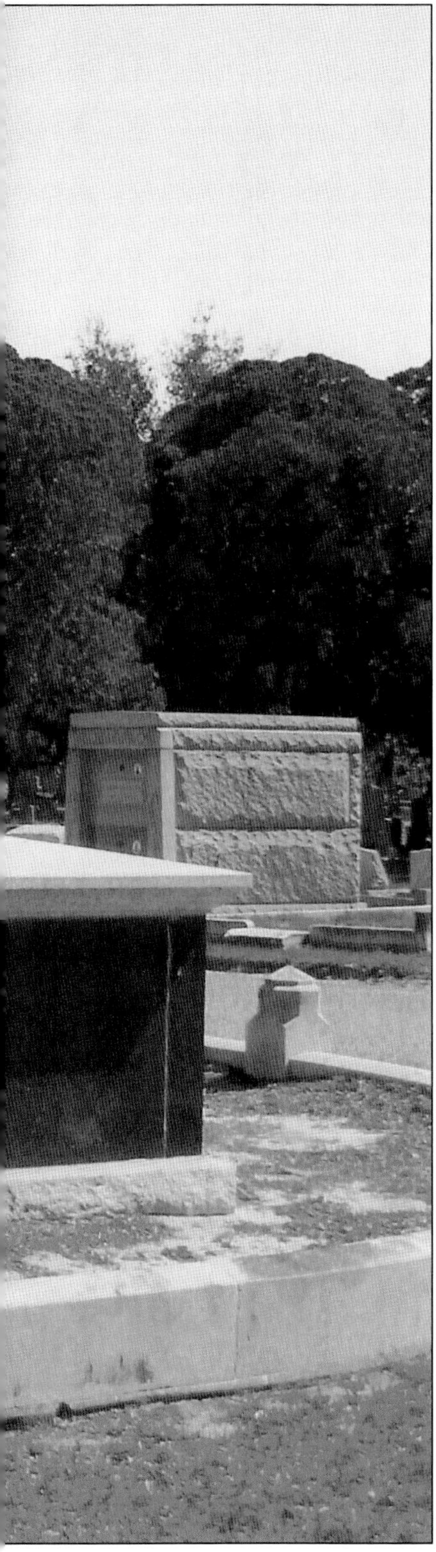

Dr. "Ham" Hampton went to Italy to have these monuments made for himself and his wife, Emma. After a dispute with city leaders, and with an electoral loss, he decided the sculptures would face west, turning his back on Tampa. Dr. Hiram J.S. Hampton (December 10, 1887–March 31, 1935) had written on his tombstone, "I love my companion and appreciate my friends on earth and crave that we may have a reunion after death." Emma "Jodie" Denham Hampton was born on September 24, 1893, and died on February 26, 1991. Her tombstone inscription reads, "Truly a beautiful Butterfly has lived among us."

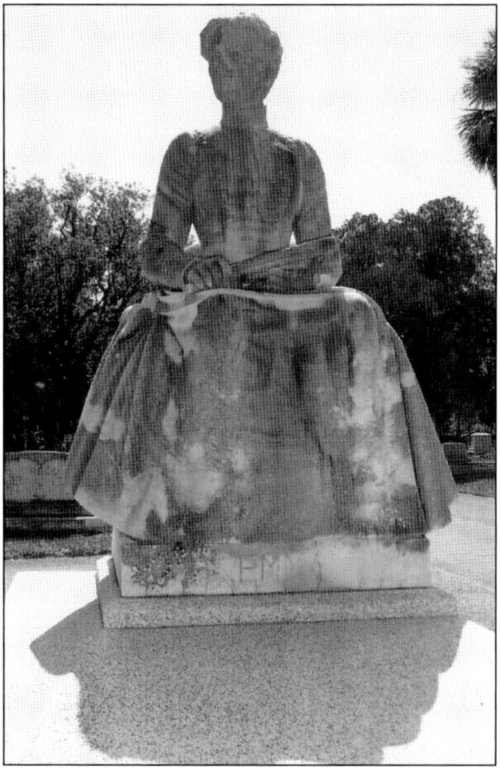

Hiram J. Hampton (below) was born in Madison County, Georgia. The 1870 US Census of Danielsville, Madison County, lists as his parents Hubbard and Mary Jane Hampton. Hiram lived with them, and his occupation was noted as a farmer. By 1880, he was a married physician, and he and his wife, Emma (left), had moved to the community of Maysville in Banks County, Georgia. The 1900 census shows them living in Tampa on Florida Avenue. Their family had expanded to include six children: Harvey J., Ham S., Howe, Hale R., Hood C., and Emma. By 1910, Hiram's wife, Emma, had died, and he was left to continue to care for the children who still lived in his household. His son Ham had become a doctor, and his son Howe worked at the hospital as a bookkeeper.

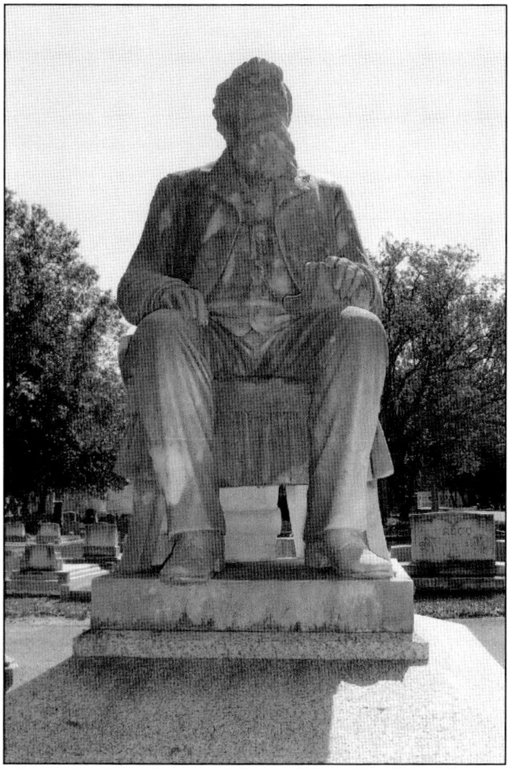

According to the *Directory of Deceased American Physicians, 1804–1929*, Dr. Hiram J. Hampton was an 1879 graduate of the Georgia College of Eclectic Medicine and Surgery. He owned and operated the Tampa Heights Sanitarium in the late 19th and early 20th centuries, advertising his services "for the cure of cancer, rupture, scrofula and kindred diseases, and all cases requiring surgical attention. No Mercury Used In This Institution. Tape Worm Positively Removed." His wife, Emma, at times assisted as his nurse. In 1903, Dr. Hampton was recognized as a member of the Eclectic Medical Examining Board for Florida by the National Eclectic Medical Association of the United States. In the photograph below, with a little black bag in hand and pistol tucked away in his pants waist, Dr. Hampton prepares to make calls, from the finest hotels in town to the most remote rural areas of the county.

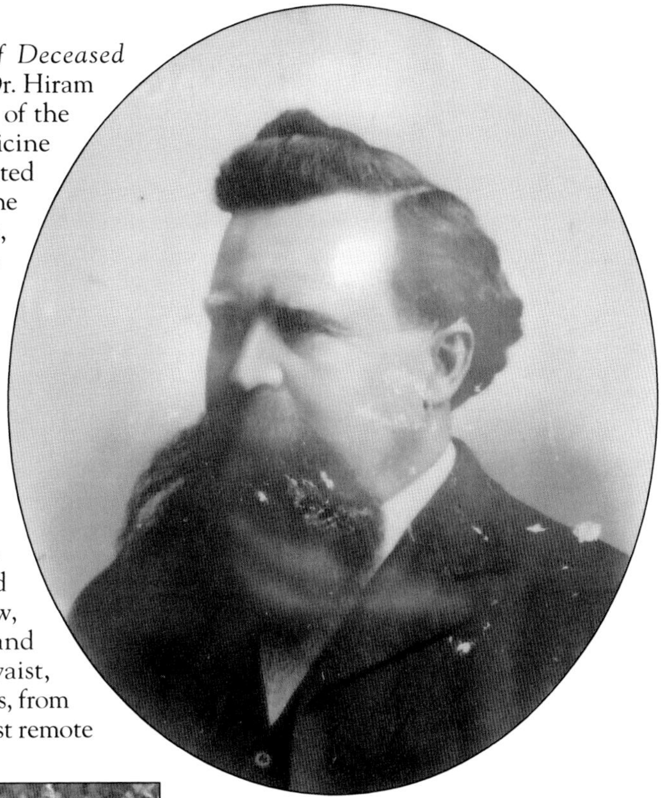

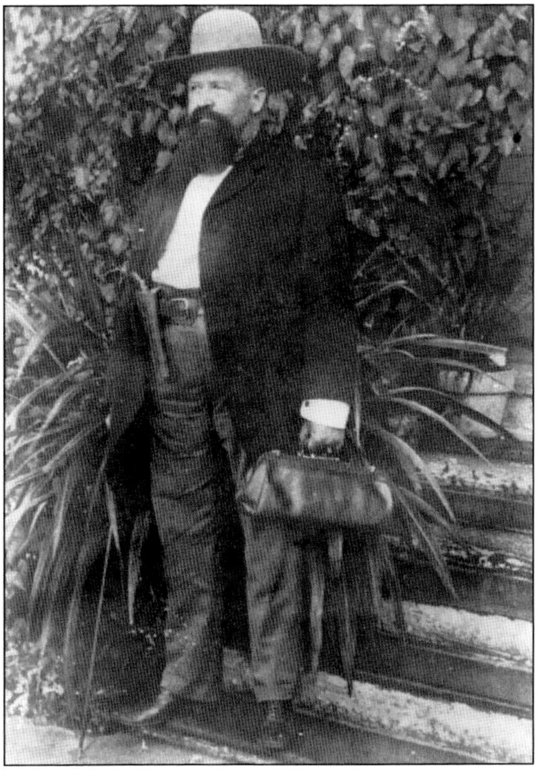

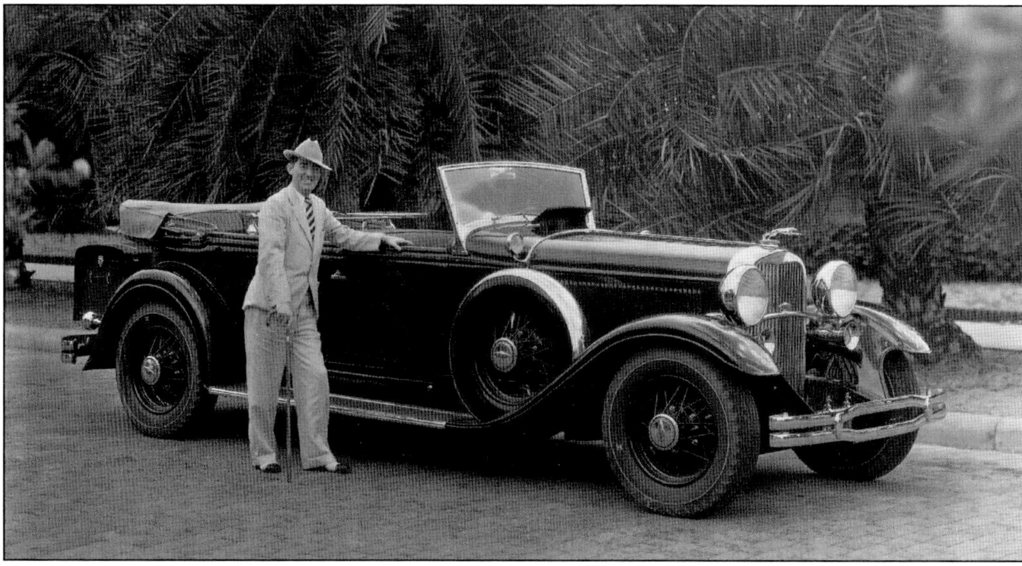

In the photograph above, Eli Buchanan Witt is seen standing next to his 1931 Model K Lincoln. Witt was born in Gates, Tennessee, in 1880. Upon completing his studies at Southwestern Baptist University, he became a salesman for the R.J. Reynolds Tobacco Co. In 1889, he was transferred to Tampa, a city that was quickly emerging as the American capital of hand-rolled cigars. In 1905, Witt rented the front window of a small Franklin Street drugstore and built a tobacco counter. To attract customers, he jangled a half-filled penny matchbox at pedestrians, offering free matches with the purchase of tobacco products. He earned $5 his first day. From the tiny storefront, Eli Witt created the nation's largest wholesale cigar, cigarette, and confection business and was referred to as the "South's most outstanding tobacco merchant." By the time he died 42 years later, his business sales had topped $100 million. The January 31, 1947, *Tampa Morning Tribune*'s banner headline saluted him: "Fabulous Eli Witt is Dead." In 1947, the *New York Times* honored Witt as "the first to clothe cigars in cellophane." The *Times* noted that Witt popularized the wooden cigar tip. Moreover, his company, Hav-A-Tampa, is arguably the most enduring and endearing brand name, honoring Tampa: the Cigar City. (THCPL.)

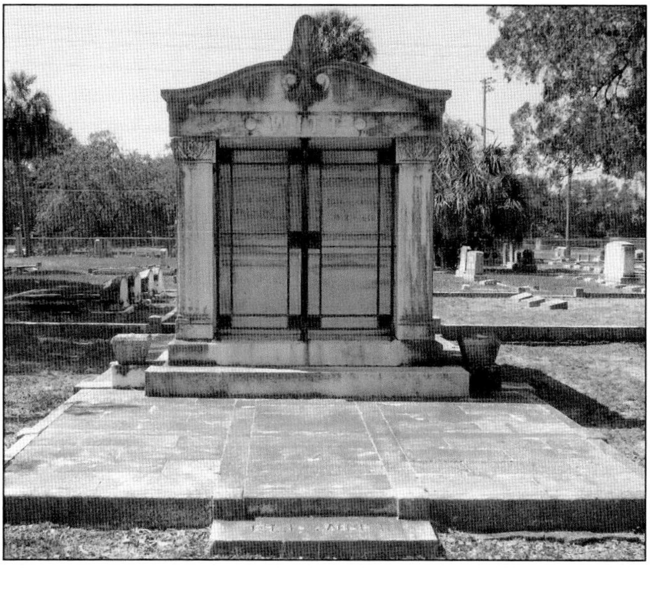

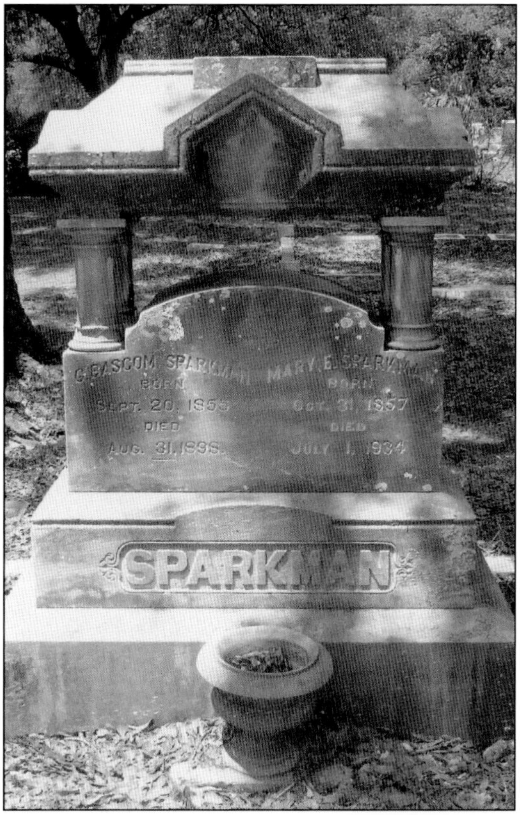

George Bascom Sparkman was born on September 20, 1855, in Simmons Hammock (Dover, Florida), the son of Elijah Bird Sparkman and Sarah Ann Mizell. George attended local schools and graduated with high honors in September 1877 from the University of Virginia Law School. He returned to Tampa, where he opened a law office with his cousin Stephen M. Sparkman. On April 26, 1883, Sparkman married Virginia-born Mary Kershaw in Madison County, Tennessee. The Sparkmans had seven children: Thomas Byrd, George B. Jr., Mary Evelyn, Lois Louise Frances, Simeon Stephen, James Kershaw, and Rose Elizabeth. While city council president, Sparkman replaced acting mayor Matthew E. Haynsworth on March 22, 1881, serving until August 14, 1883. Sparkman also served on the city council (1884–1886 and 1891–March 4, 1892) and was a judge for the Sixth Circuit Court (1893–1894). He died on August 31, 1898, in Tampa, Florida. The photograph below is of Sparkman Channel looking toward downtown Tampa with Florida Portland Cement Company in the foreground. (THCPL.)

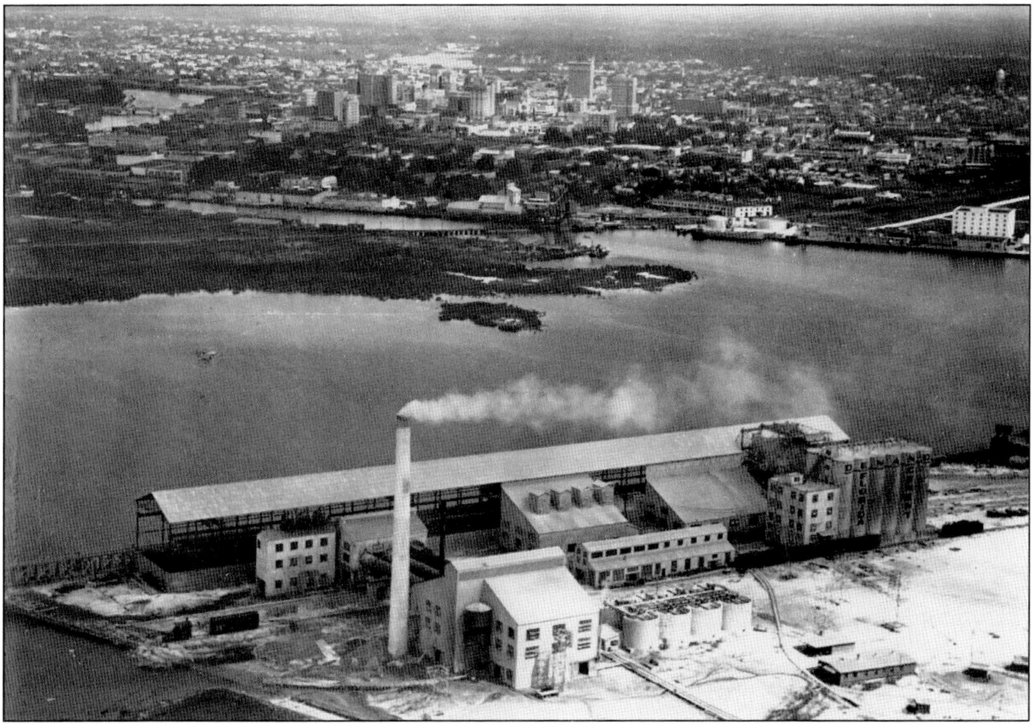

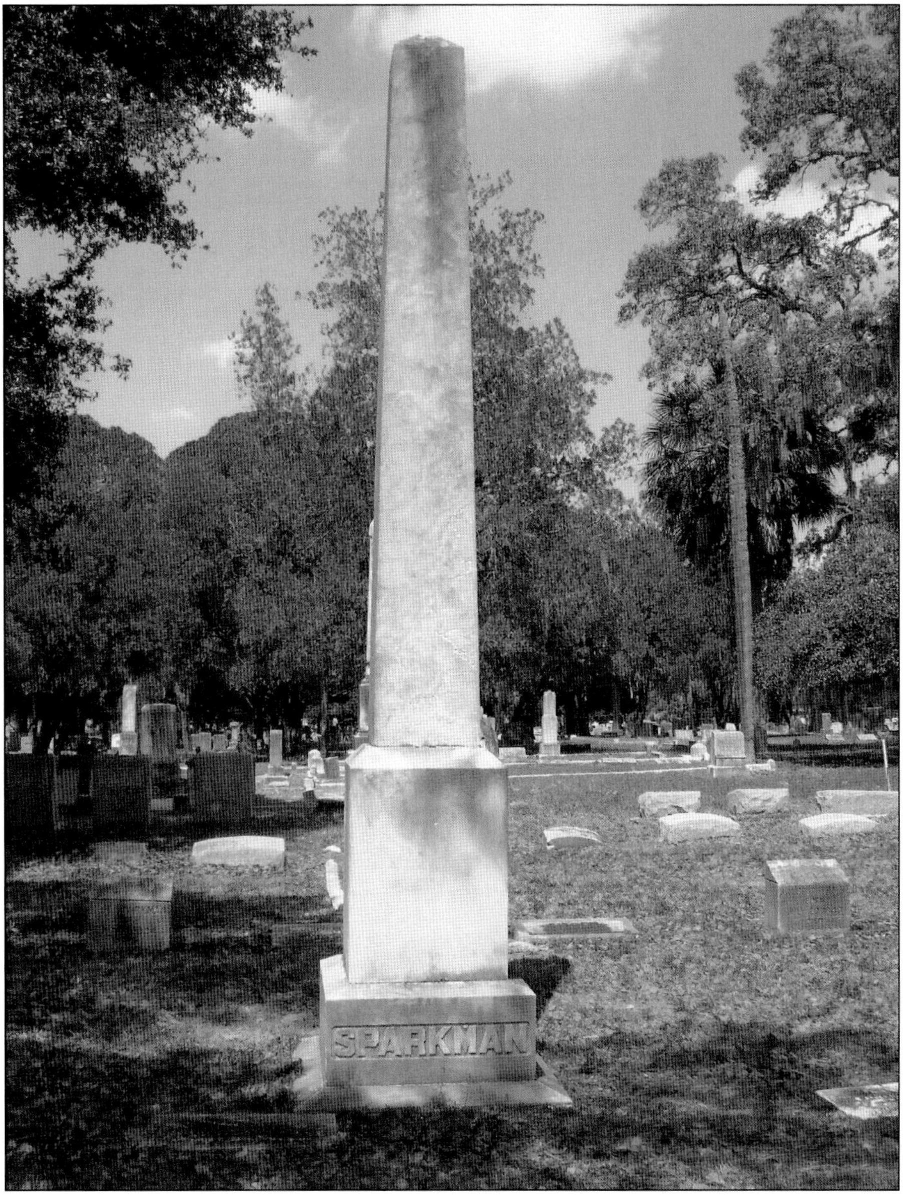

Stephen Milancthon Sparkman served as the state attorney for the Sixth Judicial Circuit from 1878 to 1887. In the early 1880s, he became counsel for the South Florida Railroad and the Plant System. Sparkman was elected as a Democrat to the 54th Congress (1895) and the 10 succeeding congresses. His many years of service to the Democratic Party included chairman and delegate to the Democratic National Convention in 1892. The Thursday, April 12, 1917, *Tampa Times* states, "Former Congressman, S.M. Sparkman was named to the chairmanship of the Bay & Harbor Bureau with a goal of securing deeper water for Tampa." He served on the Rivers and Harbors Committee for a total of 20 years, acting as chairman for the last six. During his years as a congressman, he traveled to Europe to study the waterways of European countries, bringing back valuable information to help develop the deep Gulf ports of Florida. His success in obtaining millions of dollars for these waterway developments immensely impacted the income produced by Florida's Gulf Coast ports for almost 100 years. He resumed practicing law in Tampa in 1916.

Stephen M. Sparkman Sr. was born on July 29, 1849, in Hernando County, Florida, the son of Nathaniel Keightley and Mary Cason. After being educated in country schools, he taught for several years and then studied law in the Tampa office of Henry Laurens Mitchell, who would later serve as governor. Sparkman was admitted to the bar in October 1872. He married Mary Ellen Hooker, daughter of John I. and Cuthbert Lanier, in Polk County in 1875. They had nine children: E. Lamar, Mary C., Julia, Ellie Louise, Stephen M. Jr., Cuthbert Wayne, Curtis Lanier, Francis Eugenia, and Nathaniel Keightley. Mary Ellen died on May 27, 1912, while Stephen died in Washington, DC, on September 26, 1929.

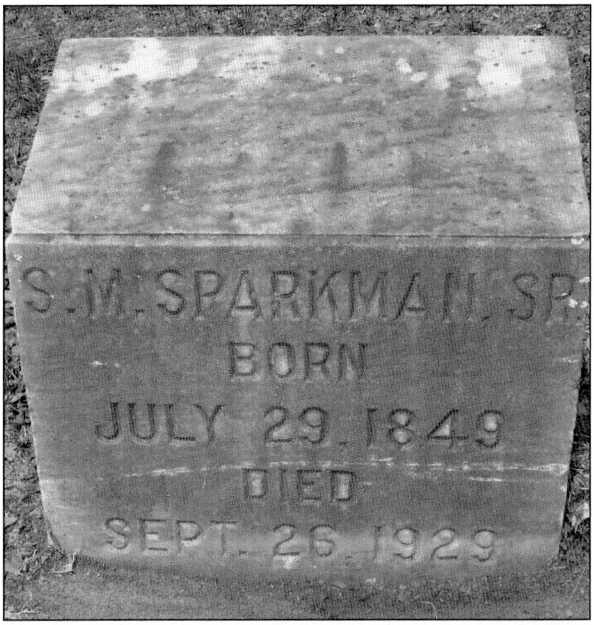

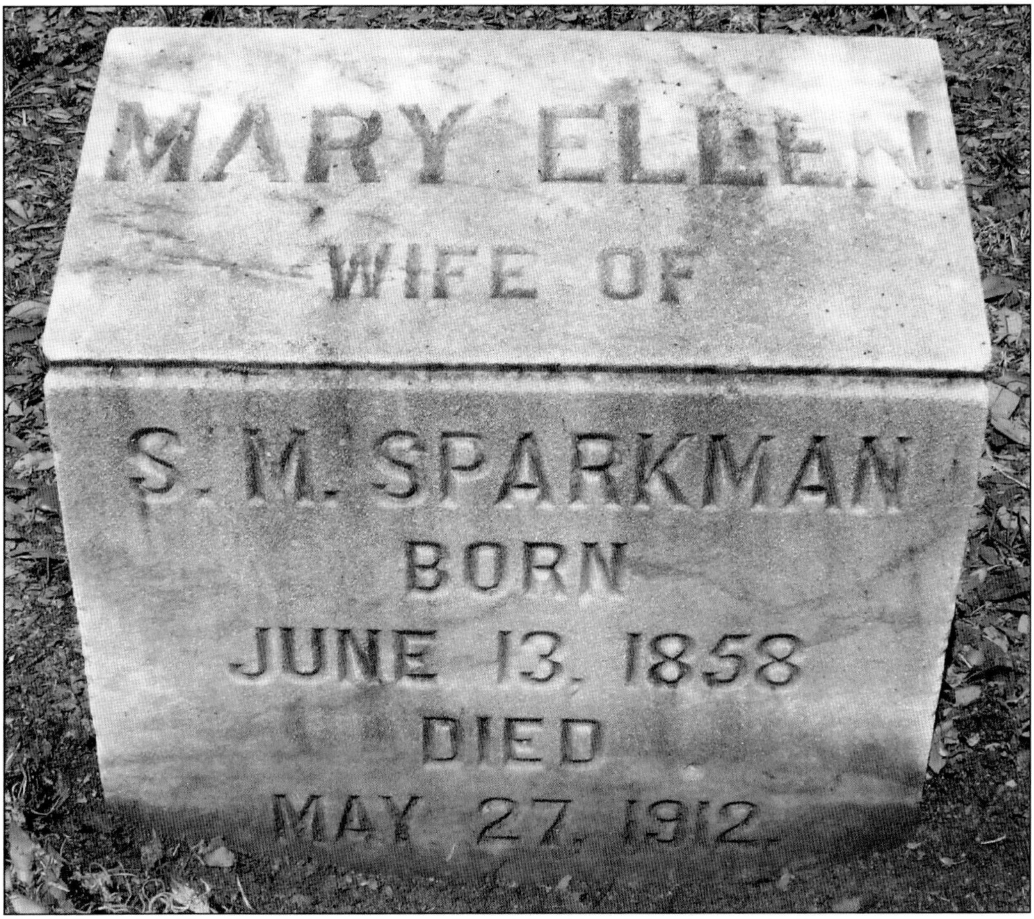

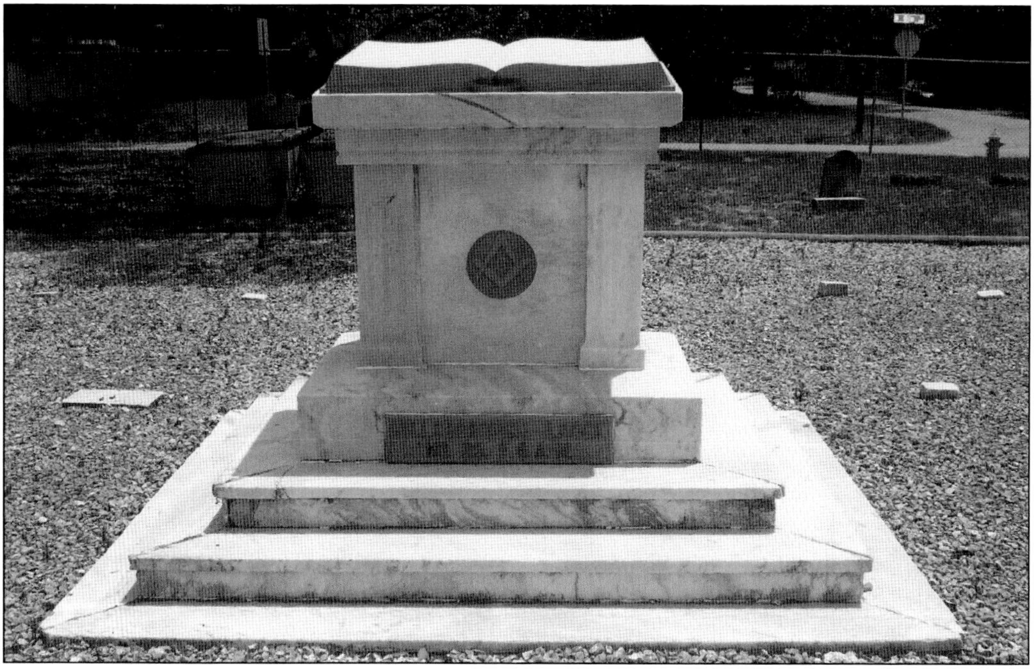

Freemason members established the first Masonic Lodge in 1850, attaining 61 "brothers" by the end of 1851. Erected in 1927–1928, Hillsborough Lodge's two-story building at 508 East Kennedy Boulevard features elaborate brick and ornamental glazed terra-cotta detailing and is a Mediterranean Revival, Beaux-Arts structure designed by member and architect M. Leo Elliott Sr. The lodge room is adorned with a 40-foot-high, hand-painted ceiling. The lodge is historically significant due to its association with early community leaders who helped in the social, economic, and political development of the Tampa area. Merchants, lawyers, engineers, and educators comprised a large part of the lodge's diverse membership, including Abe and Isaac Maas, Mayor Herman Glogowski, and Gov. Doyle Carlton. Two leading educators, Ludwig Bucholtz and Ernest L. Robinson, provided two generations of service to the lodge and their state and local school systems. The building was placed in the National Register of Historic Places in 1986.

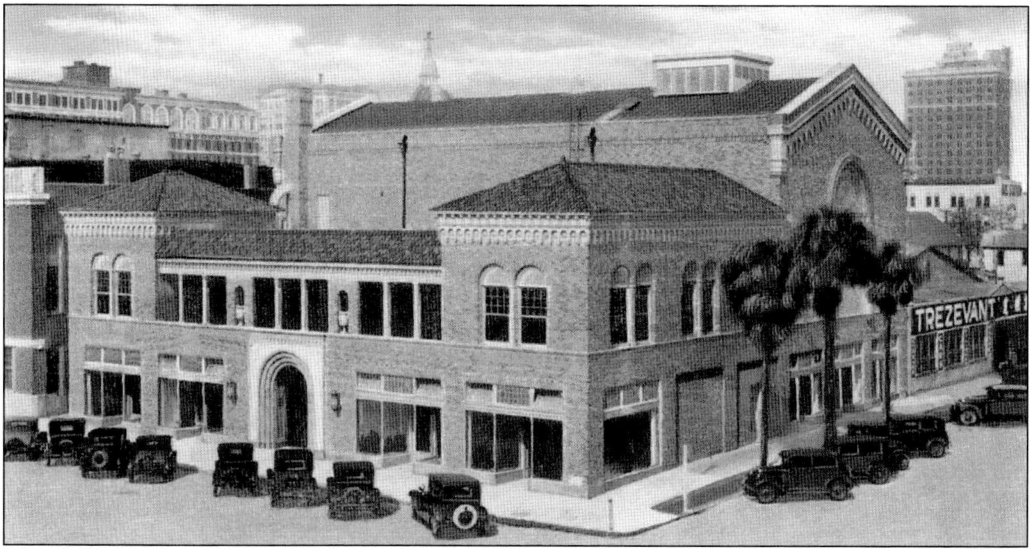

Joseph Robles, of Andalusia, Spain, served as a Confederate scout. Wounded and sent home, he joined the home guard and, while standing watch on the north shore of Old Tama Bay near a Confederate saltworks on McKay Creek north of Rocky Point, spotted a Union gunboat. Robles watched as a landing party approached to see whether the saltworks had been restored. He hid in a big boiler and waited. As the Union soldiers came ashore, Robles shouted orders to an imaginary auxiliary and fired his 10-gauge shotgun into the group. The enemy assumed there was a strong force concealed in the brush. Accounts vary as to the number of soldiers killed or wounded, but no doubt Robles disarmed the remaining Yankees. Joseph died in 1907 at the age of 89. His son Joseph P. died in 1951 at the age of 104, and the younger Robles's wife, Martha Ann, died in 1932.

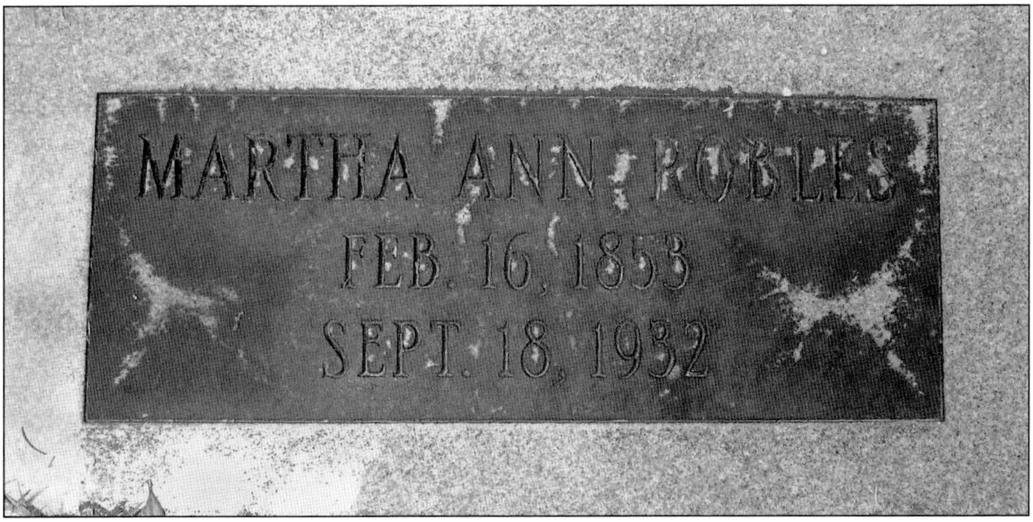

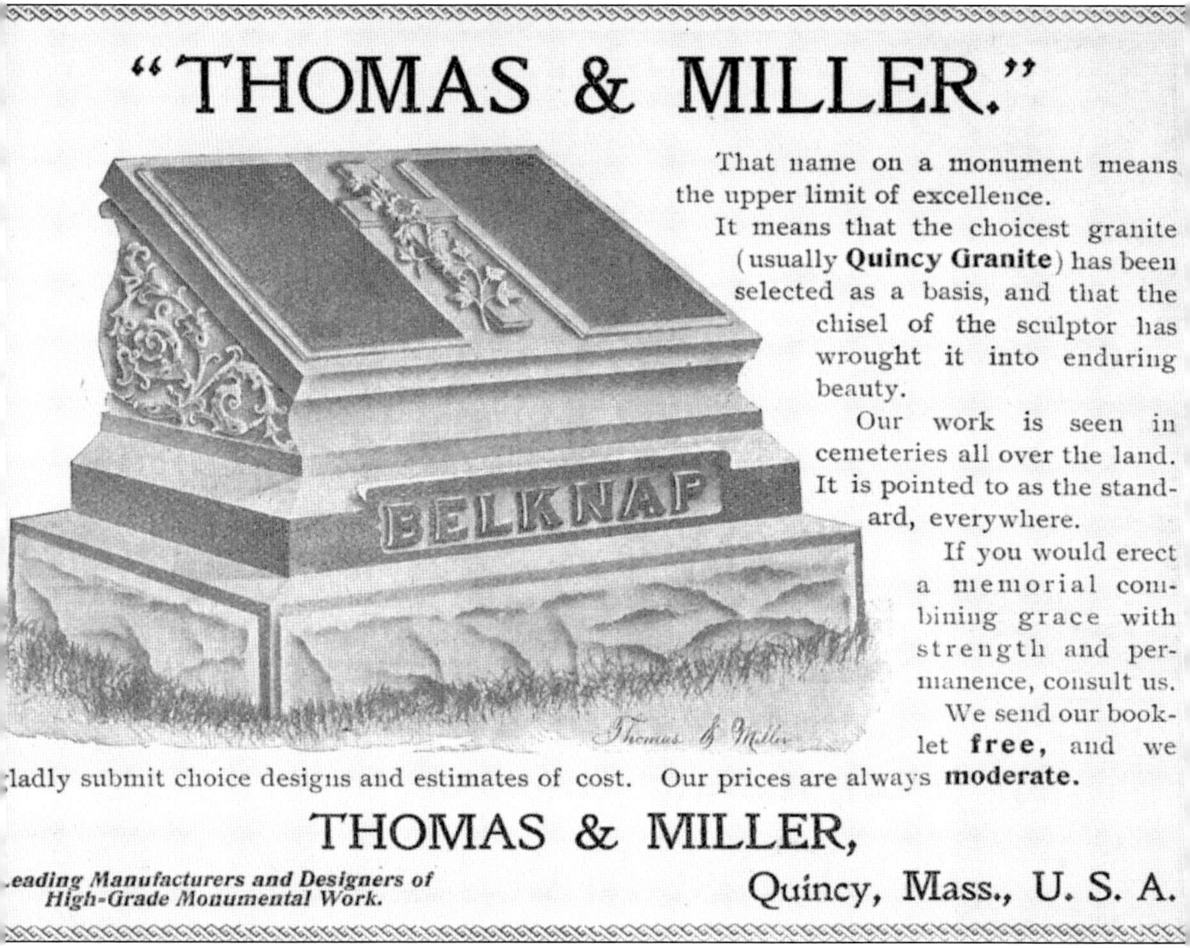

The Thomas & Miller Company plant covered an area of over 70,000 feet and was equipped with the latest machinery to facilitate the manufacture of the high-class work for which it was noted, and its monuments were sent to all parts of the United States and many foreign countries. The choicest granite, usually called Quincy Granite, had been mined and selected based on its quality. John L. Miller, a native of Truro, Nova Scotia, apprenticed to the iron foundry trade, at which he worked four years, when, on December 31, 1872, he went to Quincy, Massachusetts, and was employed by the O.T. Rogers Granite Company and Fredericks & Field before he organized the Merry Mount Granite Company, in which he held the position of manager for seven years. Miller then became associated with W.H. Thomas of Saratoga Springs, New York, and they established the firm of Thomas & Miller, which continued for 12 years, after which Miller bought his partner's interest.

The McKay and Flisch gravestones are examples of what could have been shipped to Tampa's Woodlawn Cemetery by the Thomas & Miller Company of Quincy, Massachusetts. The highest-quality stone material was selected and carved by skilled artisans in the trade. Symbolic of a person's life and accomplishments, many stones are adorned with motifs that signify eternal life, grief and sorrow, wisdom and knowledge, and the victory of death. A stalk of wheat symbolizes that the time of life is one's divine harvest, while a rising sun that shines is a symbol that one's life has been renewed in heaven. Many children's graves are adorned with lambs, the symbol of innocence.

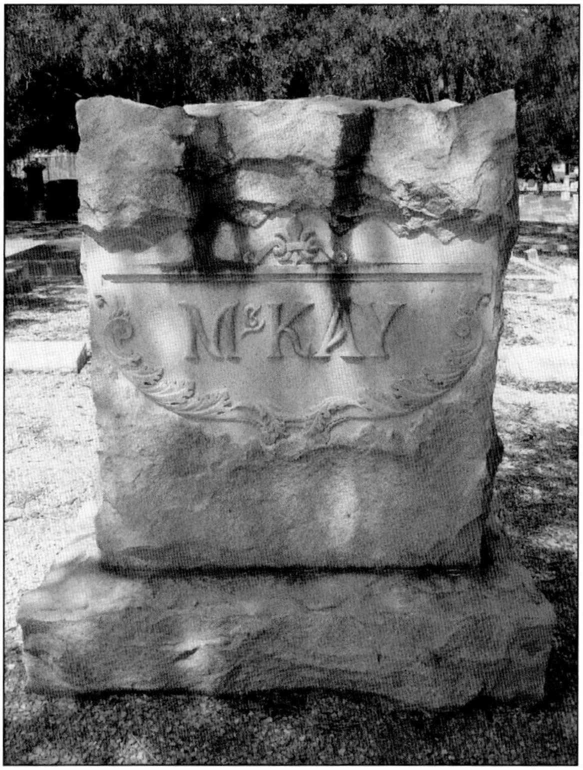

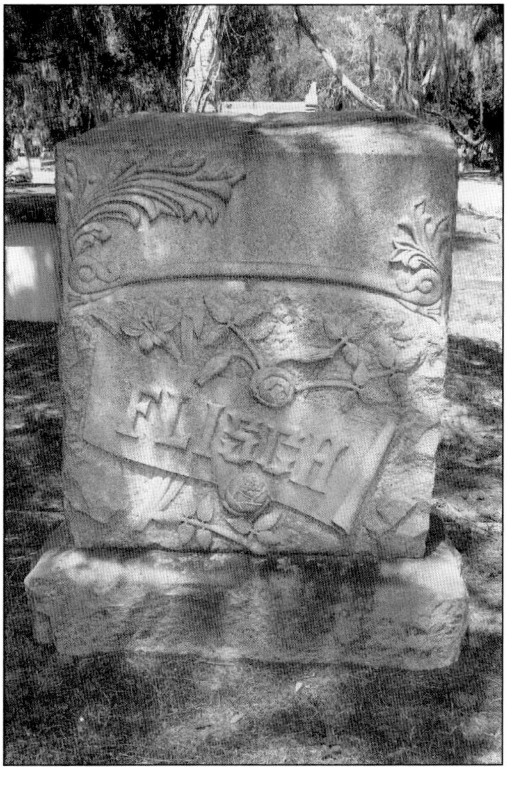

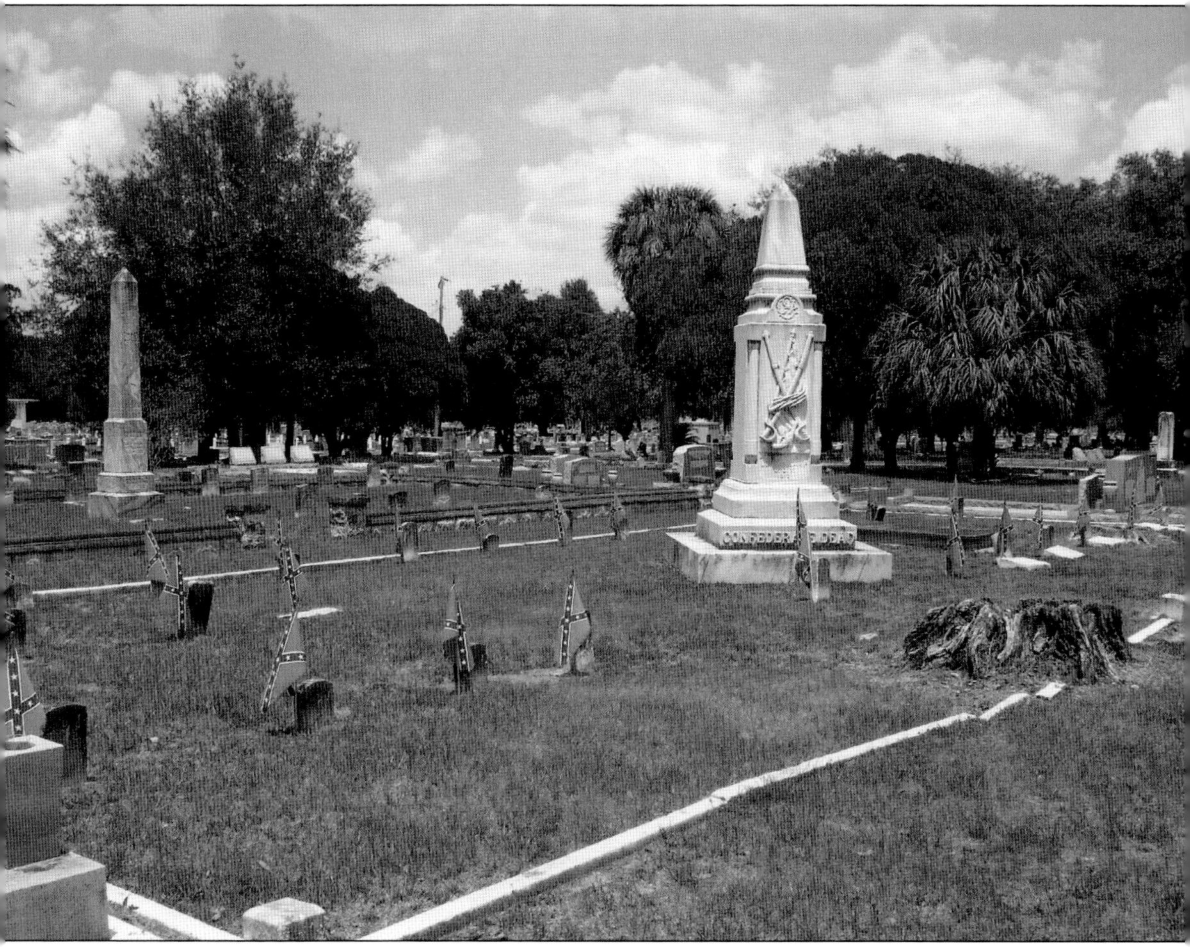

After facing one another on the battlefields, these soldiers, of both the Grand Army of the Republic (Union) and the Confederate States Army (Rebels) came to their final resting places lying side by side. The years 1861 to 1865 changed everything in this country. More than one million Southern men served in the Confederate military; nearly 300,000 died during the war. Florida, which sent more of her sons per capita into the Confederate army and navy than any other state, remembers its heroes each April 26, which by Florida state law is a legal holiday: Confederate Memorial Day. Confederate flags are placed at the gravesites of known Confederate soldiers. The Sons of Confederate Camps of Jubal Early 556 and Judah P. Benjamin 2210 and the Augusta Jane Evans Wilson chapter 2640 of the United Daughters of the Confederacy participate in these events.

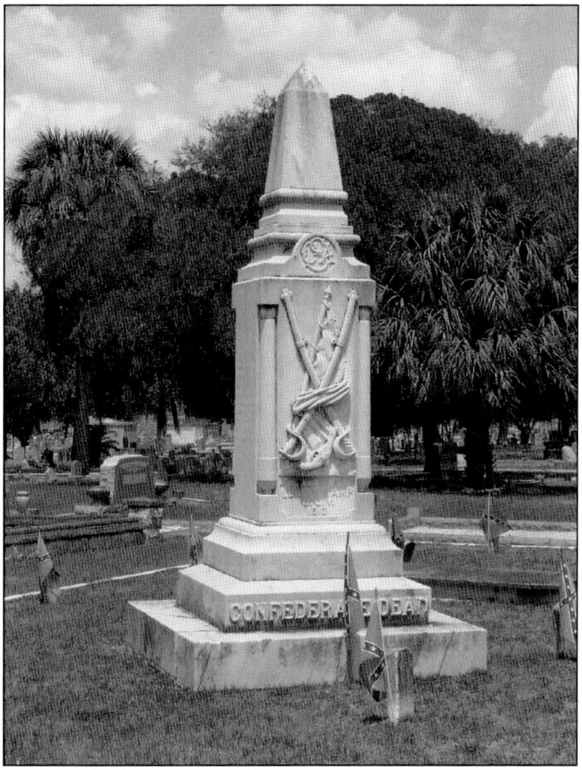

Soldiers listed on this *Confederate Dead* memorial marker include W.F. Bailey, J.B. Bannister, John Brain, J.C. Bravo, L.W. Campbell, S.J. Cochran, C.W. Conway, John Coyne, D.L. Cutling, J.E. Fillman, F. Franklin, C.C. Gant, F.T. Goss, A.T. Hamilton, S.M. Hankins, A.I Hurd, A.R. Joyner, Wm. M. Lockett, Chas. McNealy, H.C. Mills, L. Mourgeon, J.J. Nesbitt, G.W. Rice, J.G. Robles, W.H. Stafford, Wm. Switzer, B.F. Taylor, Fred Turner, and Geo. B. Wilds. The GAR soldier area contains the graves of Thomas B. Malone, Capt. Richard H. McIntire, Thomas A. Price, W.H. Weisner, and others.

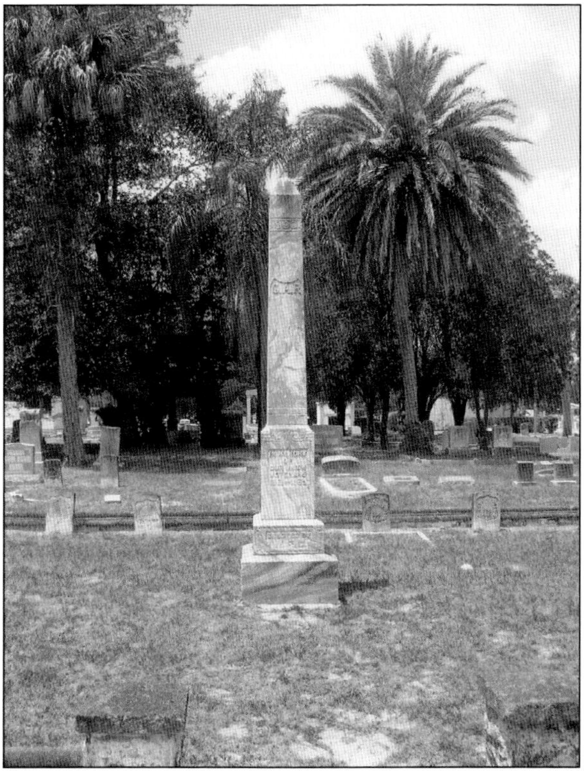

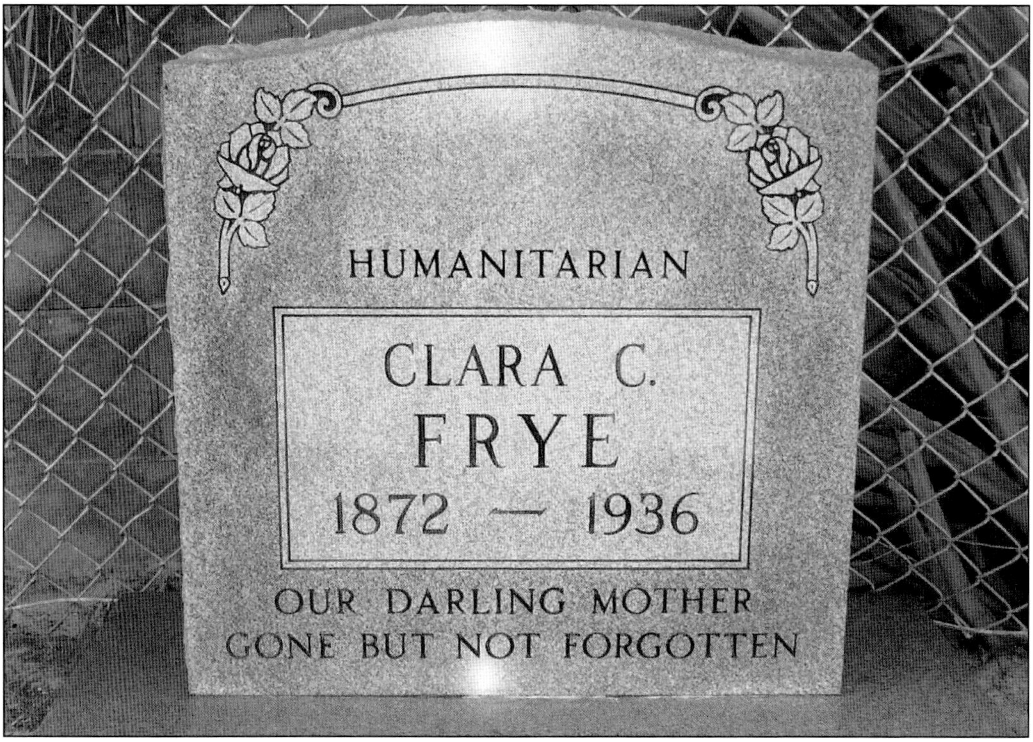

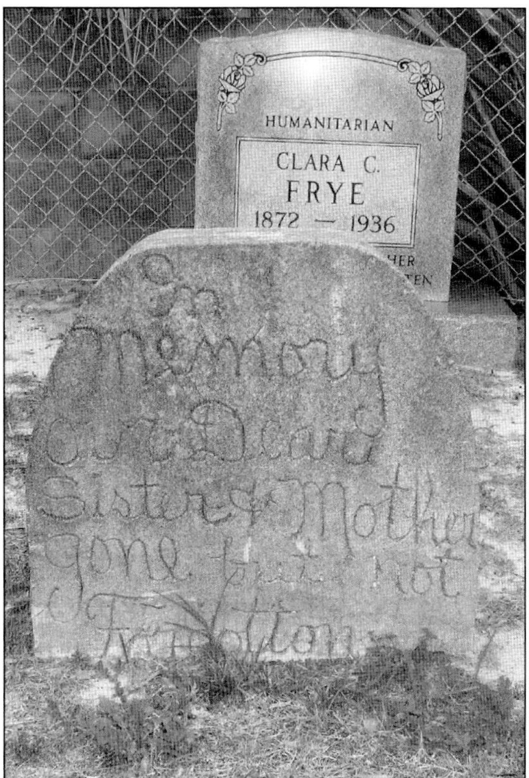

Clara C. Frye was born in Montgomery, Alabama, and trained in nursing care. She began a lifelong commitment to the care of sick and injured African Americans in her small Tampa home in 1908. In 1938, the Tampa Negro Hospital in Roberts City was dedicated as the Clara Frye Memorial Hospital. Howard W. Blake High School was later built on the site. Clara C. Frye is buried in Woodlawn Cemetery. Until 1991, her grave was marked by a simple homemade stone (left) that read, "In memory of our dear sister and mother. Gone but not forgotten." A new headstone (above) was dedicated by the Wilson Funeral Home in 1991 for the woman who had given so much of herself, for so many, and at such a great price. She was a charter inductee into the Hillsborough County Women's Hall of Fame in 2011.

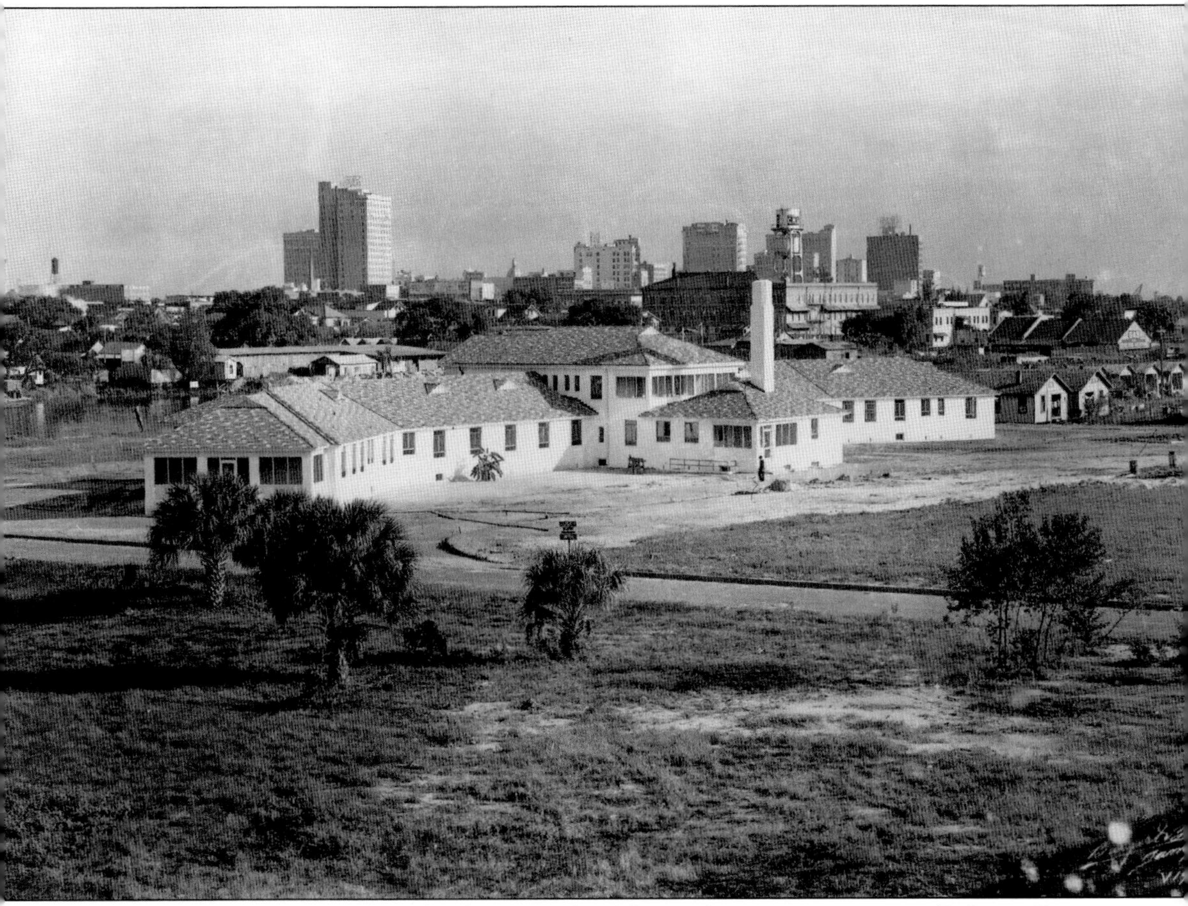

The Clara Frye Hospital, built by the WPA for African American patients in Roberts City on the west bank of the Hillsborough River, is shown here in 1938 with the Tampa skyline in the background. Clara Frye Memorial Hospital existed in West Tampa from 1938 to 1967 and was named for Frye, who admitted patients of all races, African American or otherwise, to her hospital. The Tampa Municipal Hospital did not admit African American patients until the 1950s. In 1967, the same year Tampa General Hospital integrated, Clara Frye's hospital was closed and demolished due to poor and unsanitary conditions. (THCPL.)

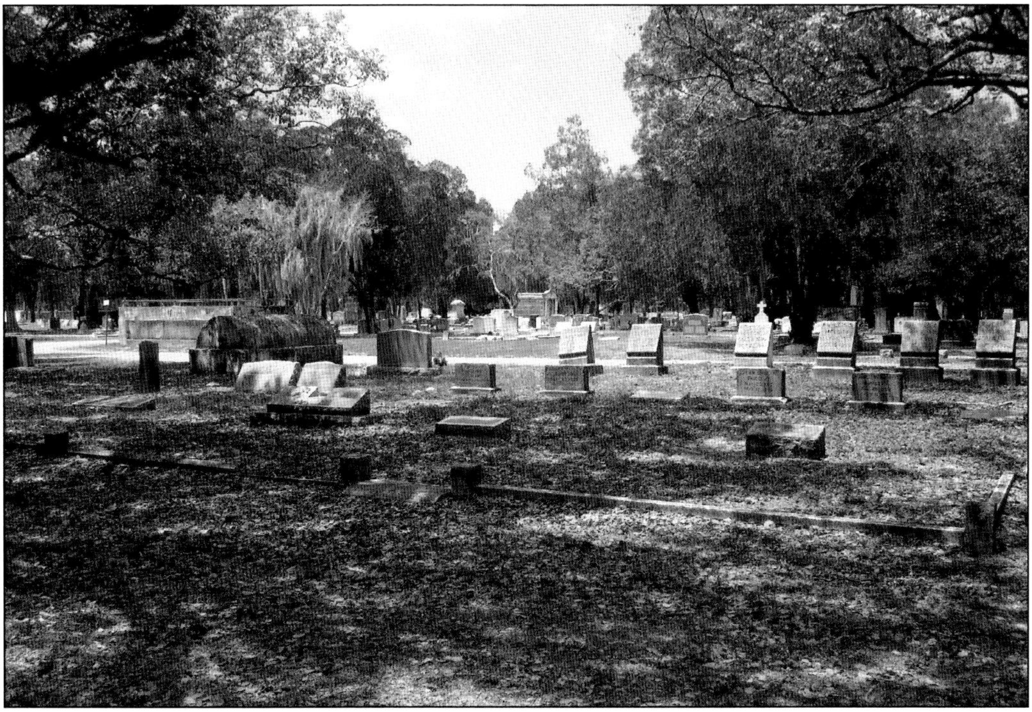

One must wonder why, with all the photographs taken by the Burgert family, none seem to have been taken of their family graves in Woodlawn Cemetery. The Burgert family's impact on commercial photography began in 1899, when S.P. Burgert & Son first opened a photographic studio in Tampa. By 1918, the Burgert Brothers Commercial Photography Studio, with brothers Jean and Al Burgert at the helm, was firmly established in Tampa, providing commercial photography services to the west coast region of Florida. The firm continued in operation until 1963. During this time, the brothers took over 80,000 photographs for their clients. Burgert Brothers photographs appeared in *Life* and *National Geographic* magazines as well as in local newspapers, advertisements, promotional brochures, and displays for stores and offices. In the photograph below, Al Burgert is shown on location for a photography job in 1925. (THCPL.)

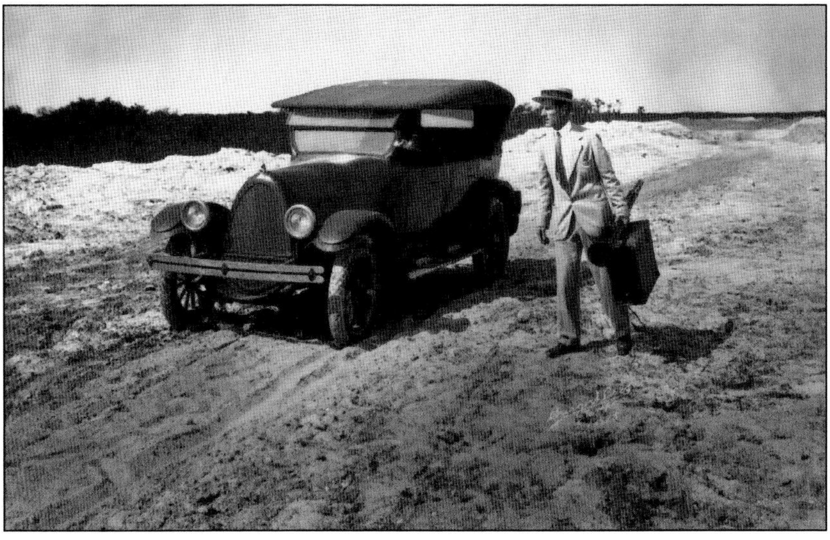

The first Burgerts came to the United States in the second quarter of the 19th century from Alsace-Lorraine. Samuel P. Burgert was born in 1849 in Cincinnati, Ohio. He married Adelina Jane Barlow, a native of Shreveport, Louisiana, and they had four sons while living in Ohio: Willard, Harold, Walter, and Jean. During the 1880s, Samuel moved his family to Florida, where he worked in Jacksonville as a photographer and where he and Adelina became parents of twin boys, Alfred and Albert, in 1887. By 1898, the Burgert family had moved to Tampa and was engaged in the photography business as S.P. Burgert & Son, Photographers. Images would continue to be taken by members of the Burgert family for almost 70 years, who photographed weddings, funerals, parades, business openings, fires, hurricane damage, and almost any event that one could imagine impacting the Tampa area. The example seen to the right is of Samuel P. Burgert. (THCPL.)

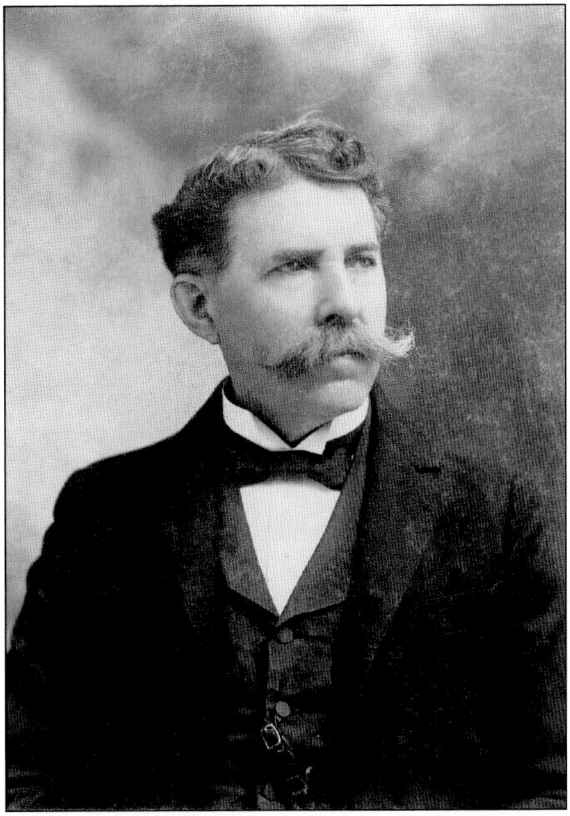

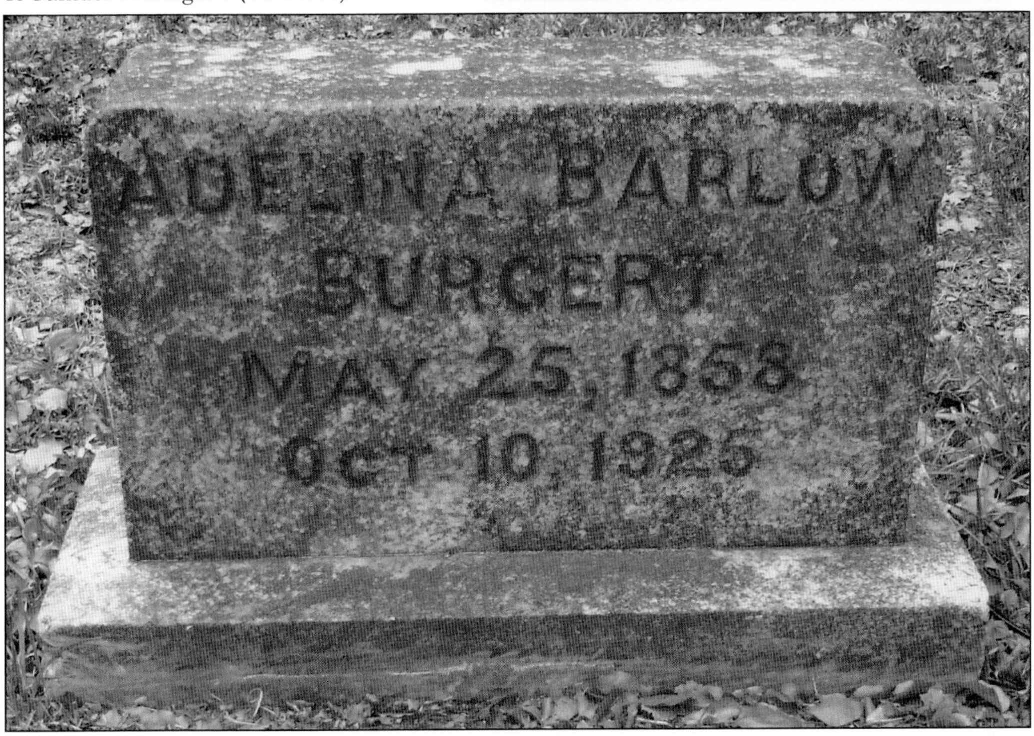

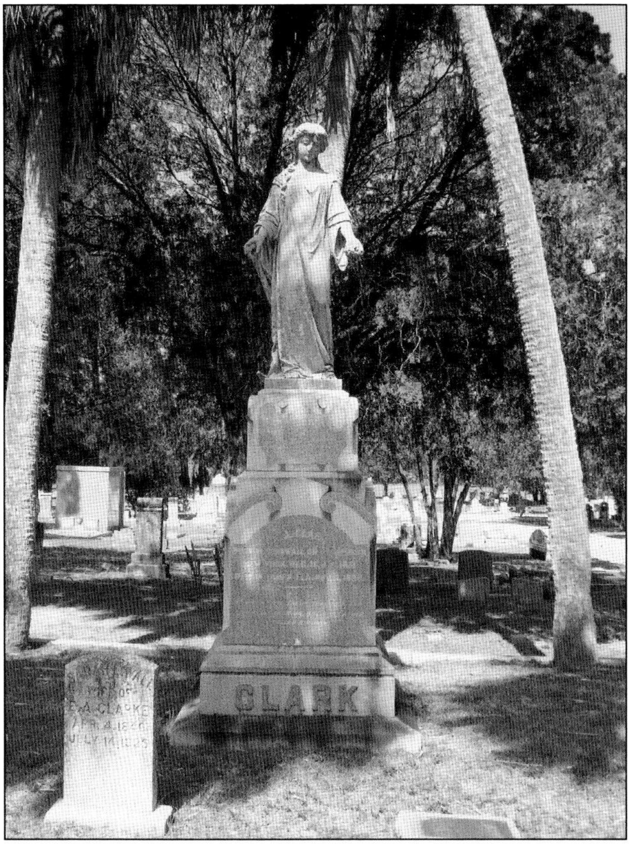

Edward A. Clarke was born in 1827 in Cornwall-on-the-Hudson, New York. He arrived in Tampa in 1853, opening a general store at the corner of Washington and Marion Streets. He served as a blockade-runner during the Civil War, was captured at Anclote Keys, and imprisoned until the end of the war. Returning to Tampa, he opened his store and began to amass real estate holdings, including a 33-acre tract he acquired from an African American servant named Fortune Taylor. His first wife, Helen Mary Branch, and daughter Clara Vashti were victims of yellow fever epidemics in 1858 and 1857. Clarke and his second wife, Sarah L. Wall, had one daughter, Flossie, who married Andrew J. Knight. Clarke died in November 1886. Belarmino Vallejo's membership in the Woodmen of the World Society allowed him the privilege of a stone symbolic of the organization.

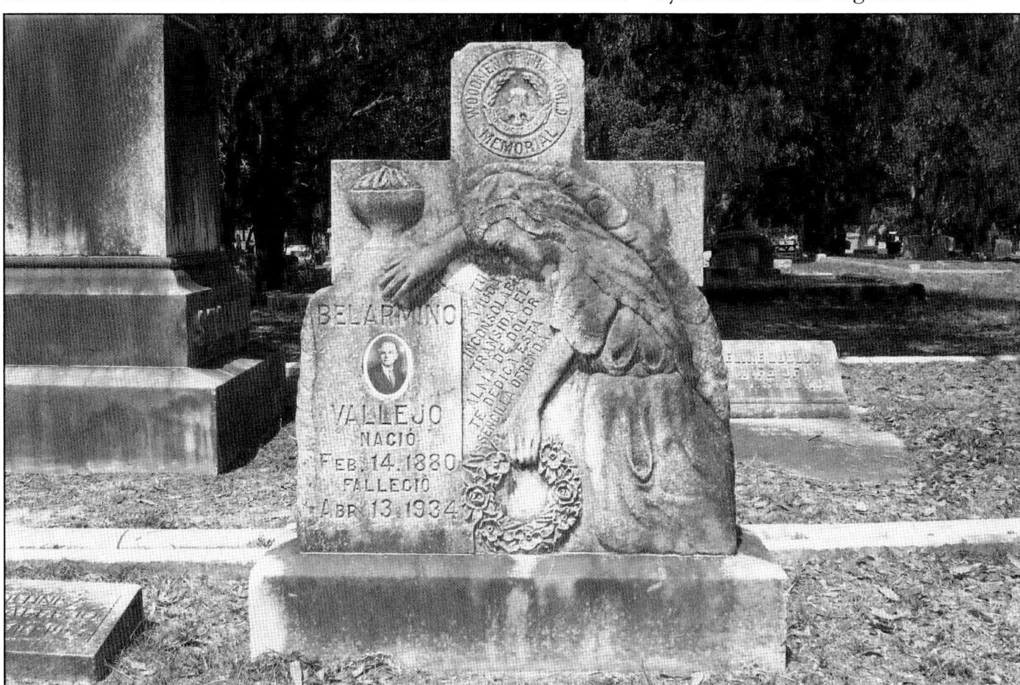

The parents of Joseph Grimaldi, John A. and Mary Stella Ardolino, were both born in Italy. Their oldest children were born in Massachusetts and, upon moving to Tampa, Florida, their son Joseph and his younger siblings were born. Father John started working as a barber and railroad ticket agent and later became a solicitor before going into the fire insurance business. He was one of the first presidents of the Italian Club and, in 1910, organized a second Italian Club, becoming its president. Mary Stella's parents, Antonio and Theodora Ardolino, immigrated to the United States in 1890 and, according to the 1910 census, were living with their daughter and her family.

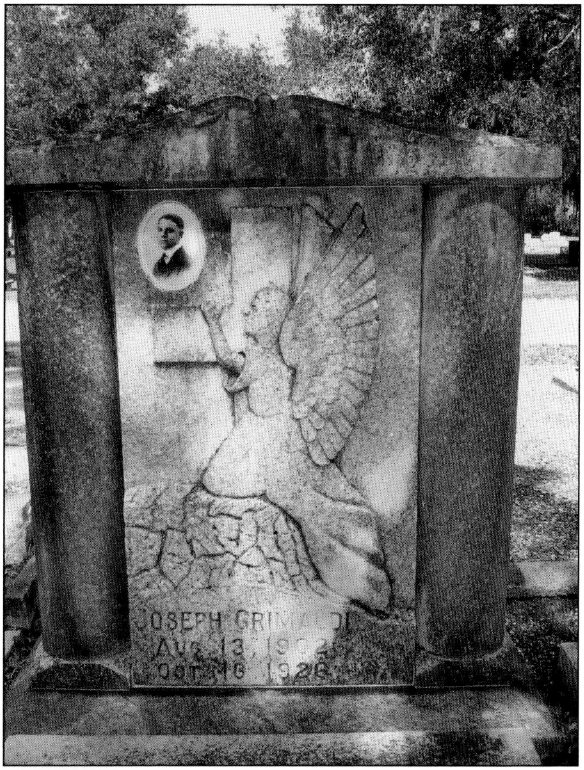

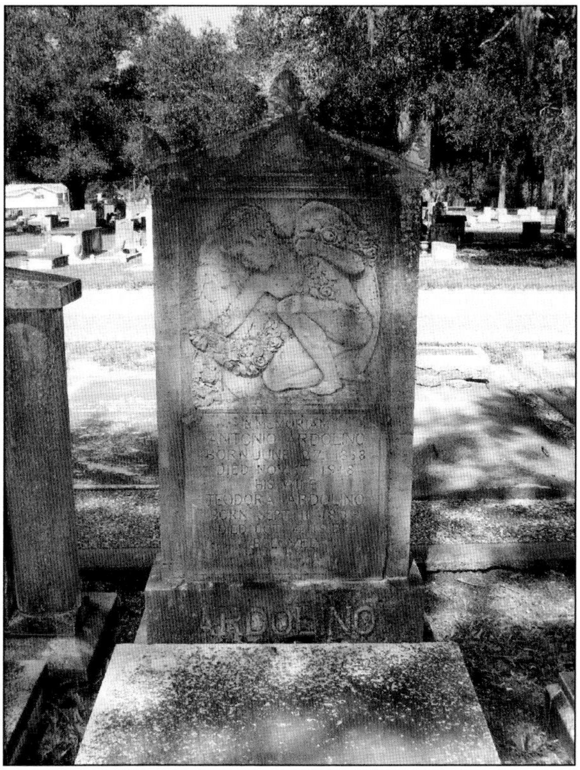

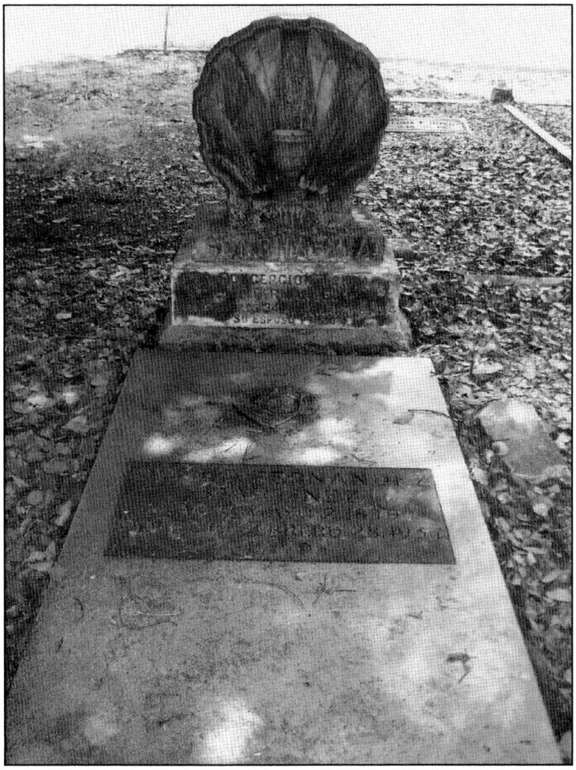

Ovidio Fernandez Martinez was born on May 2, 1879, and died on February 28, 1937. Part of the inscription written on this gravestone is in Italian. The large shell atop the headstone symbolizes birth, life, and baptism. He was a member of the Woodmen of the World, and his membership is symbolized on the bed stone.

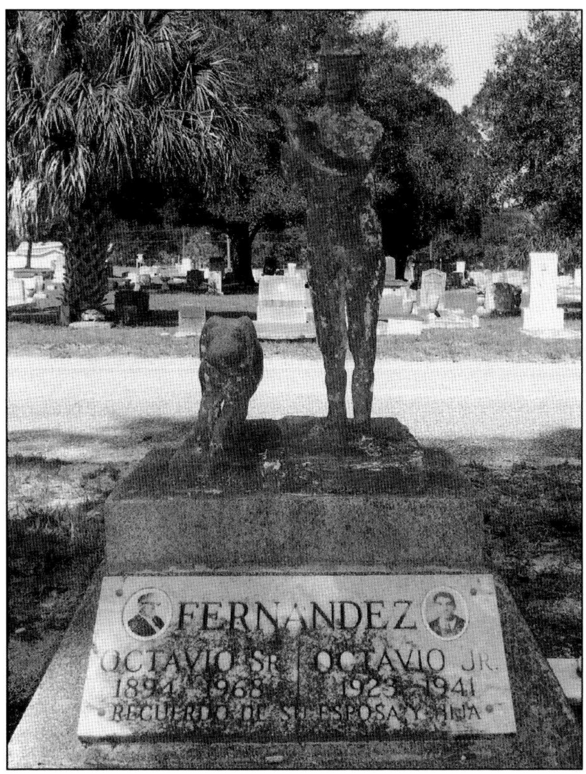

Father and son, Octavio Fernandez Sr. and Octavio Fernandez Jr., were laid to rest side by side. The concrete statute of the man with his dog and gun could be expressing his hobby as an outdoors sportsman. Ever faithful in life, his companion dog is still at his side. Octavio Sr., a cigar maker, was born in Jesus del Monte, Cuba. He married Ana Luisa Diaz on April 6, 1894. They had two children, Madeline and Octavio Jr.

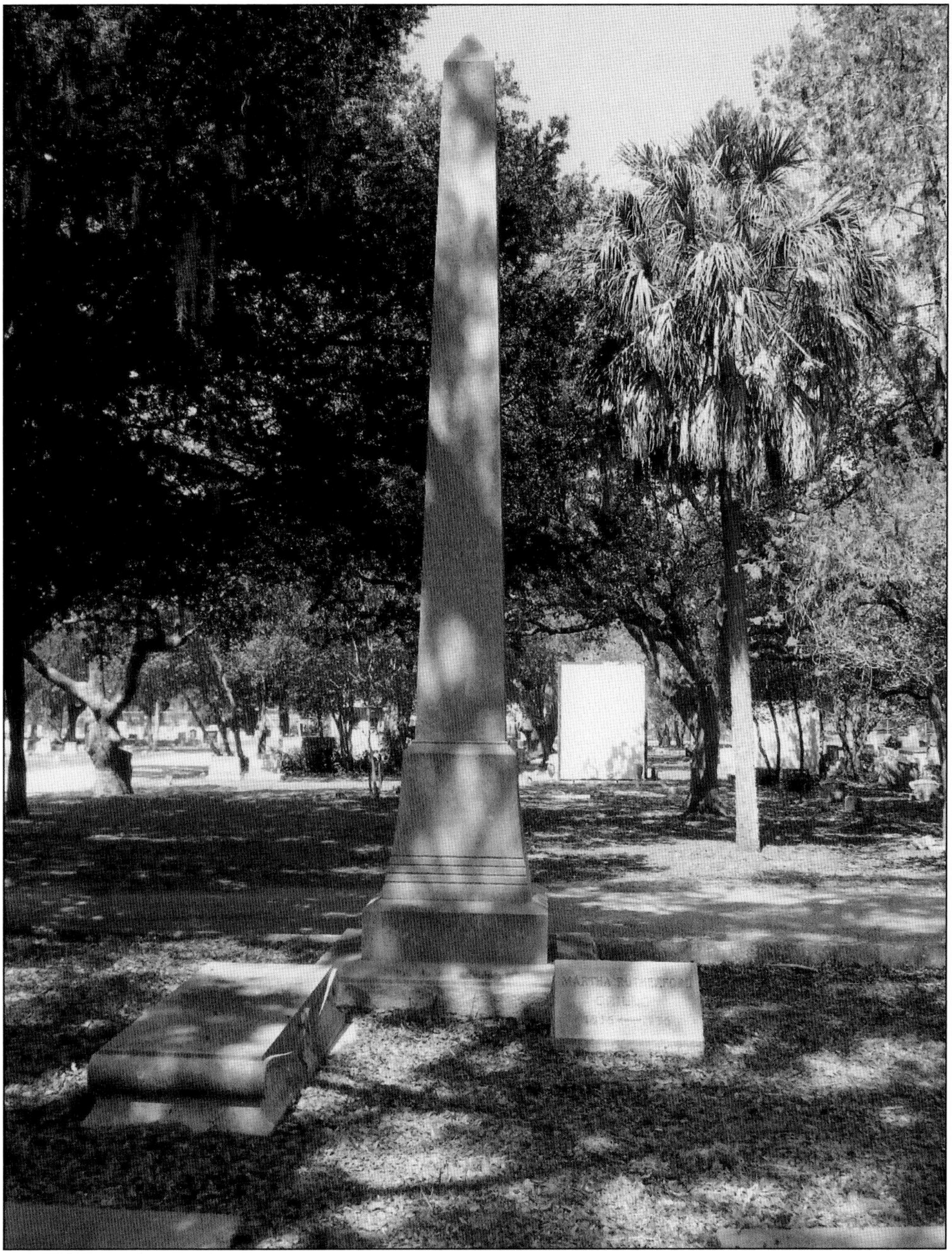

Odet Grillon was the son of John Grillon and Charlotte Septima Marie Phillippi, who was the daughter of Odet Phillippi. Odet was born on November 12, 1846, and died on October 28, 1913. Martha Rutherford Grillon was born in 1855 and died in 1936. The US Census records indicate that the Grillon family was of French descent. As early as 1860, the family lived in Key West and is enumerated with the keeper of the lighthouse. In 1870, Odet and his wife, Alice, had a three-year-old son, Henry. By 1885, they were living in Tampa alone, just two doors away from H.L. Mitchell. Odet was one of many men who were appointed to a relief committee for the 1887 yellow fever epidemic. The 1920 census lists Martha Grillon as a widow living on Bayshore Boulevard next door to the Clewis family.

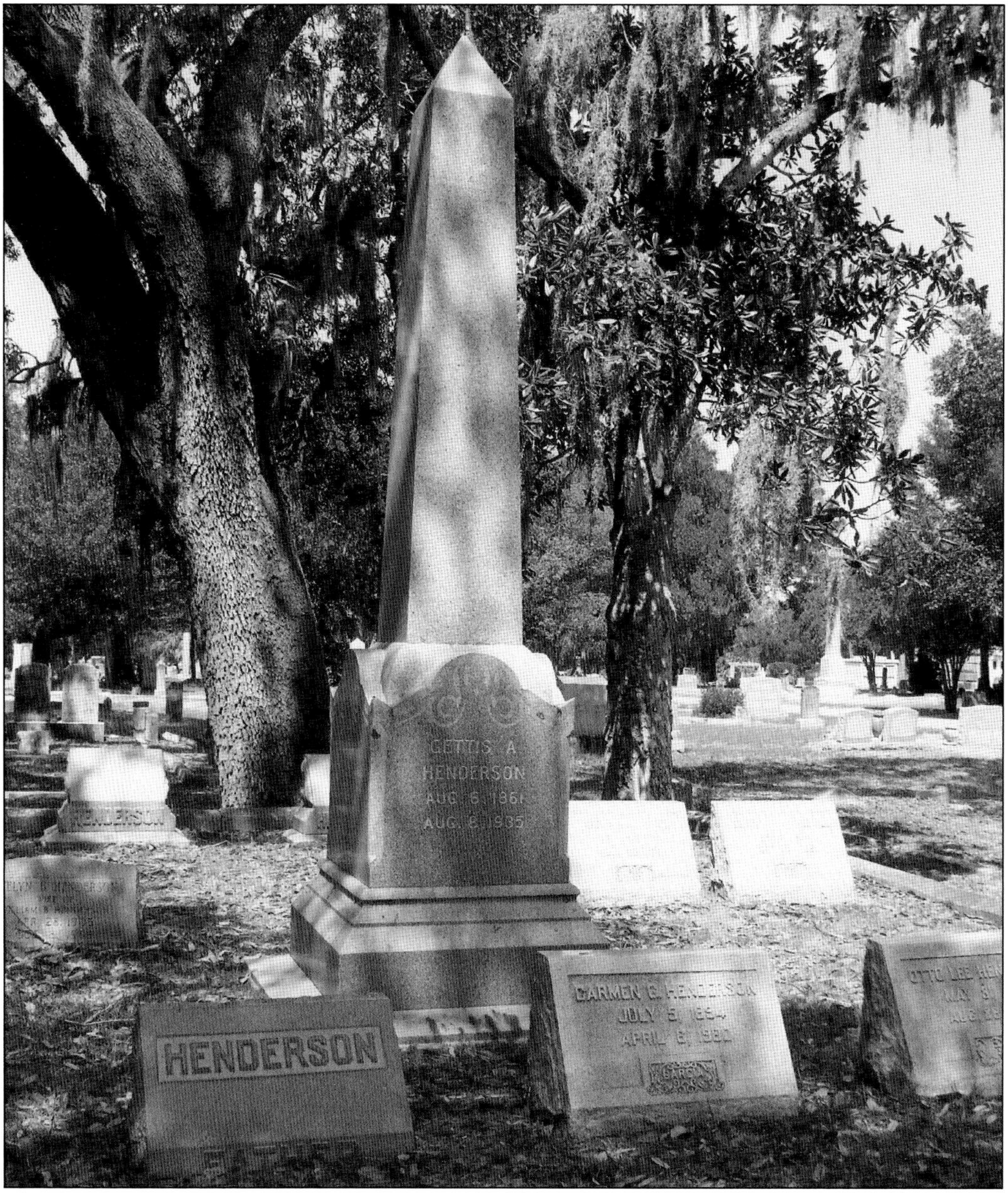

Gettis A. Henderson, of Oxford, Georgia, stated on his passport application of May 25, 1883, that he was born on the sixth day of August 1861 to parents William Benton Henderson and Caroline Elizabeth Spencer. He was applying for a passport to travel abroad to Europe. At the time, he was 21 years of age; five feet, five inches tall; and of fair complexion, with light hair and hazel eyes. His passport, which he had paid for with money order no. 3059, was issued on June 7, 1883. Wedding photographs of both he and his first wife, Harriet Evelyn Stallings, were taken at a photography studio in Atlanta. From this marriage came the following known children: Parks Augustus, Otto D., Cora Amanda, John, William B., Fannie M., and Emma. Hattie died on February 28, 1904. Sometime around 1905, Gettis married his second wife, Cassie, and they had the following children: Walter H., Gettis, and Elizabeth. Henderson died on August 8, 1935, in Atlanta and was brought back to Tampa and interred next to his first wife, Hattie.

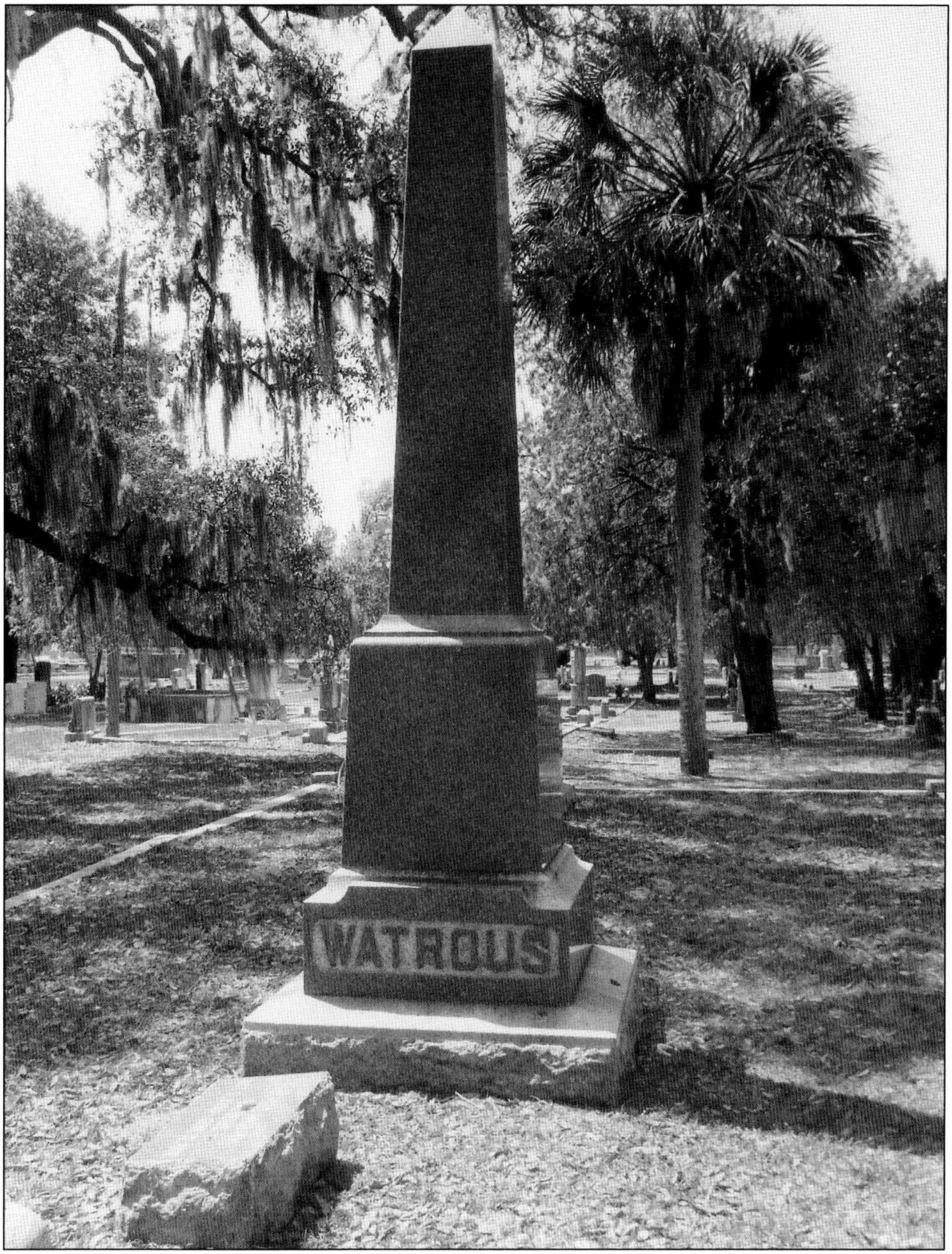

Harry James Watrous and his wife, Mary Nannie Givens of Alabama, were the parents of five children: Mary, Margaret, Louise, Harry, and Thomas Monroe. Harry's father, James M. Watrous, married Jennie "Jane" Elizabeth Robinson in Elmira, New York, on December 26, 1854. She died in Tampa on May 16, 1916. The Watrouses came to Tampa in 1876 and purchased a tract of land totaling 150 acres in the southwest section of the city along the shore of Hillsborough Bay. This land, which he had planted in orange and peach trees, is now a part of "Suburb Beautiful." Harry Sr. was college educated and involved in the real estate business. Their family lived on Morrison Avenue in the Hyde Park neighborhood. One daughter, Margaret, was a trained nurse, and a son, Thomas M., was a lawyer. According to the 1920 US Census, the senior Watrous was living next door to his son's family. He died on March 24, 1922.

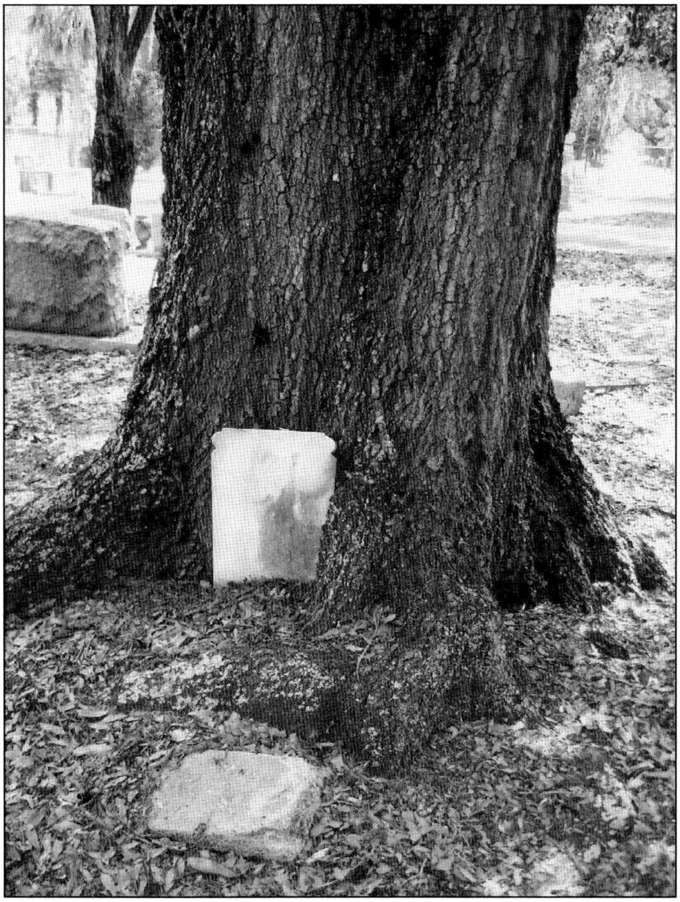

So many times, people hear the expression that a picture is worth a thousand words. Such is the case with this photograph, showing a small marble stone that has become enclosed by the growth of a large oak. All that remains readable on the stone is the name on the top, Victor. The size of the stone indicates that perhaps this is the grave of a child or young adult.

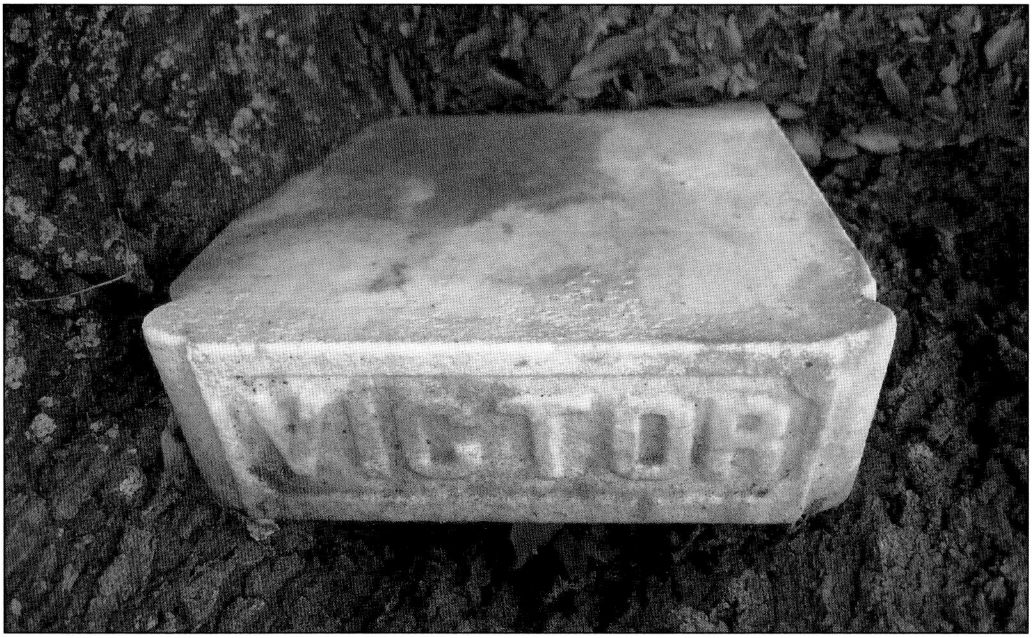

Four

Rodeph Sholom, Beth (Bet) Israel, and Schaarai Zedek

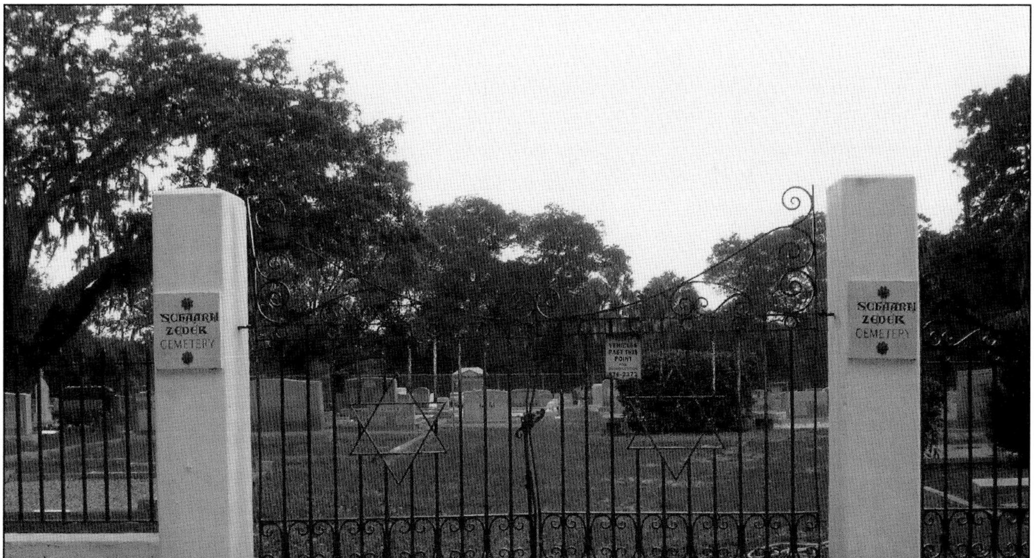

Schaarai Zedek, Tampa's first Jewish synagogue, counts as a founder Tampa's first Jewish mayor, Herman Glogowski. The Schaarai Zedek Cemetery was established in 1896. Many Jewish graves contain stones on top of the headstone. The placing of small stones using the left hand, a mitzvah, is a custom that indicates someone has visited the gravesite. In ancient times, graves were marked with mounds of stones; in placing or replacing them, one is perpetuating the existence of the gravesite.

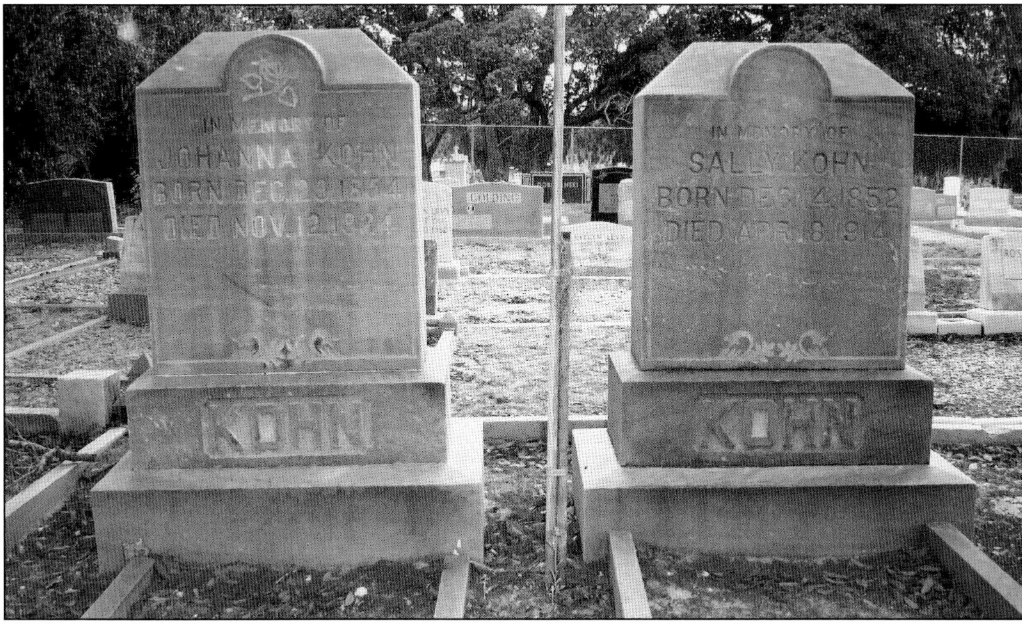

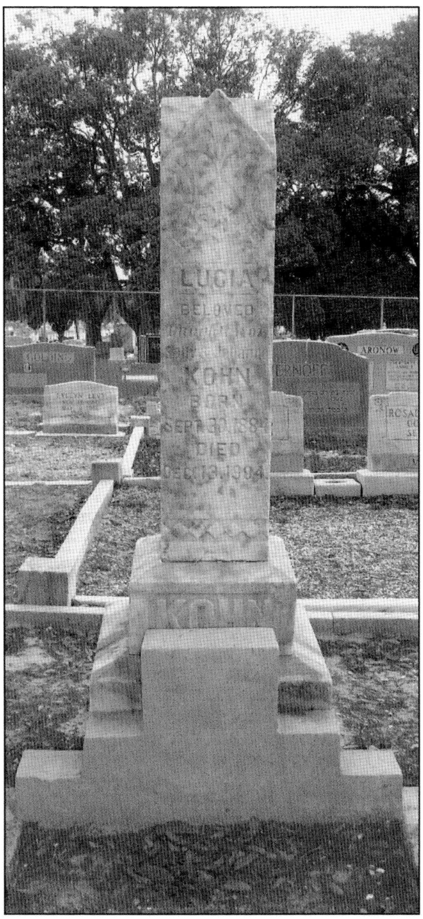

Sally (Saloman) Kohn (December 14, 1852–April 18, 1914) and his wife, Johanna Kohn (December 29, 1854–November 12, 1924), were married in 1872 and were the parents of two daughters, Rosabelle (b. October 1872) and Lucia (September 30, 1884–December 13, 1904). According to the *Polk's 1906 City Directory for Tampa*, Sally was a superintendent at the E'burg Gunst. Co., and by 1910 she was working at a cigar factory as a superintendent. Their family lived at 305 Azeele Street. After Sally's death in 1914, Johanna lived with their daughter Edna and her husband, Dr. Louis Levy, and their two children, Lawrence and Anita.

The family of little five-year-old Leon Perez had a photograph of him in boxing shorts and gloves framed within the headstone on his grave. The lamb is a symbol of innocence, and the pebbles placed on the stone indicate that someone has visited the grave—an old Jewish custom.

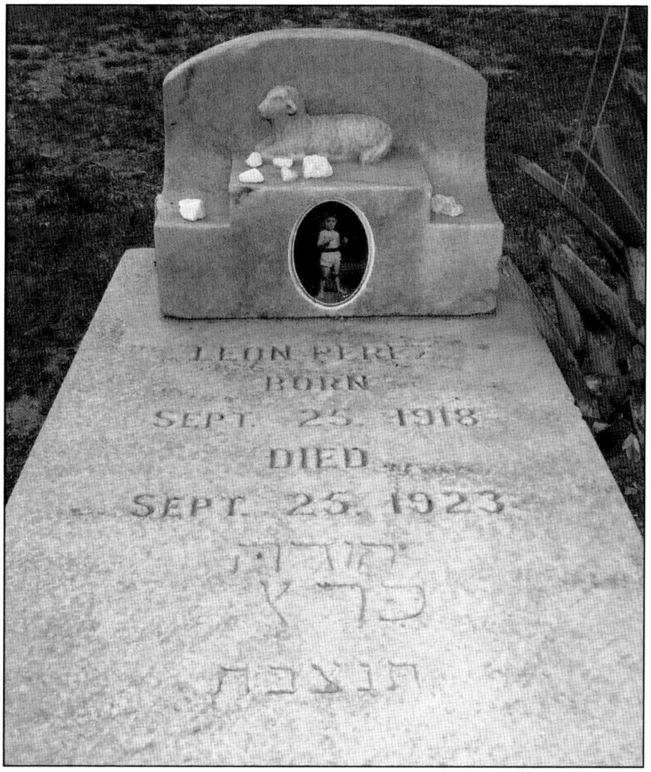

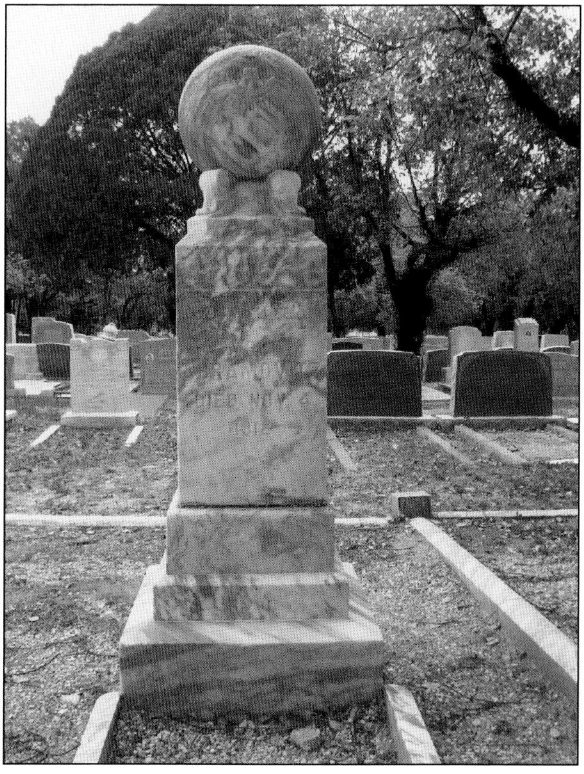

The Woodmen of the World emblem atop the orb on the footed pedestal signifies membership in this society for Wolf Arramovitz, who died on November 4, 1912. On October 14, 1894, thirty-one men and women met in the home of M. Henry Cohen to form the first synagogue in Tampa. Shaarai Zedek (Gates of Righteousness) was selected as the name. The corporate charter was granted on December 15, 1894. Rabbi D. Jacobson became the first rabbi.

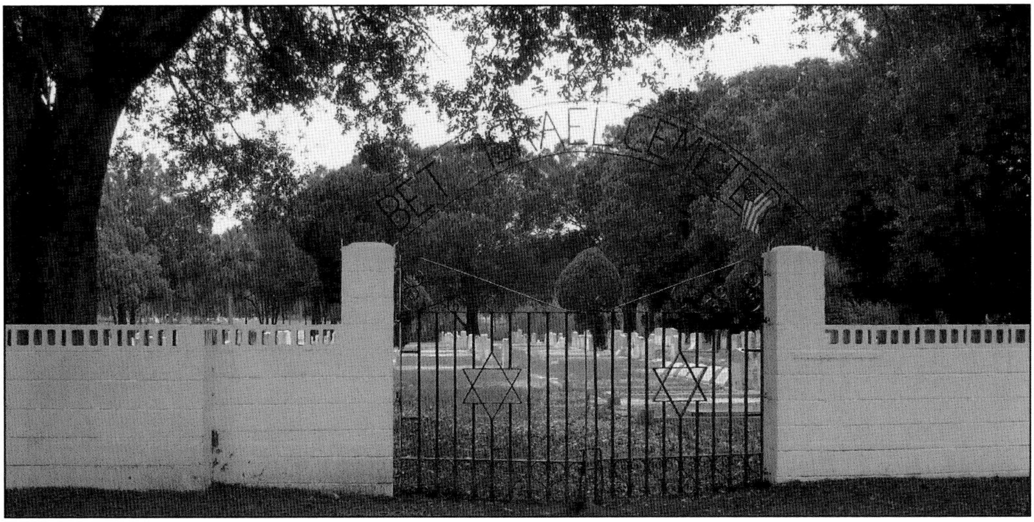

The Rodeph Sholom Cemetery was established in 1881, two years before the official establishment of Woodlawn. It expanded into a nonadjacent space known as Beth (Bet) Israel. The Beth (Bet) Israel Synagogue was established in 1952.

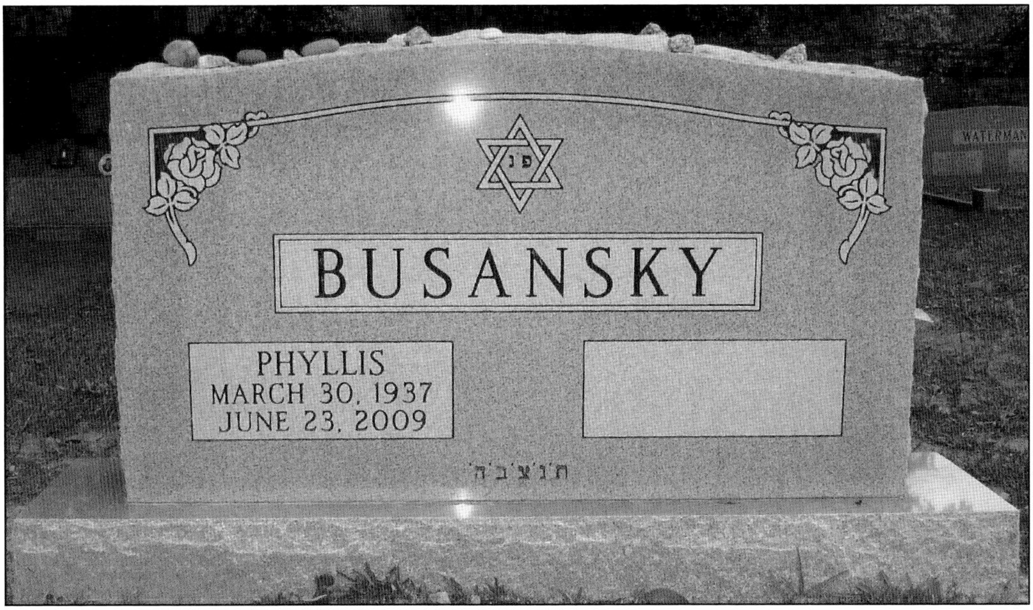

Phyllis Hendler Busansky was born in Hartford, Connecticut, on March 3, 1937, and graduated from Wheaton College with a bachelor's degree in English literature. She earned her MBA from the Heller School at Brandeis University and served on the faculty at Columbia University. In 1996, she became the first Heller alum to run for Congress (Florida District 11). In 1962, Phyllis and Sheldon Busansky moved to Florida, where she served as a Hillsborough County commissioner (1989–1997). She was the first executive director of Florida's welfare-to-work agency (WAGES) under governors Lawton Chiles and Jeb Bush. She won election in 2008 for Hillsborough County supervisor of elections. She passed away unexpectedly while attending a supervisor of elections conference and is survived by her husband, Sheldon, sons Alex and Edward, daughter Rebecca, and nine grandchildren. She was inducted into the Hillsborough County Women's Hall of Fame in 2012.

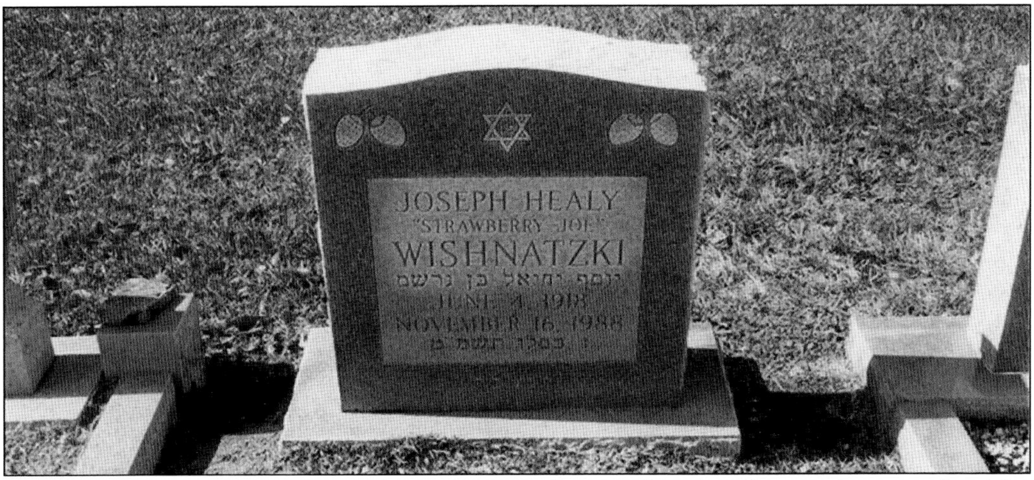

Joseph Healy Wishnatzki, or"Strawberry Joe," is well remembered in the strawberry market. The forerunner of Wishnatzki Farms, Wishnatzki and Nathel, was founded in 1922 in New York City by pushcart owners Harris Wishnatzki and Daniel Nathel. Wishnatzki, a Russian immigrant who arrived in New York City in 1900, had been selling fresh fruits and vegetables from his pushcart for several years. By the late 1920s, Wishnatzki was making regular trips to Florida to purchase produce. In 1929, he relocated permanently to Plant City, Florida, to set up a shipping operation while Nathel remained in New York City. In Florida, Wishnatzki envisioned bringing fresh strawberries to fruit-deprived consumers in the northern states during the winter months. Challenges with transporting perishable goods were eventually overcome, and the company's New York City hub began distributing fresh fruit. Thanks to Wishnatzki, Plant City growers gained access to large American markets.

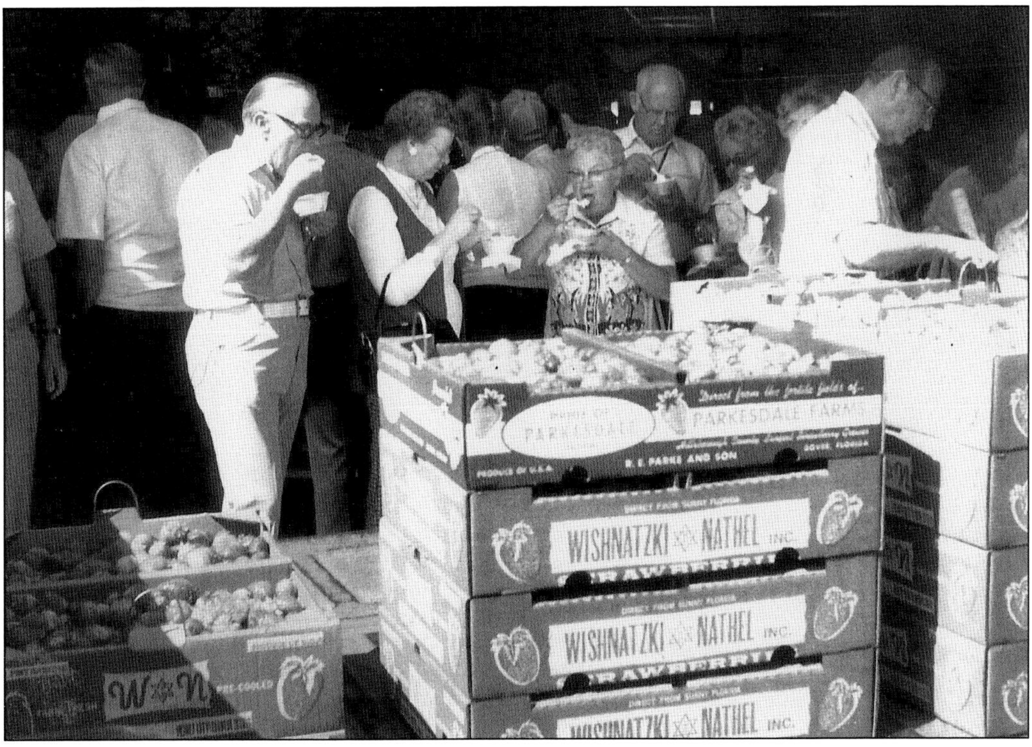

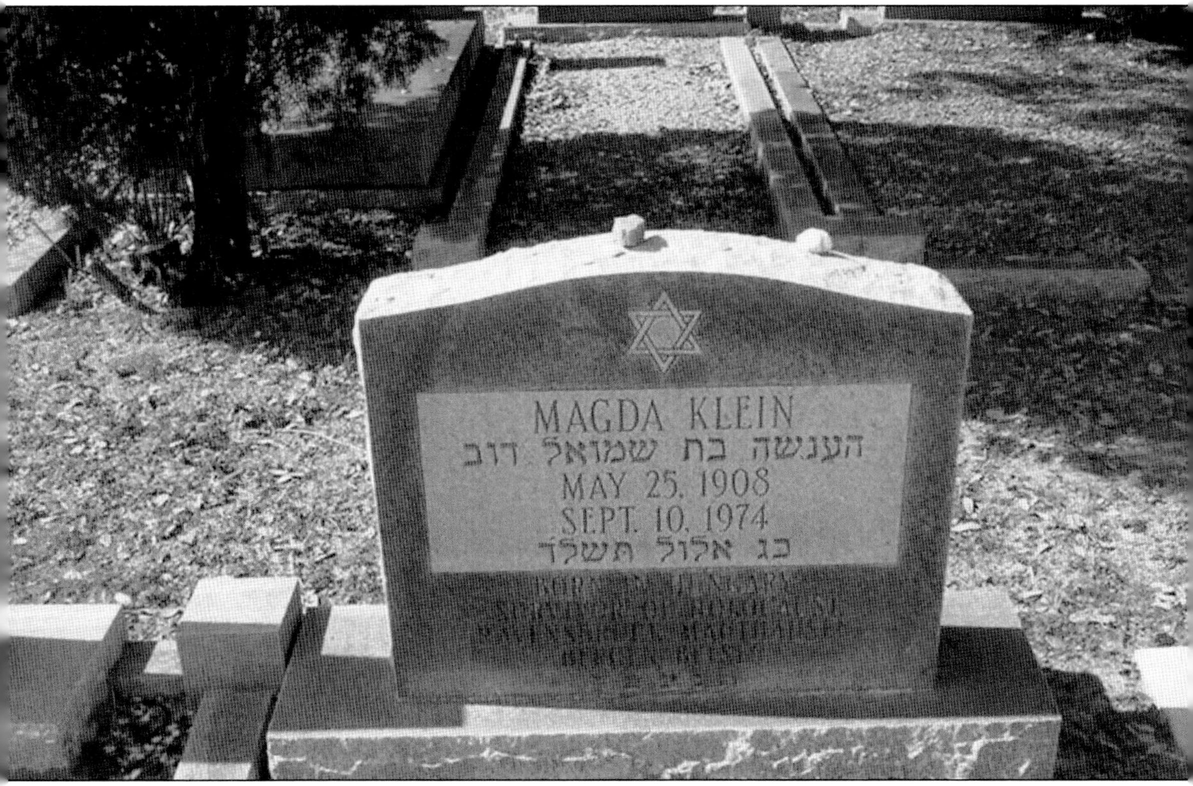

Magda Klein (May 25, 1908–September 10, 1974) was a survivor of the Holocaust. Telling, teaching about, and writing memoirs of the Holocaust recalls the painful past in order to assure future generations of children an innocent and happy childhood free of menacing violence.

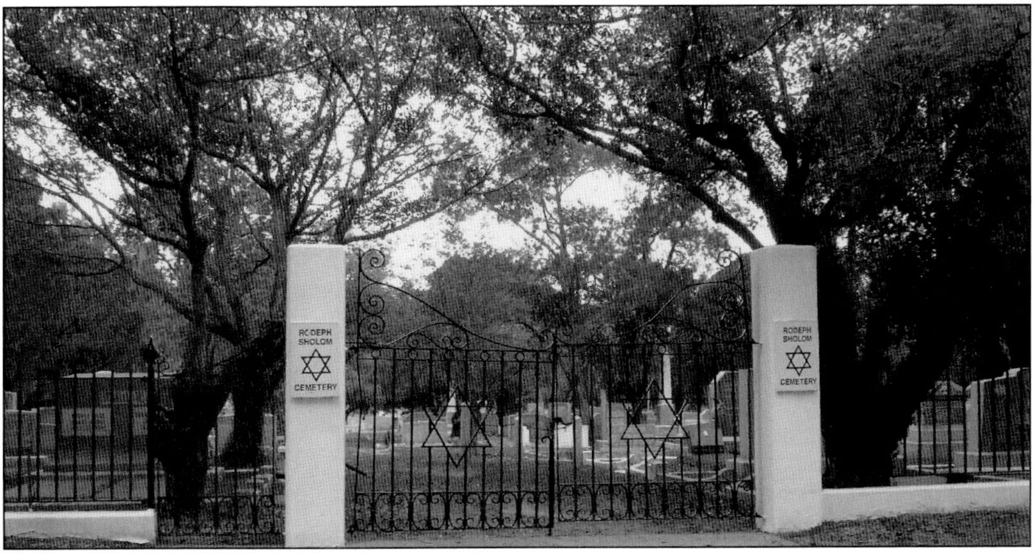

The Rodeph Sholom Cemetery was established in 1881, two years before the official establishment of Woodlawn. In 1903, a group of men met at the home of J.L. Mairson to organize a synagogue. The name Rodeph Sholom (Pursuers of Peace) was proposed by S.S. Zelnicker. The birth of Tampa's new congregation was met with great enthusiasm. Starting with 26 families, it grew rapidly, and within a few years there were 100 families.

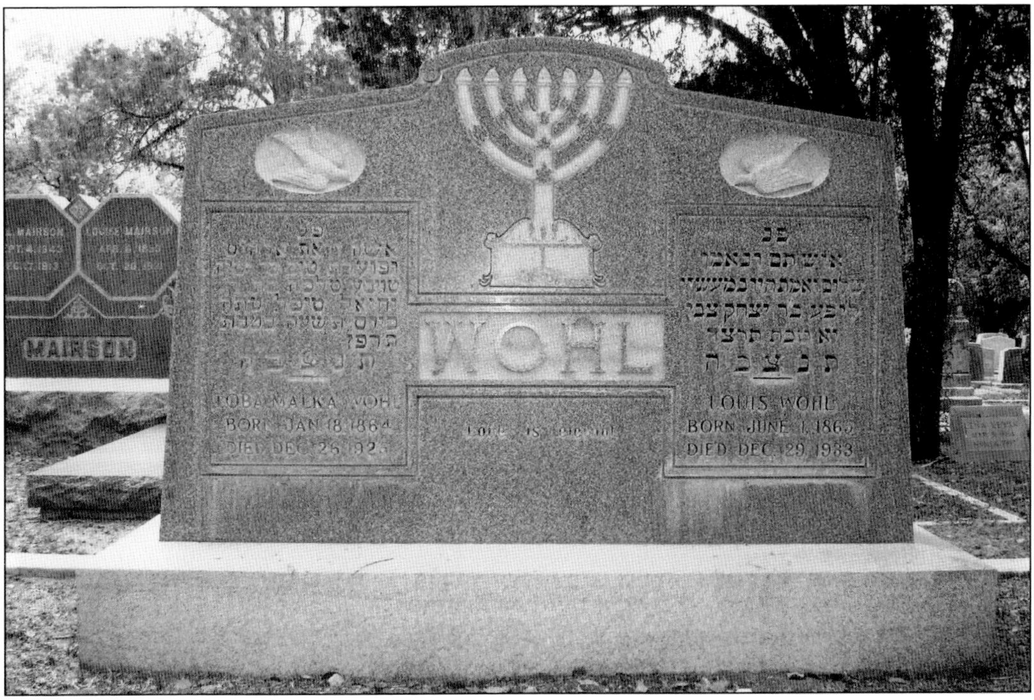

Louis Wohl was born in Iasi, Romania, on June 1, 1865, the son of Isidor and Leah Wohl. He was educated in schools in his native country and immigrated to the United States in 1888. He married Toba Malka Kasriel, also a Romanian, on August 10, 1891, in New York. Eventually settling in Tampa, their family grew to include six children. After his first store was destroyed by fire, he opened up his new "racket store" in Ybor City, which today is known as Louis Wohl & Sons.

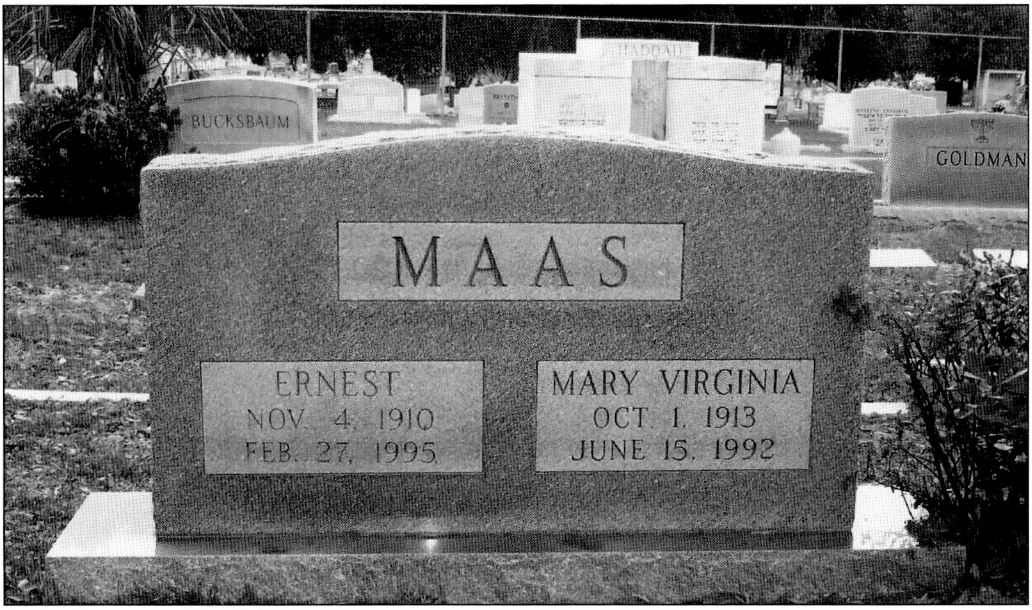

Ernest Maas, born in 1910, was the son of Ernest Maas and Maude Baer, who were married in 1909. The elder Maas stated he was born in Dolgrsheiere, Germany (Dolgesheim, Mainz-Bingen, Rheinland-Pfalz, Germany), and had traveled to the United States from Bremen on September 15, 1895. He listed his father as being Joseph Maas of Hessen-Kassel. They were involved with their family department store, Maas Brothers, which sold a fine line of clothing and home furnishings.

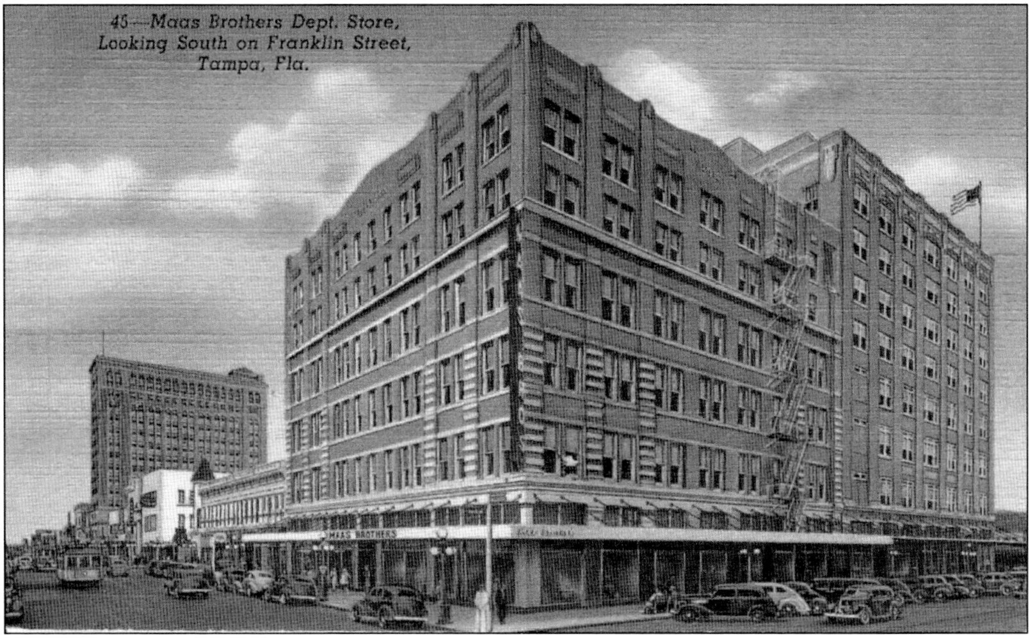

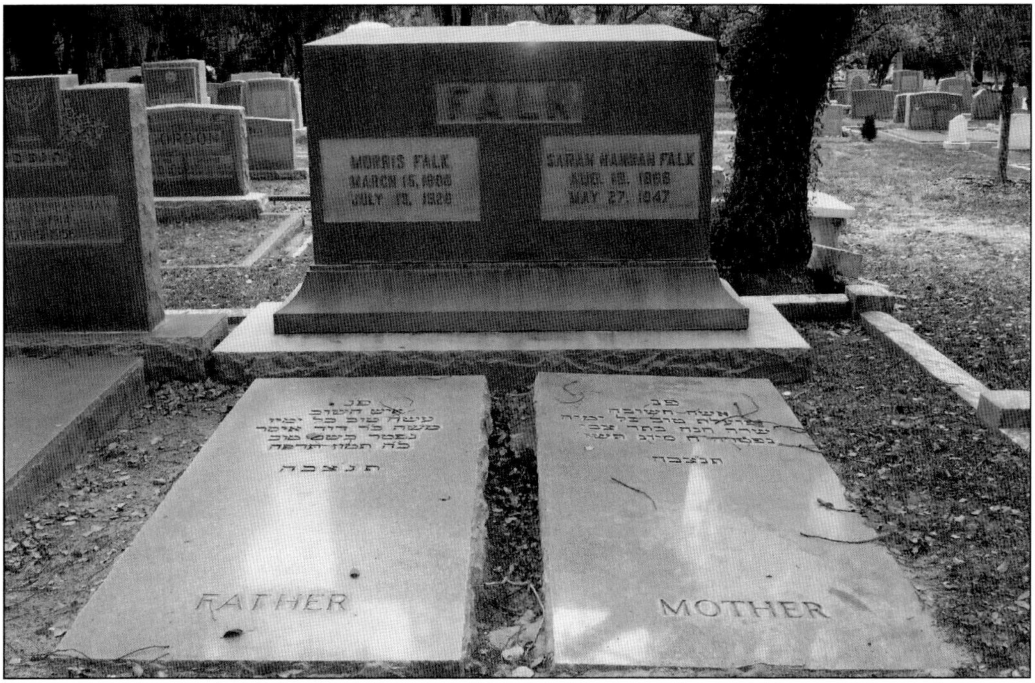

Morris and Sarah Hannah Falk and their daughter, Lizzie, shared their home on Florida Avenue with Morris's brother Offin and his wife, Emma, and son David. David A. Falk was born in Tampa in 1896, the only son of a Polish immigrant father. He graduated from Hillsborough High School, attended Washington and Lee University, and served in World War I. When he returned to Tampa, he joined his father in the family business, O. Falk's Department Store, which was downtown on Franklin Street. His volunteer service on the University of Tampa Board of Trustees, from 1948 until his death in 1960, earned him the commemoration of the David Falk Memorial Theater. The 1928 theater is directly across Kennedy Boulevard from the University of Tampa. The photograph below, taken on June 4, 1924, shows the Falk Building at the corner of Tampa and Polk Streets. The crossing gates on the right were probably used by streetcar and railroad lines. (THCPL.)

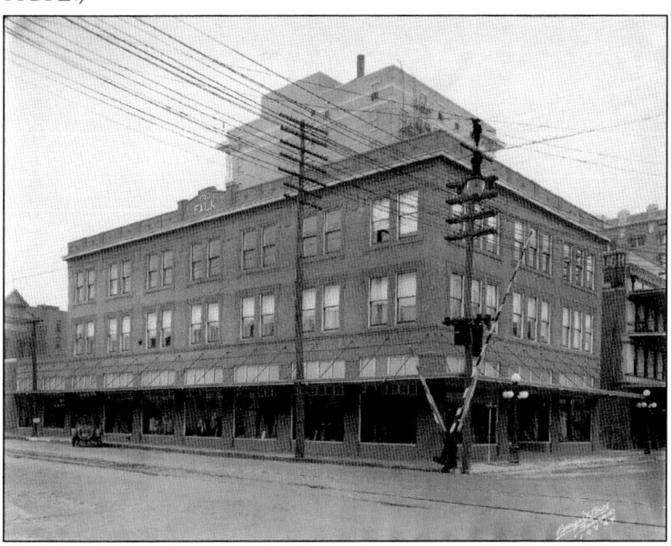

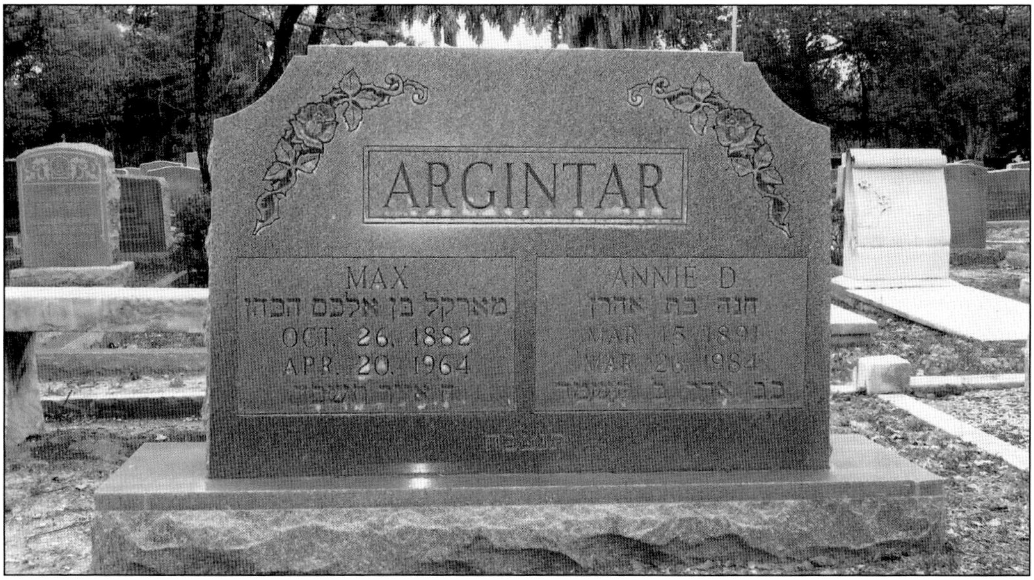

Max and Annie Argintar were both immigrants from Romania. From page four of the *Key West Citizen* newspaper dated Monday, October 24, 1932, "Mrs. Max Argintar, formerly Miss Annie Davis, of Key West, who was spending several weeks as the guest of her uncle and aunt, Mrs. D. Aronovitz & other relatives, left Saturday over the East Coast for a short visit in Miami before returning to her home in Tampa." The clothing store of Max Argintar featured everything a well-dressed gentleman would desire. (THCPL.)

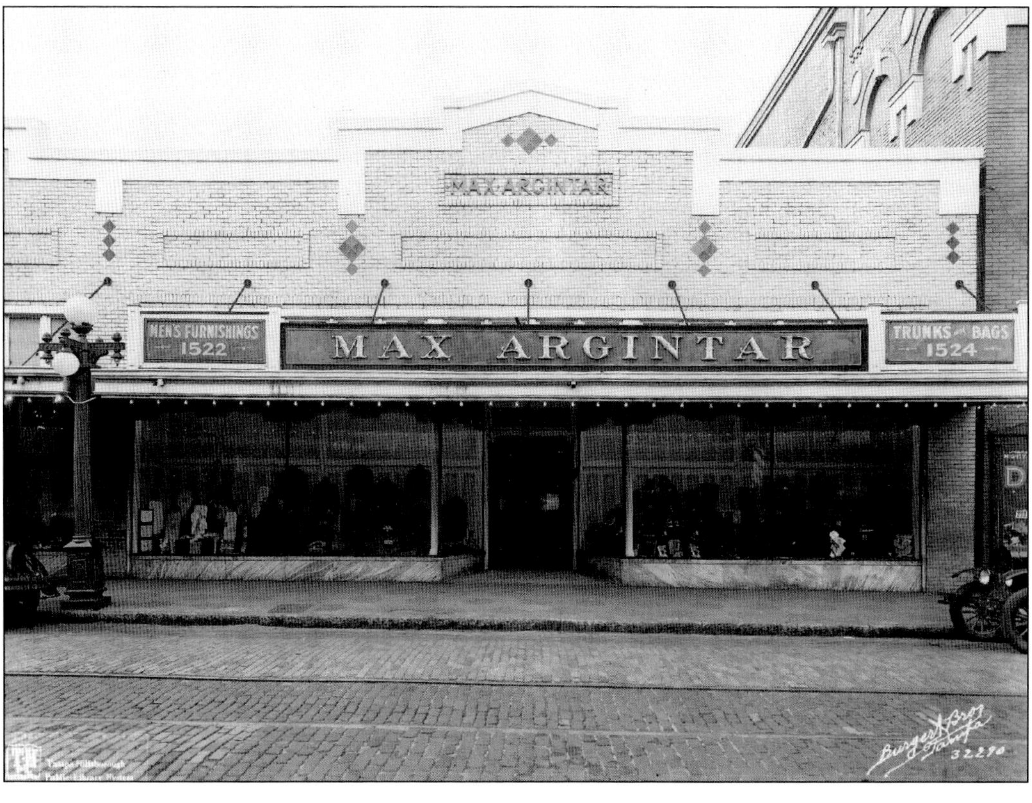

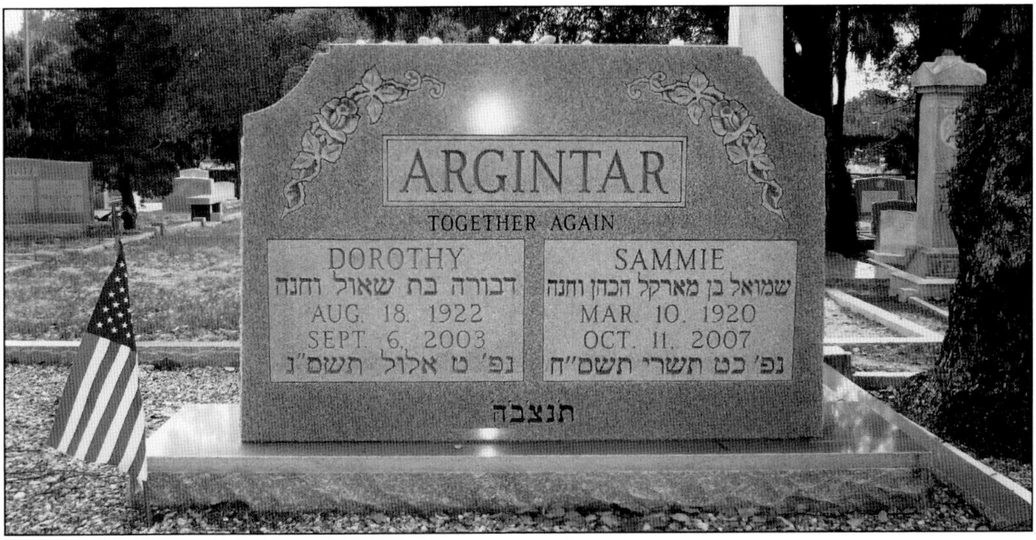

Sammie Argintar and his wife, Dorothy, were affiliated with the family store. According to the 1935 State of Florida Census, they lived at 2309 Nebraska Avenue, and Sammie was a merchant. His sister Florence and her husband, Dr. Fred Lebos, who was a dentist, were living in the same household.

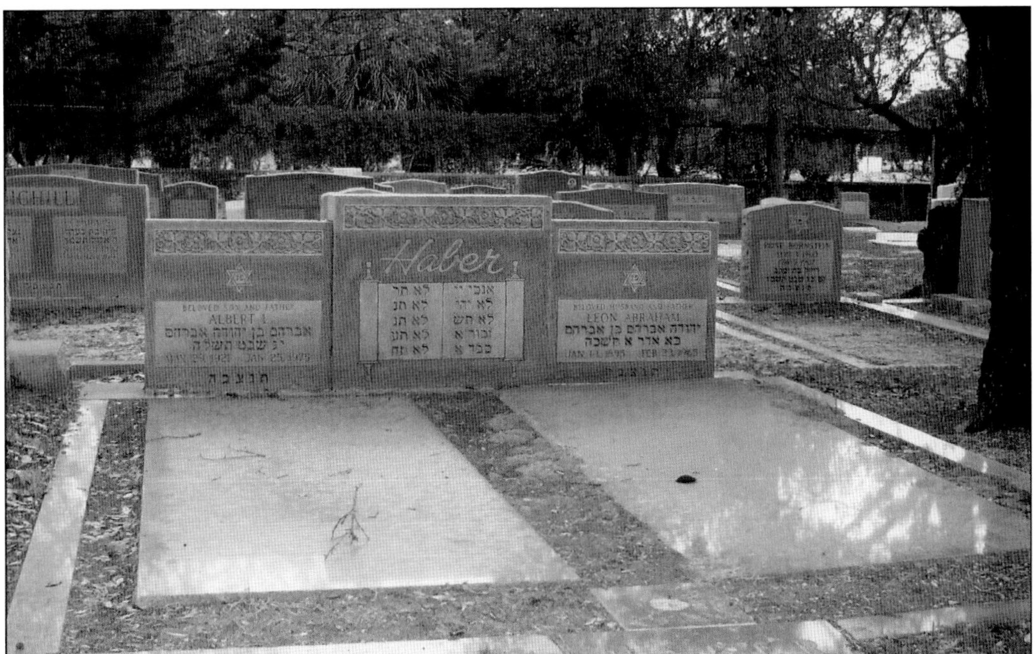

In 1975, at the time of his death at the age of 52, Albert Haber owned stores in Tampa and St. Petersburg. Joseph Brandt, age 39, who pleaded guilty to murdering department store magnate Albert Haber, told police he was hired by Haber's wife, 39-year-old Betty Lou Haber, and her 22-year-old son Arnold Jefferson McEver III. He testified against the pair at their trial. With Brandt as the star prosecution witness, mother and son were both convicted of first-degree murder and sentenced to life in prison. Brandt testified that he was offered $15,000, to be paid when Mrs. Haber received her life insurance benefits.

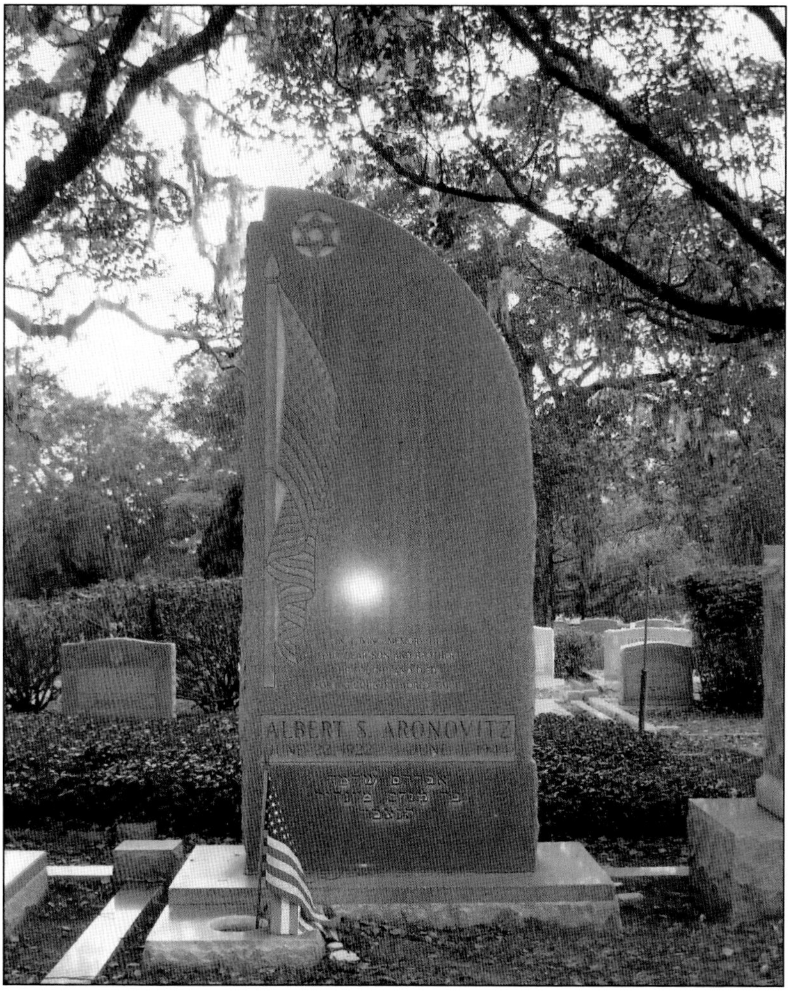

Sgt. Albert S. Aronovitz was the son of Mr. and Mrs. Manuel Aronovitz. According to the National Jewish Welfare Board Bureau of War Records, he was killed in action on June 1, 1944, in Italy. His parents resided at 848 South Willow Street in the Hyde Park neighborhood.

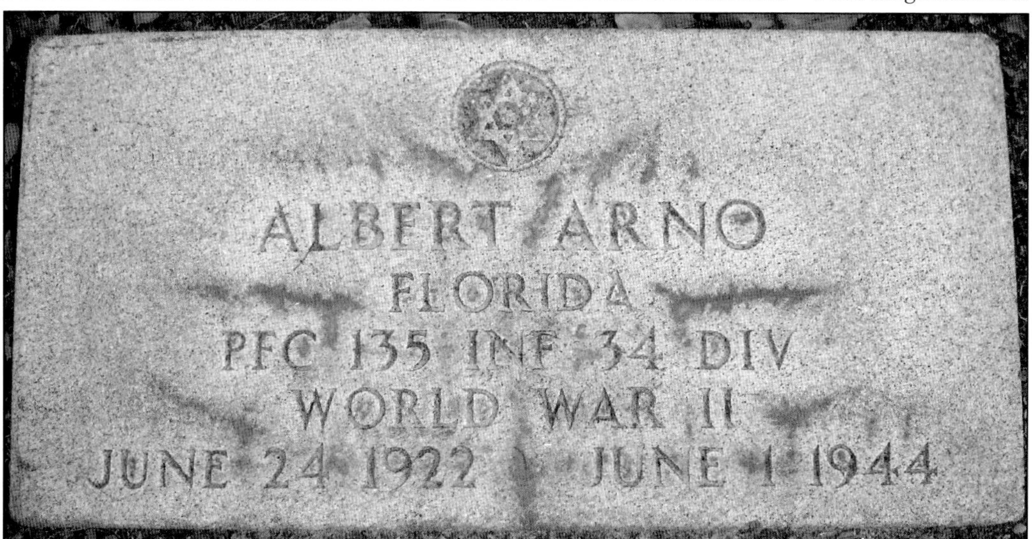

Five

Centro Asturiano Memorial Park, Centro Asturiano (Old), and El Centro Español

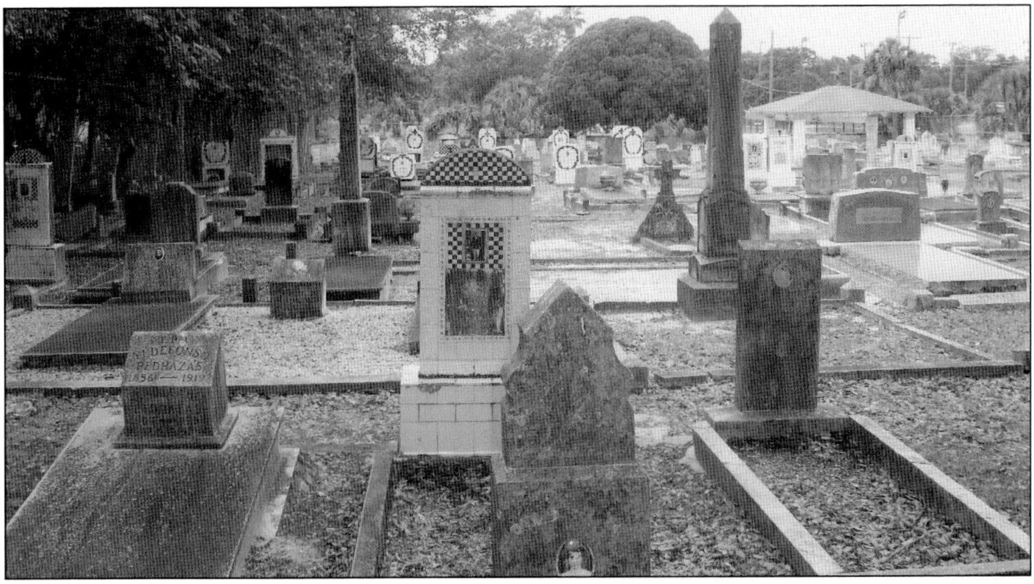

Two cemeteries were established for members of El Centro Asturiano de Tampa and their families. The "Old" Centro Asturiano Cemetery was established in 1904 after the cemetery land was donated for the club's use by the City of Tampa. Among the 601 persons interred at the Old Centro Asturiano Cemetery is club founder Antonio Gonzales Prado, who was buried there in 1904.

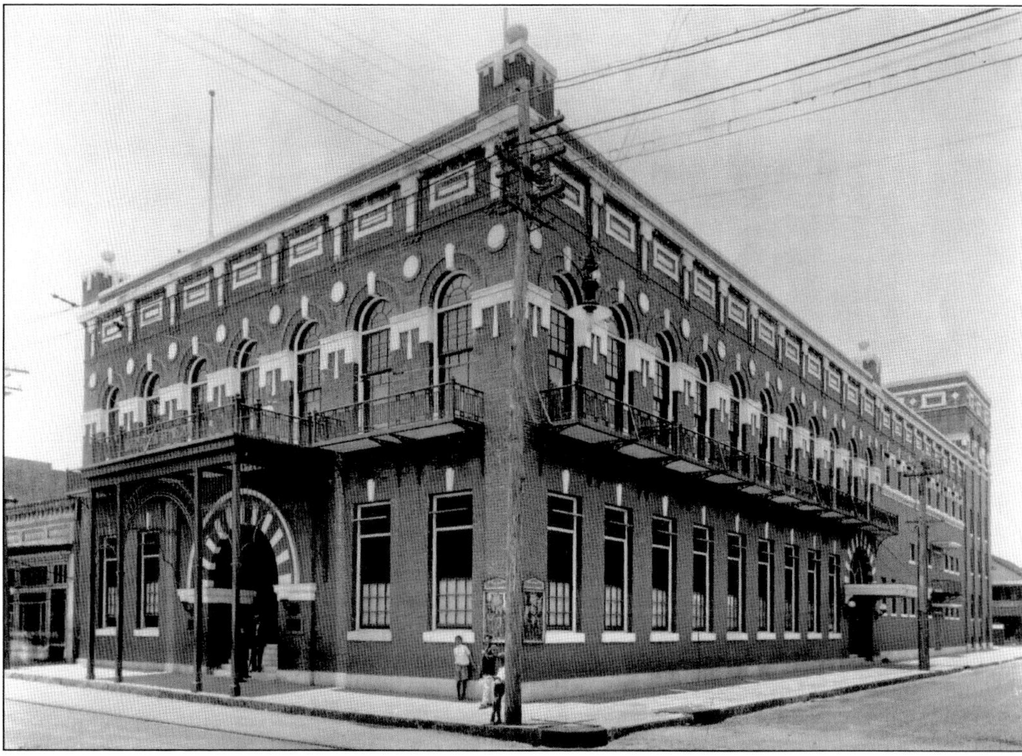

El Centro Español de Tampa is a social club for immigrants and the descendants of immigrants. Chartered on September 7, 1891, El Centro Español was the first Latin club organized in Ybor City, Tampa's "Latin Quarter." The society opened the first club building in June 1892 on land purchased by Ignacio Haya at Sixteenth Street and Seventh Avenue. By 1909, club officers embarked on a building campaign to build two new clubhouses: one in Ybor City and one to accommodate members in West Tampa. Complete in 1912, El Centro Español de Tampa sits on the site of the original structure on Seventh Avenue. The Centro Español building received recognition as a U.S. National Historic Landmark on June 3, 1988, and is included in the National Register of Historic Places. (THCPL.)

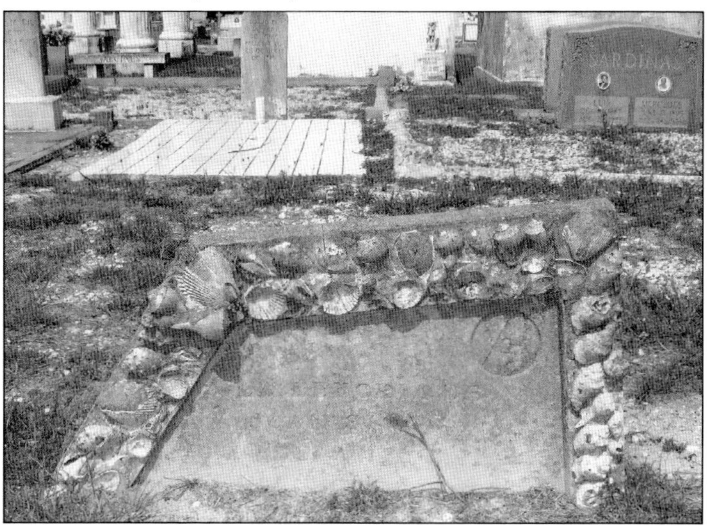

This homemade grave marker using scallop and conch shells is commonly seen in cultural and rural cemeteries. The shells are a symbol of birth, baptism, and life. The concrete base appears to have had names inserted by letter stamps but is no longer easy to read. The method of gravestone rubbing (attaining traces of names by the use of paper and pencil) is highly discouraged and is often prohibited by cemetery rules.

Like everything else in life, even the cemetery has rules. *The Cementerio del Centro Español* booklet was provided to members of the social club explaining the benefits and services. (USFSPC.)

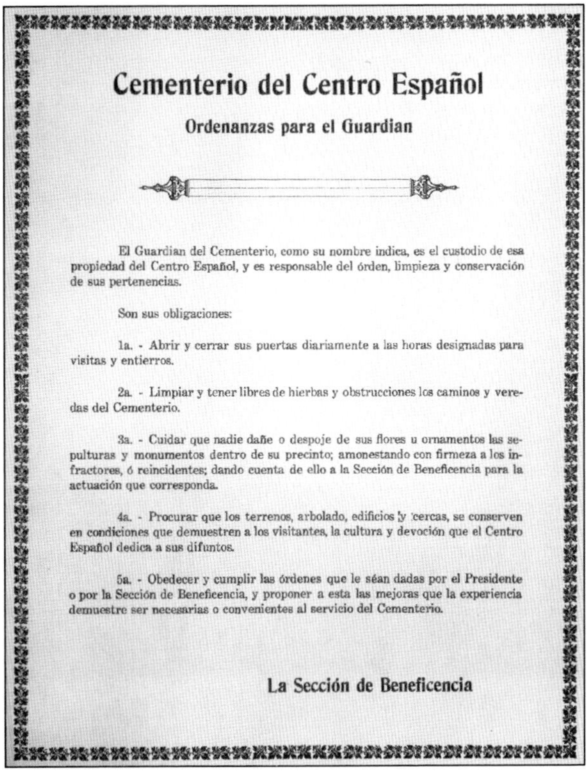

Cementerio del Centro Español

Ordenanzas para el Guardian

El Guardian del Cementerio, como su nombre indica, es el custodio de esa propiedad del Centro Español, y es responsable del órden, limpieza y conservación de sus pertenencias.

Son sus obligaciones:

1a. - Abrir y cerrar sus puertas diariamente a las horas designadas para visitas y entierros.

2a. - Limpiar y tener libres de hierbas y obstrucciones los caminos y veredas del Cementerio.

3a. - Cuidar que nadie dañe o despoje de sus flores u ornamentos las sepulturas y monumentos dentro de su precinto; amonestando con firmeza a los infractores, ó reincidentes; dando cuenta de ello a la Sección de Beneficencia para la actuación que corresponda.

4a. - Procurar que los terrenos, arbolado, edificios y cercas, se conserven en condiciones que demuestren a los visitantes, la cultura y devoción que el Centro Español dedica a sus difuntos.

5a. - Obedecer y cumplir las órdenes que le séan dadas por el Presidente o por la Sección de Beneficencia, y proponer a esta las mejoras que la experiencia demuestre ser necesarias o convenientes al servicio del Cementerio.

La Sección de Beneficencia

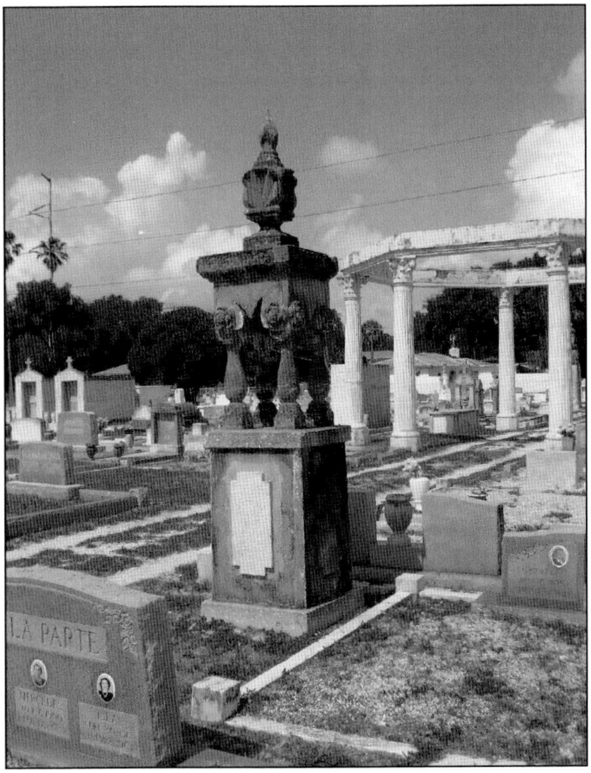

This table-style monument at the grave of Antonio Pagron can be interpreted as the preparation for the heavenly feast that is awaiting his passing into heaven. Typical of the early 20th century, this prime example contains an urn atop the table, signifying an occupied grave and mortality. The roses signify brevity of life, grief, and sorrow.

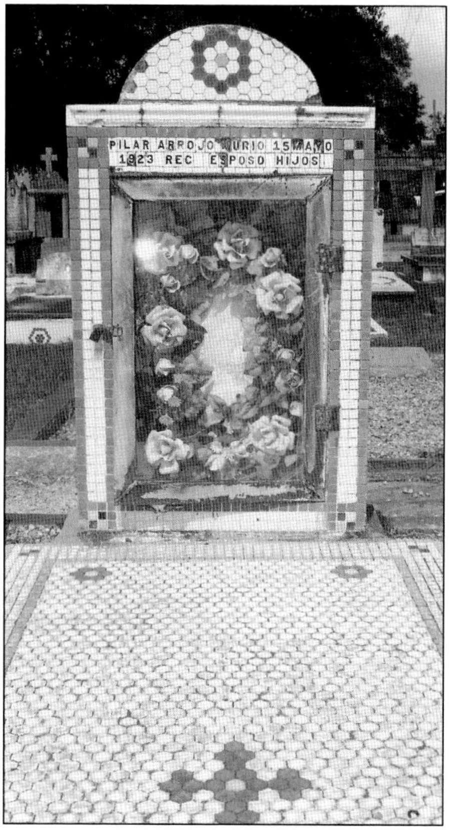

Typical of many of the gravestones in the Centro Español Cemetery are these two examples of hand-laid tile placed in geometric patterns, including the spelling out of the departed person's name, birth and death dates, and any inscriptions of endearment. Quite often, the front of the upright portion of the monument had a glass enclosure for placement of floral arrangements, as seen on the stone for Pilar Arrojo Murio (left). The stone for Carmela Sardegna (below) appears to have had another concrete symbolic element atop the upright column, which has been broken. The oval inset with portrait remains intact.

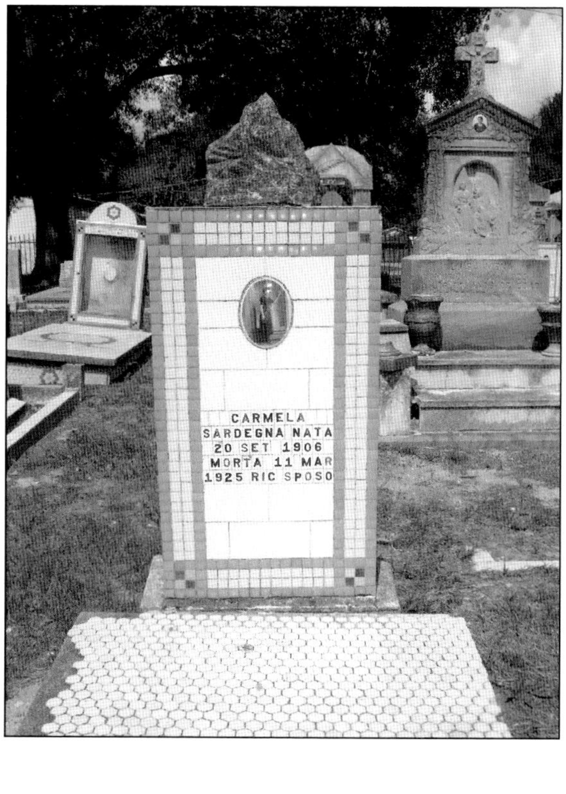

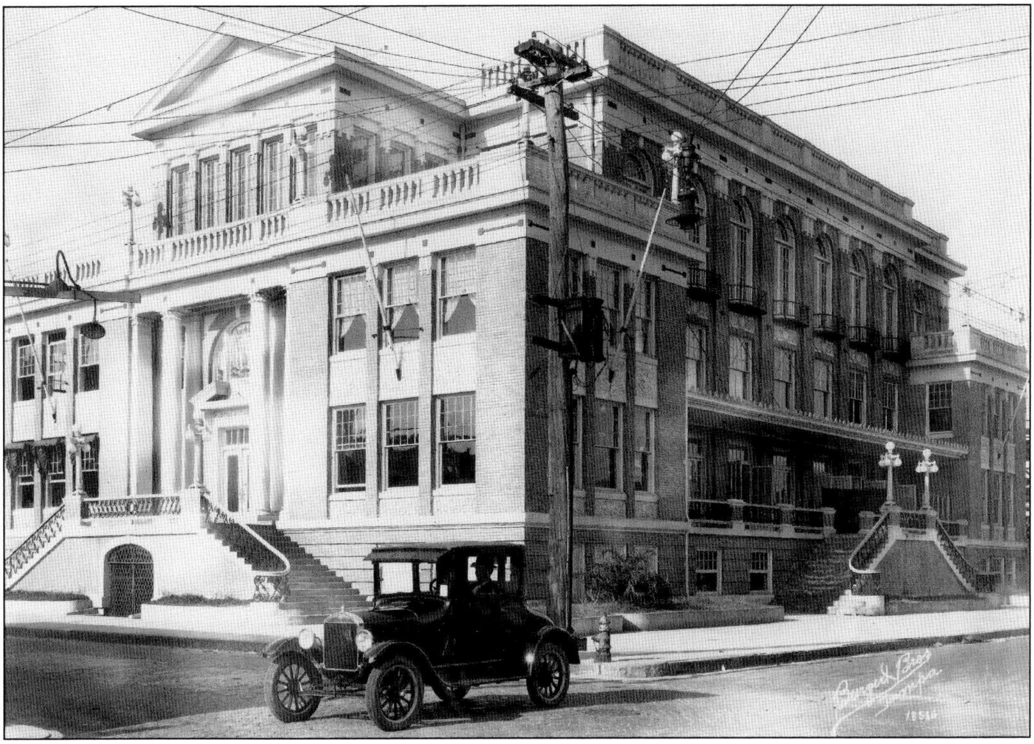

El Circulo Cubano de Tampa (also known as the Cuban Club) is a historic site in Ybor City located at Palm Avenue and Fourteenth Street. On November 15, 1972, it was added to the National Register of Historic Places. On April 18, 2012, the AIA's Florida chapter placed the building on its list of Florida Architecture: 100 Years. 100 Places as Cuban Club, Ybor City. (THCPL.)

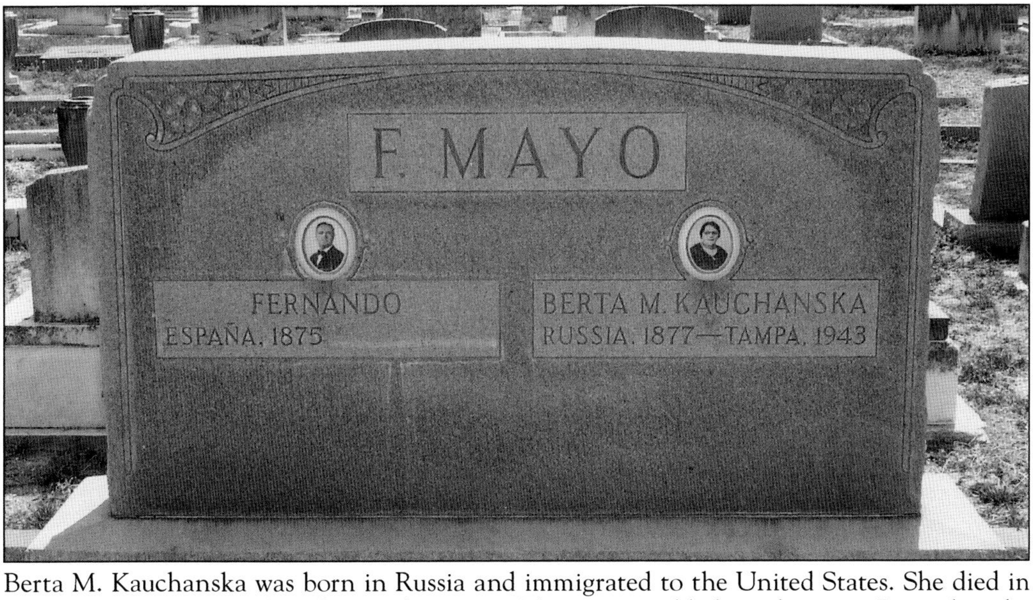

Berta M. Kauchanska was born in Russia and immigrated to the United States. She died in Tampa in 1943. Fernando, who was born in 1875, is presumably buried next to Berta, but the date of his death has not been added. Perhaps they have no local family remaining to assist in the maintenance of their final resting site.

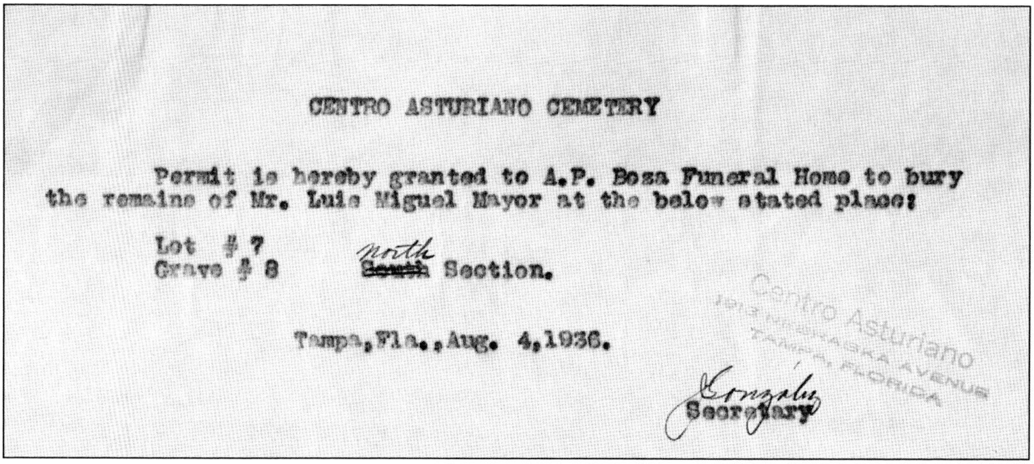

CENTRO ASTURIANO CEMETERY

Permit is hereby granted to A.P. Boza Funeral Home to bury the remains of Mr. Luis Miguel Mayor at the below stated place:

Lot # 7
Grave # 8 ~~South~~ north Section.

Tampa, Fla., Aug. 4, 1936.

Gonzalez
Secretary

Centro Asturiano
1913 Nebraska Avenue
Tampa, Florida

The Special Collections Department at the University of South Florida has items that pertain to different subject areas, including local cemetery records and ledgers. This cemetery card (above) is a noncirculating item. At times, researchers may find a ledger entry or paper document indicating burial at a location at which a gravestone marker has or has not been placed. In some cases, maps are discovered that identify all of the known occupied burial lots at a given point in time. The mayor marker (below) and entry card are a good example of this correlation between the written records and the physical markers. (USFSPC.)

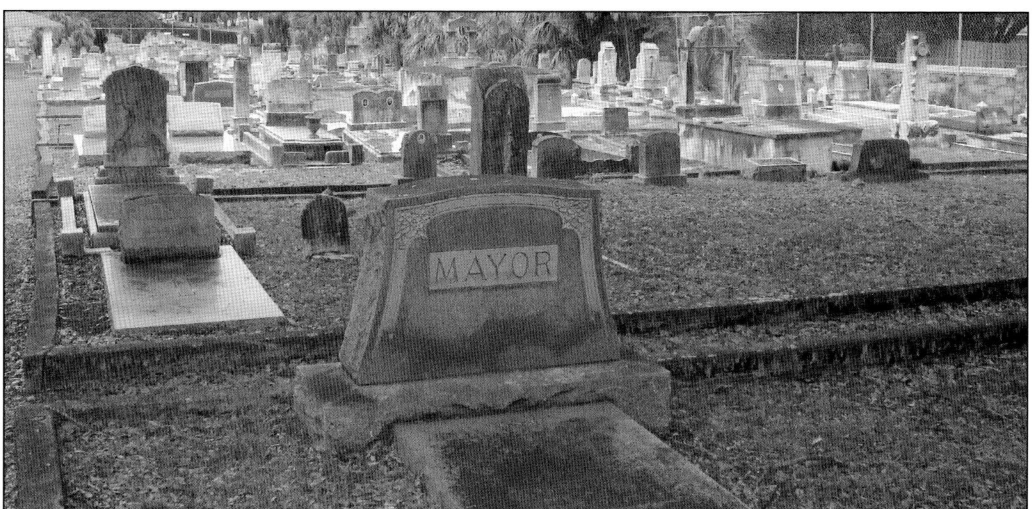

Another example of a written record is this ledger book (below) for Centro Asturiano Cemetery that verifies the stone of Maria Perez (born (nacio) March 1877, died (murio) August 8, 1921). Quite often, the carving and inscriptions on a gravestone are written in a person's native language. (USFSPC.)

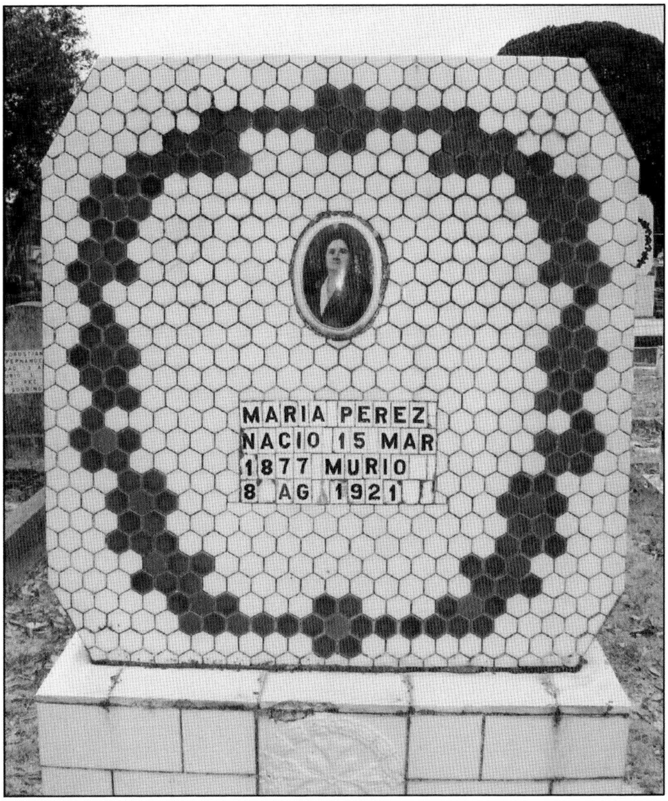

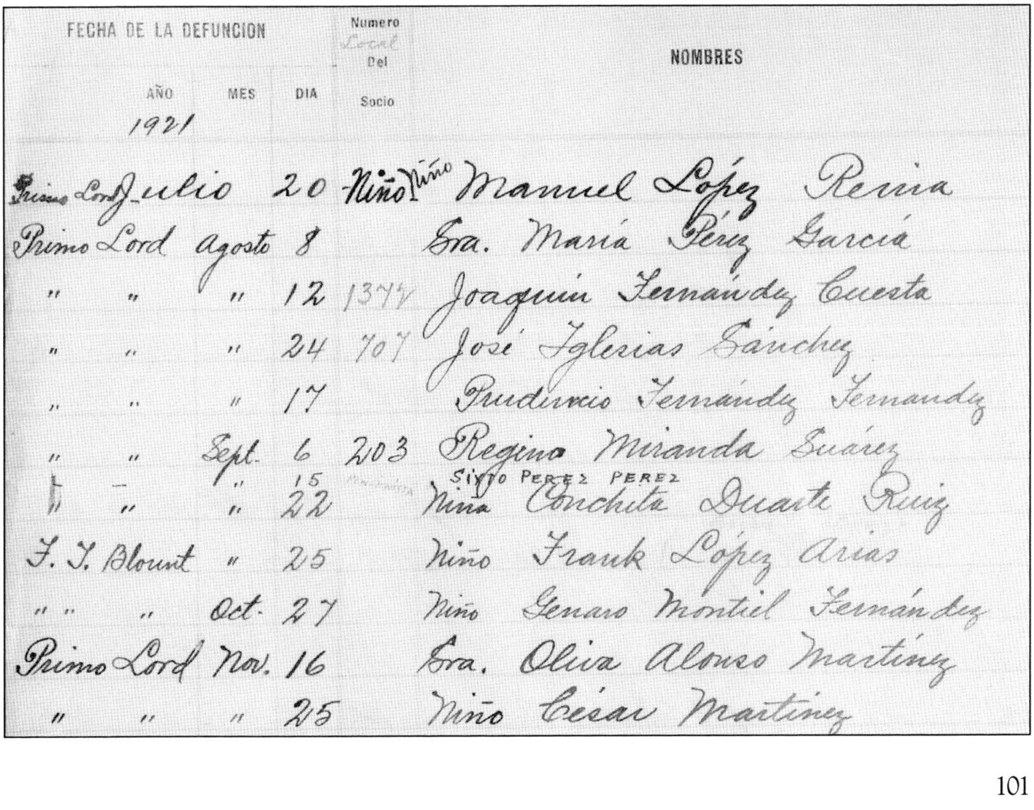

FECHA DE LA DEFUNCION AÑO	MES	DIA	Numero Local Del Socio	NOMBRES
1921				
Primo Lord	Julio	20	Niño Niño	Manuel López Reina
Primo Lord	agosto	8		Sra. María Pérez García
" "	"	12	1377	Joaquín Fernández Cuesta
" "	"	24	707	José Iglesias Sánchez
" "	"	17		Prudencio Fernández Fernández
" "	Sept.	6	203	Regino Miranda Suárez
	"	15		SIXTO PEREZ PEREZ
" "	"	22		Niña Conchita Duarte Ruiz
F. T. Blount	"	25		Niño Frank López Arias
" "	Oct.	27		Niño Genaro Montiel Fernández
Primo Lord	Nov.	16		Sra. Oliva Alonso Martínez
" "	"	25		Niño César Martínez

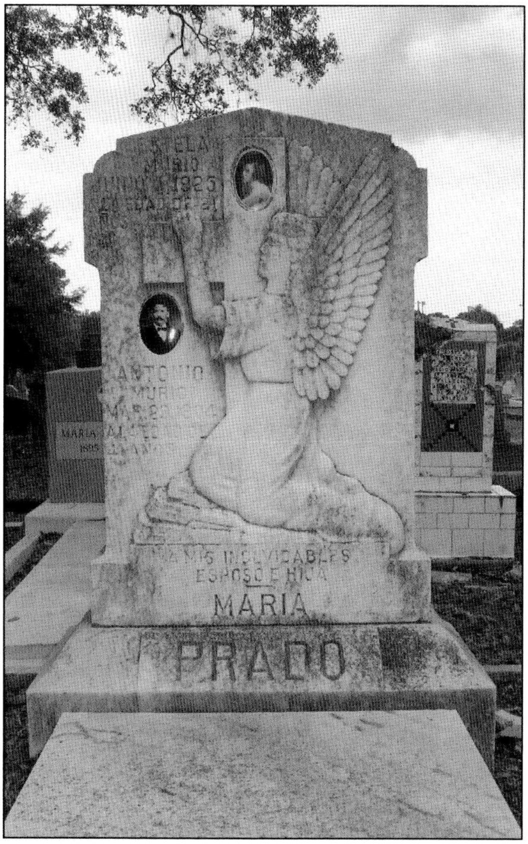

Antonio Prado died (murio) on March 29, 1904, at the age of 41. Estela died on June 3, 1925, at the age of 21. As mentioned on page 94, Antonio Prado was the founder of the El Centro Asturiano Club, which is one of Tampa's early Spanish social clubs.

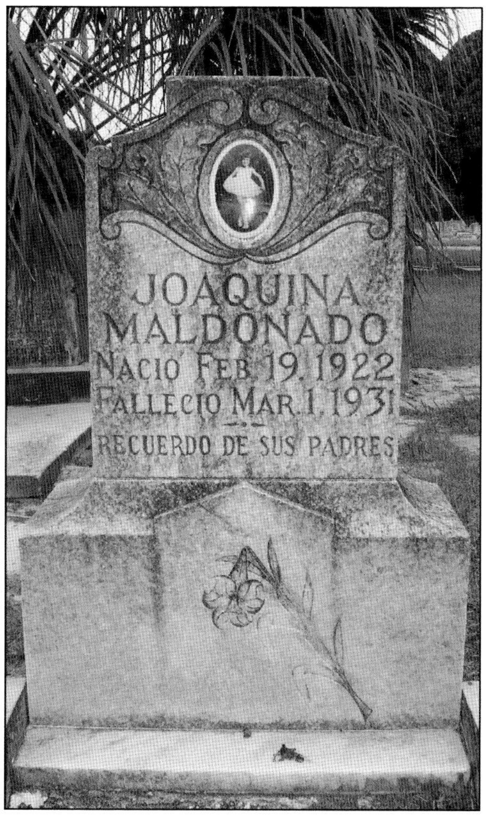

Joaquina Maldonado was born (nacio) on February 19, 1922, and died (fallecio) on March 1, 1931. Her gravestone features an oval photograph of her in a dance costume. The inscription "*recuerdo de sus padres* ("rescued by the father") could be interpreted by a visitor as meaning that she was free from pain or suffering.

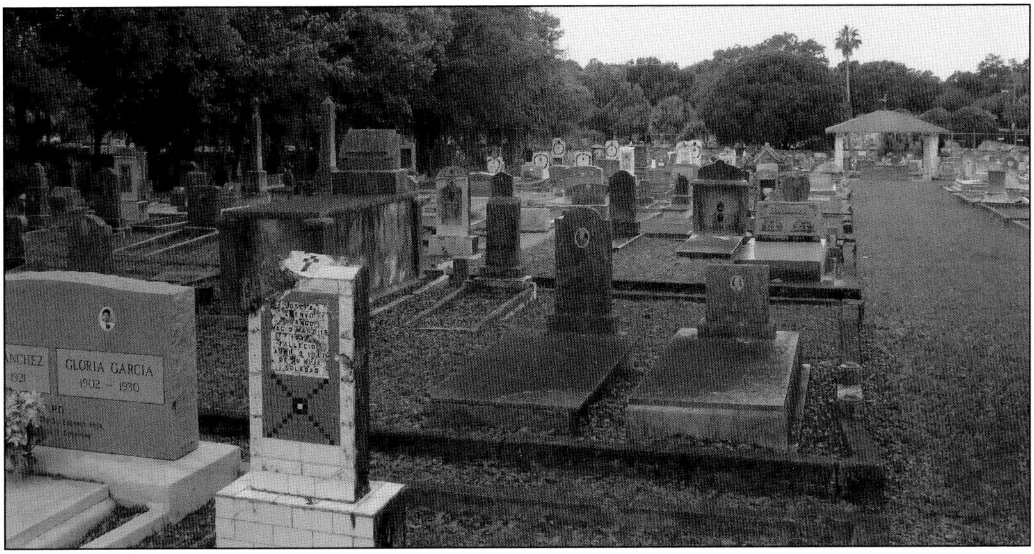

El Centro Asturiano Cemetery is laid out in a block and lot grid with very narrow pathways between. As one can see from this view, the cemetery is occupied to capacity, thus necessitating the opening of an additional cemetery for club members.

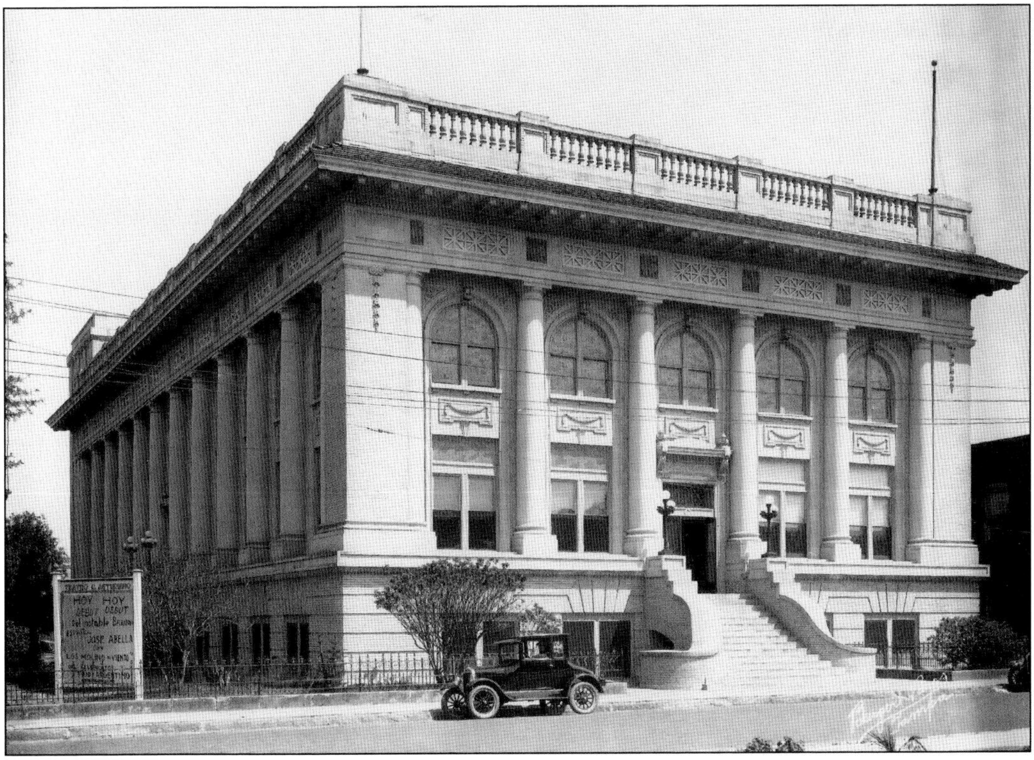

El Centro Asturiano de Tampa, listed in the National Register of Historic Places in 1974, is also a designated heritage structure in the Ybor City Historic District. Founded in 1902, the club featured a cantina, offices, library, ladies parlor, auditorium with stage, and grand ballroom. The club catered to Latin males, most of whom were immigrant workers in Ybor City's cigar factories. Member dues included health insurance and club and burial privileges. (THCPL.)

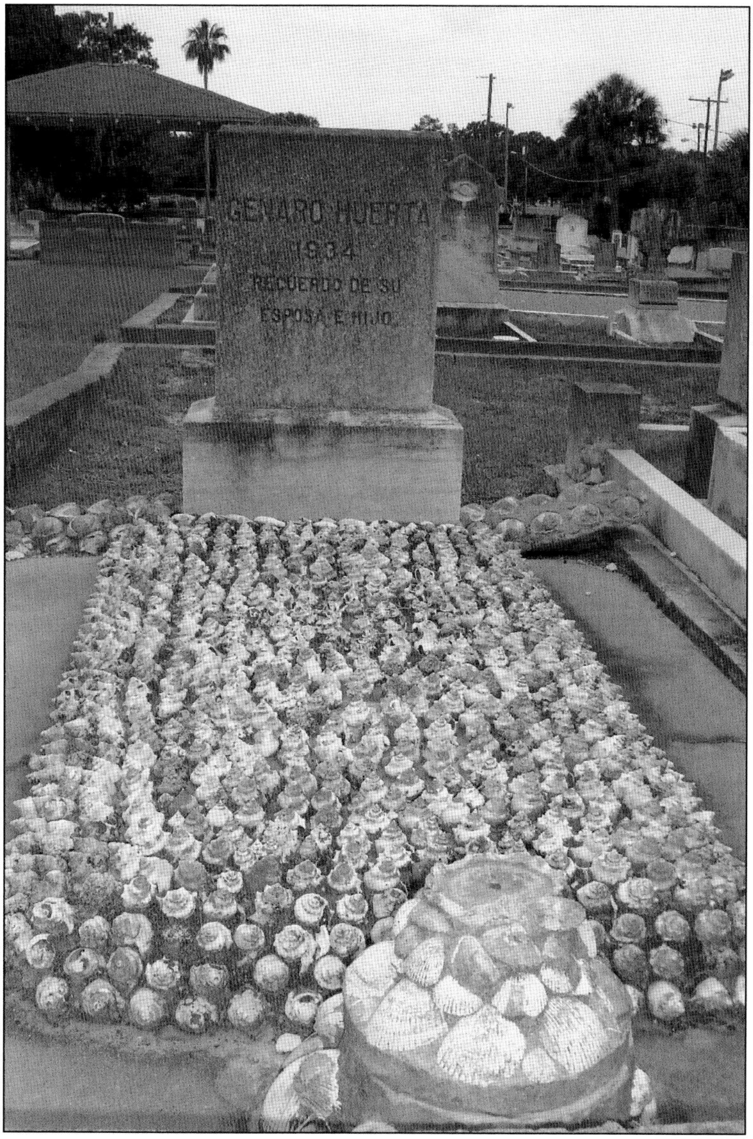

The 1934 gravesite of Genaro Huerta (left) is marked with a bed stone of conch shells. Hand-laid with loving care, this is another example of expression for the dearly departed. The shells' symbolic meanings are of life, birth, and baptism. The ledger sheet (below) is from the cemetery internment register located in the noncirculating Special Collections Department at the University of South Florida. The person's family, home, and other related information are entries in the record. Sometimes, it is only by these written records of cemetery burials that the location of a person's final resting place can be determined. Headstones at times are aged beyond legibility or have been misplaced or vandalized. (USFSPC.)

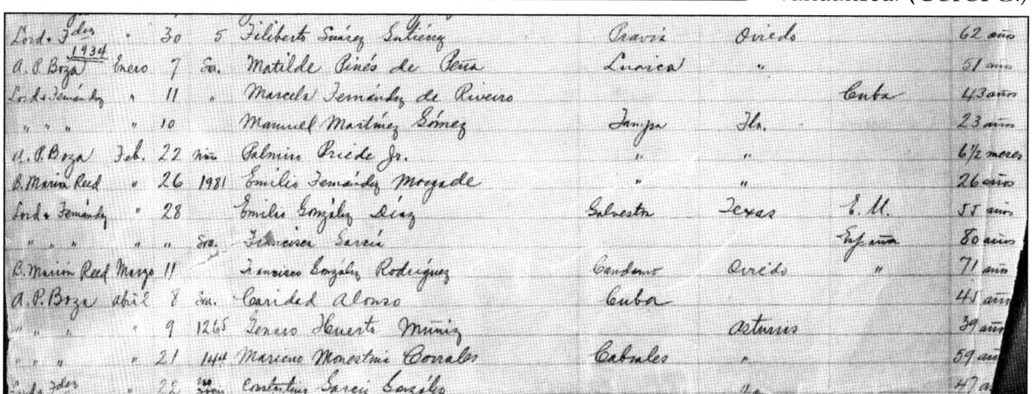

Lord + Fdez	"	30	5	Filiberto Suárez Gutiérrez	Pravia	Oviedo		62 años
A. P. Boza 1934	Enero	7	Sa.	Matilde Piñés de Peña	Luarca	"		51 años
Lord + Fernández	"	11	"	Marcela Fernández de Rivero			Cuba	43 años
" " "	"	10		Manuel Martínez Gómez	Tampa	Fla.		23 años
A. P. Boza	Feb.	22	niño	Palmiro Priede Jr.	"	"		6½ meses
B. Marion Reed	"	26	1981	Emilio Fernández Moyade	"	"		26 años
Lord + Fernández	"	28		Emilio González Díaz	Galveston	Texas	E. U.	55 años
" " "	"	"	Sra.	Francisca García			España	80 años
B. Marion Reed	Marzo	11		Francisco González Rodríguez	Candamo	Oviedo	"	71 años
A. P. Boza	Abril	8	Sa.	Caridad Alonso	Cuba			45 años
" " "	"	9	1265	Genaro Huerta Muñiz		Asturias		39 años
" " "	"	21	144	Mariano Monestrio Corrales	Cabrales	"		59 años
Lord + Fdez	"	22	[illegible]	Constantino García González		"		47 a[illegible]

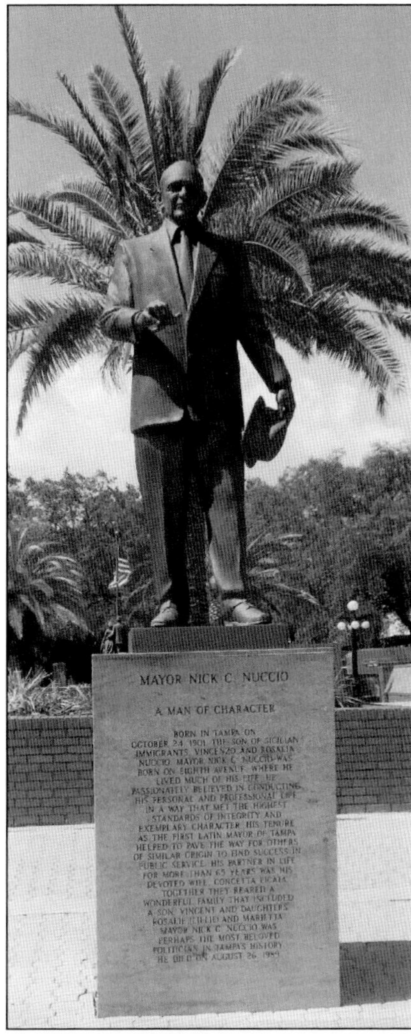

Nick Nuccio was born on October 24, 1901, in Ybor City the son of Sicilian immigrants Vincenzo (Vincent) and Rosalia Nuccio. He attended Hillsborough High School until his sophomore year and then went to work during the war years as a ship fitter. He later operated a real estate and insurance business, and in 1926 he began work as a clerk at the post office. Nuccio married Concetta Licata, his partner for 65 years, on July 6, 1924, and they had three children: Vincent, Rosalie "Lillie," and Marietta. He became the first Latino to be elected mayor of Tampa and served two terms (1956–1959 and 1963–1967). Nuccio died on August 26, 1989. The Ybor Immigrant Park statute of Mayor Nick C. Nuccio (right), honoring his life and legacy and recognizing all the contributions that he had made to the city, was dedicated in October 1999.

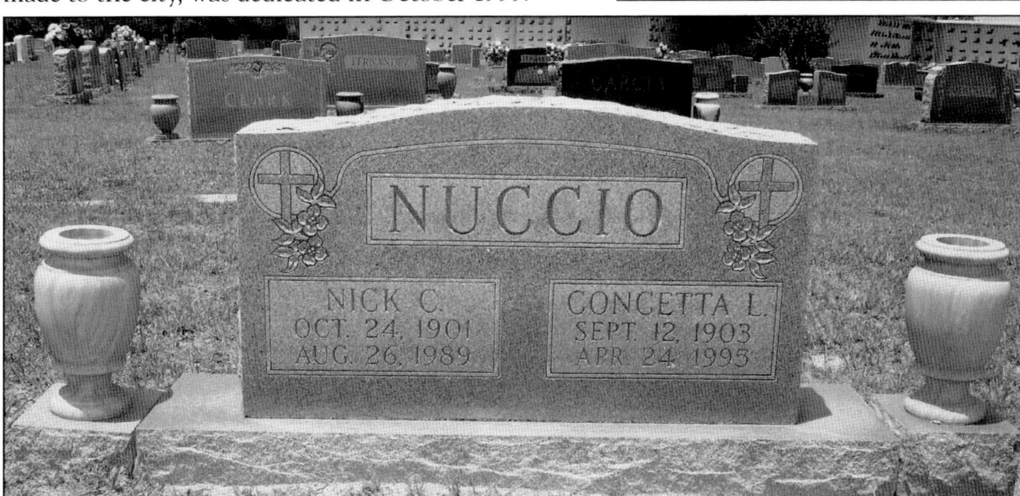

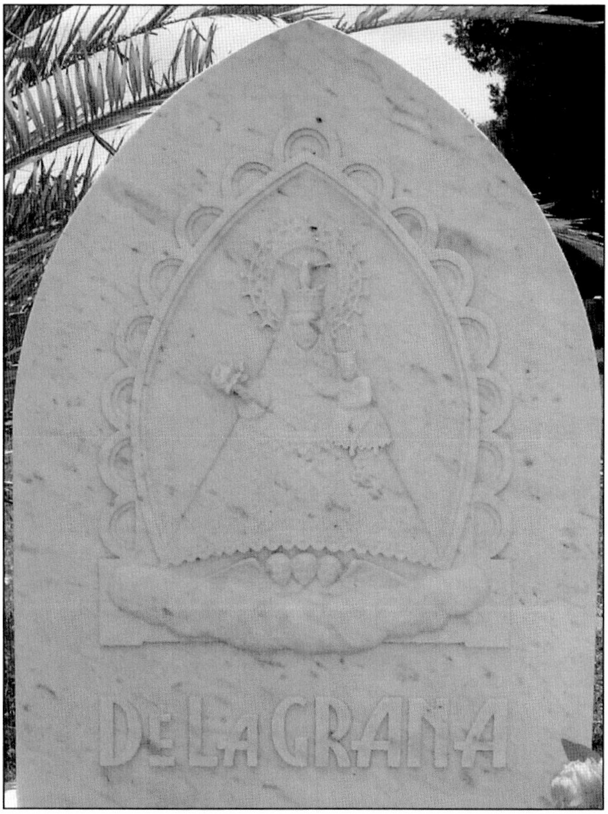

The gravestone marker for Frank and Carmen De La Grana is made of a light marble with an intricately carved relief. The symbolism can take on various meanings. The baby held safely in the arms of the angelic woman, and the three angels watching over them, clearly offers a feeling of comfort to those in their time of sorrow.

The Fernandez mausoleum is a stand-alone structure for their family burials. Also located in Centro Asturiano Memorial Park is a larger mausoleum, added in 1970 and enlarged in 1998, in which over 2,400 persons are buried. For a donation, The Las Damas volunteers will place flowers for loved one(s) four times a year on the gravestone or mausoleum plaque. Flowers are put out by the first week of the following months: March, June, September, and December.

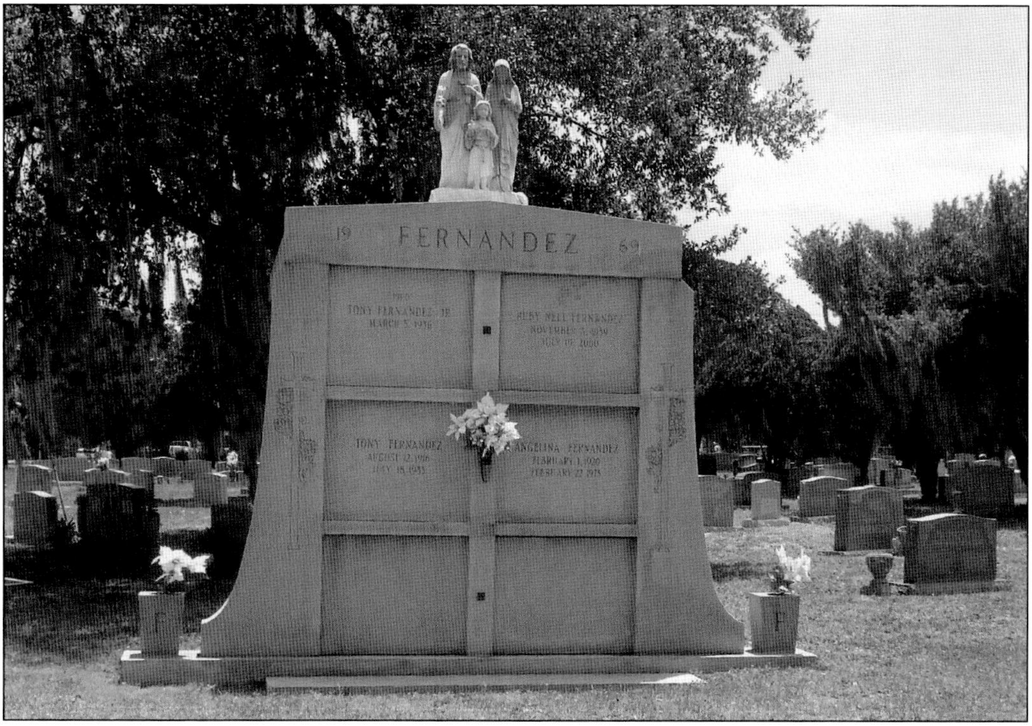

Six

L' Unione de Italiana

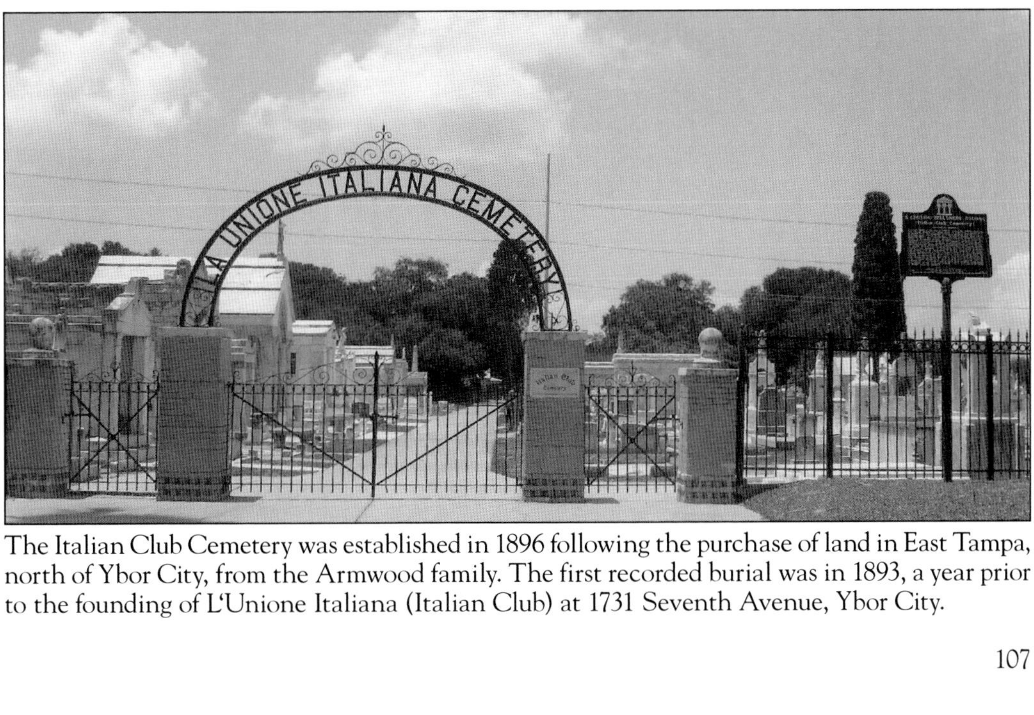

The Italian Club Cemetery was established in 1896 following the purchase of land in East Tampa, north of Ybor City, from the Armwood family. The first recorded burial was in 1893, a year prior to the founding of L'Unione Italiana (Italian Club) at 1731 Seventh Avenue, Ybor City.

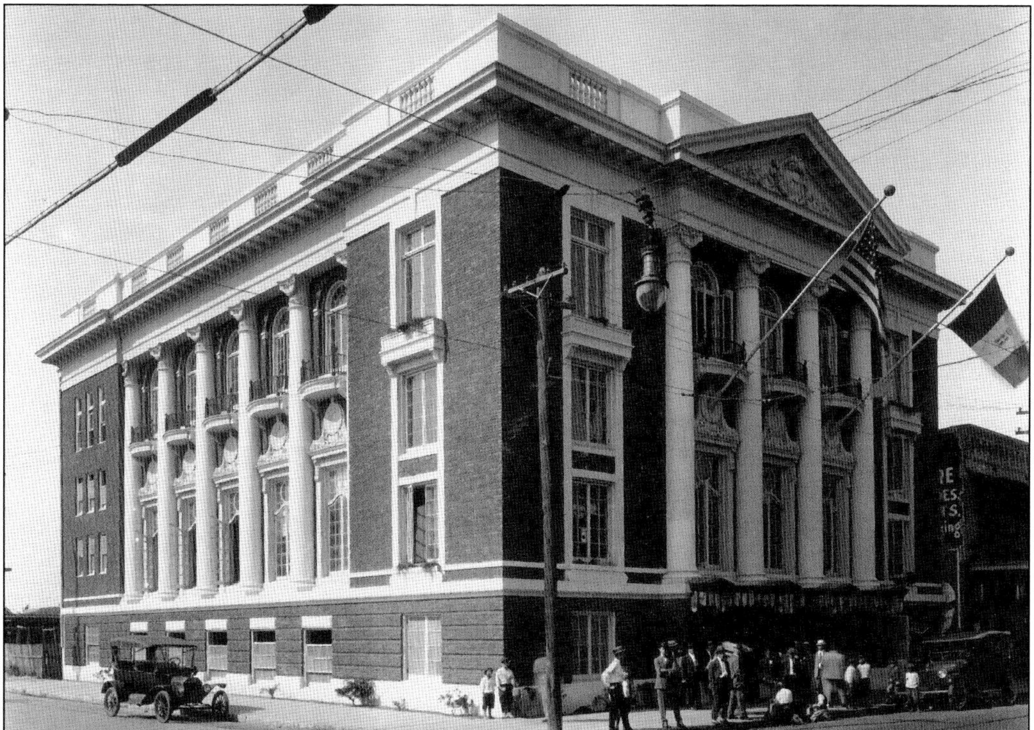

According to one historian, the L'Unione Italiana (Italian Club) was founded to serve Italian immigrants who left New Orleans because of the gang warfare there and others who migrated from the Sicilian villages of Alessandria della Rocco, Cianciana, Bivona, and Santo Stephano. Designed by the architectural firm of Bonfoey and Elliott, the Italian Club (above) was paid for by subscriptions, benefit dances, and other fundraising events. The cemetery (below) is one of great pride to the members and the community. Over 100 years old, the Italian Club Cemetery still serves Tampa's Sicilian community. Throughout the cemetery, one can see imported ceramic photograph markers, inscribed in Sicilian and Italian, which pay service to Sicilian stonecutters. (THCPL.)

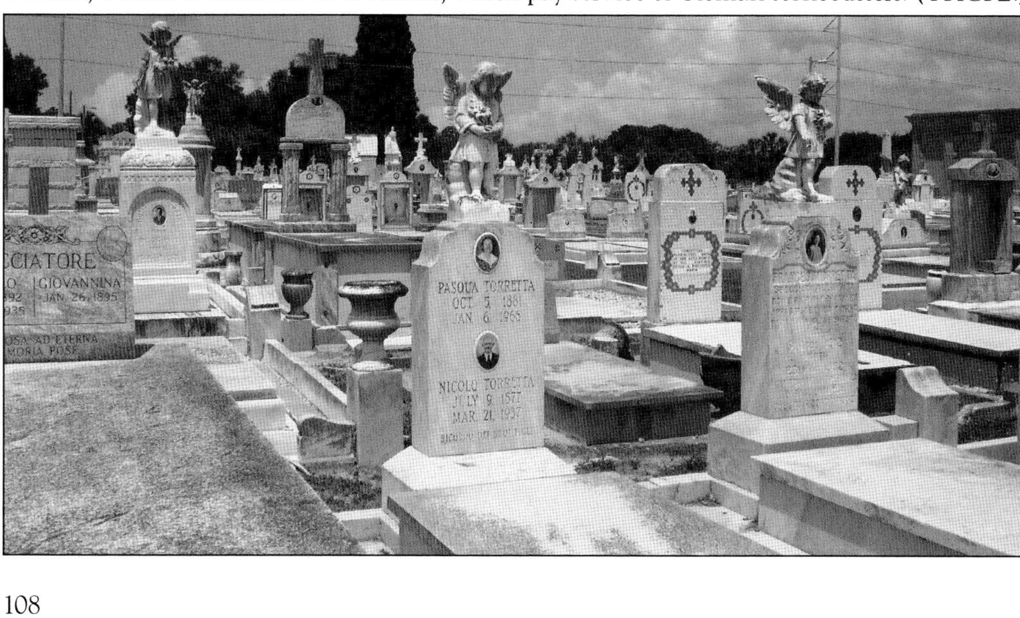

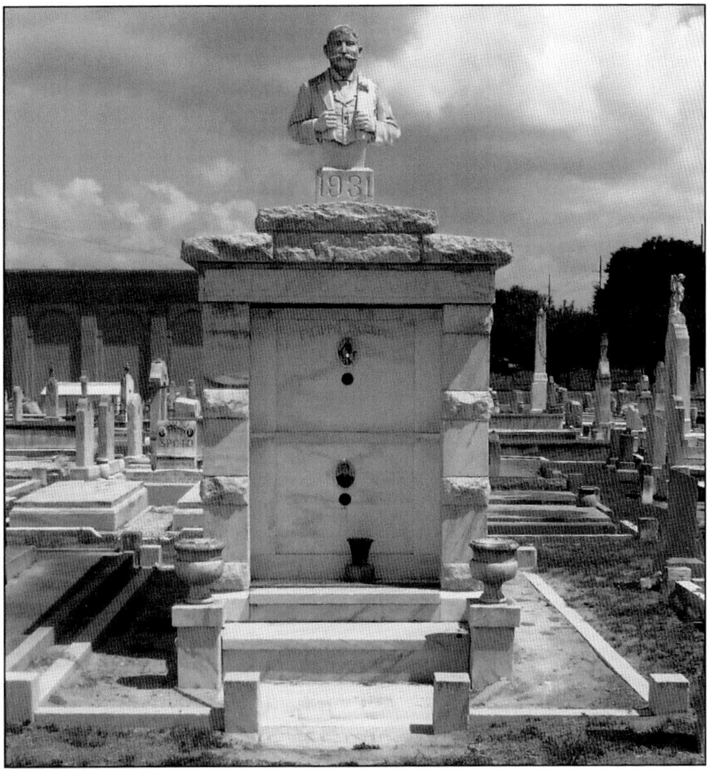

The private mausoleum for Filippo Cagnina (April 10, 1869–December 17, 1945) features a marble bust of his likeness. Cagnina worked at the Italian Club as a "billiard man" and relied mostly on tips for his income and survival. It was a surprise after his death that he had commissioned this marble bust of himself, the only one at the cemetery.

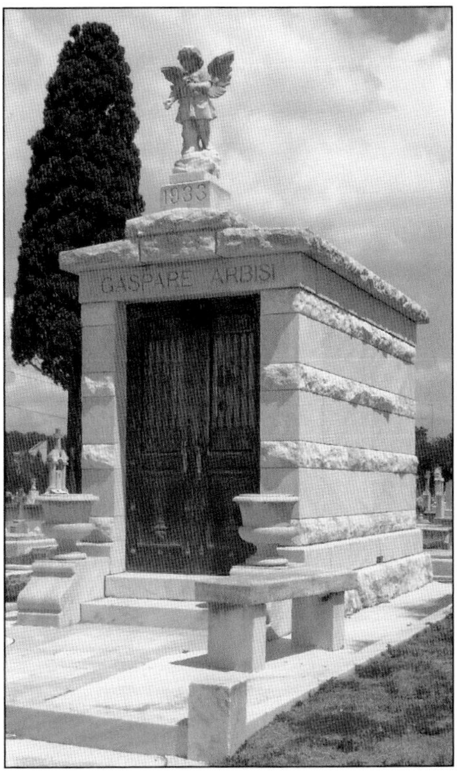

According to the 1920 US Census, Gaspare Arbisi, an Italian, first came to the United States in 1893. His wife, Teressa, stayed in Italy with their son Angelo, coming to this land in 1901. Their family, including five children—Angelo, Maria, Nicola, Marguretta, and Frances—lived on Tenth Avenue in the Ybor City neighborhood. Arbisi was a peddler of general merchandise. Son Angelo was a cigar maker, and son Nicola was a produce salesman.

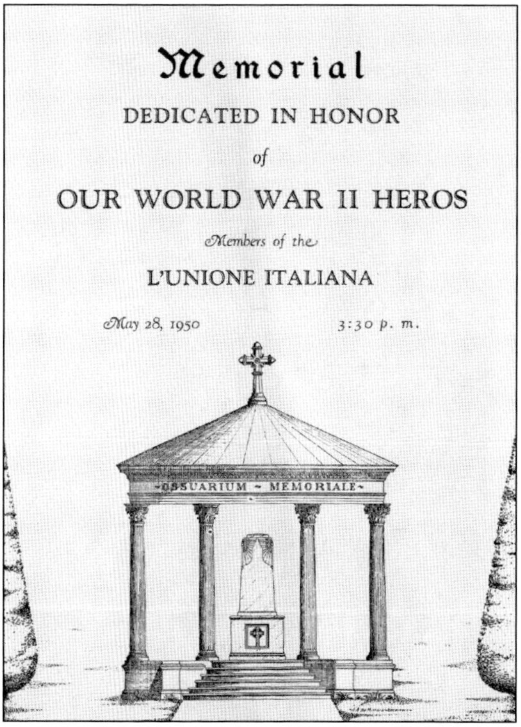

Memorial

DEDICATED IN HONOR

of

OUR WORLD WAR II HEROS

Members of the

L'UNIONE ITALIANA

May 28, 1950 3:30 p. m.

On May 28, 1950, the members of the L'Unione Italiana dedicated this *Ossuarium Memoriale* to World War II heroes. The grand event was attended by many members of the Italian Club, many whose loved ones had made the ultimate sacrifice. The memorial is made of the finest marble, and engraved are the names of the soldiers honored: Pfc. John W. Boatwright Jr., Pfc. Helson L. Cucumano, USMC Joe M. Dominguez, 2nd Lt. Tony E. Emanuel, 2nd Lt. Cilio S. Guerriere, Pfc. Frank Ippolito, Sgt Ignazio Italiano, Pfc. Joe Lazzara, T/Sgt Gaetano F. Perrone, Pfc. Peter Tagliarini Jr., and Pvt. Sam Tagliarino. (USFSPC.)

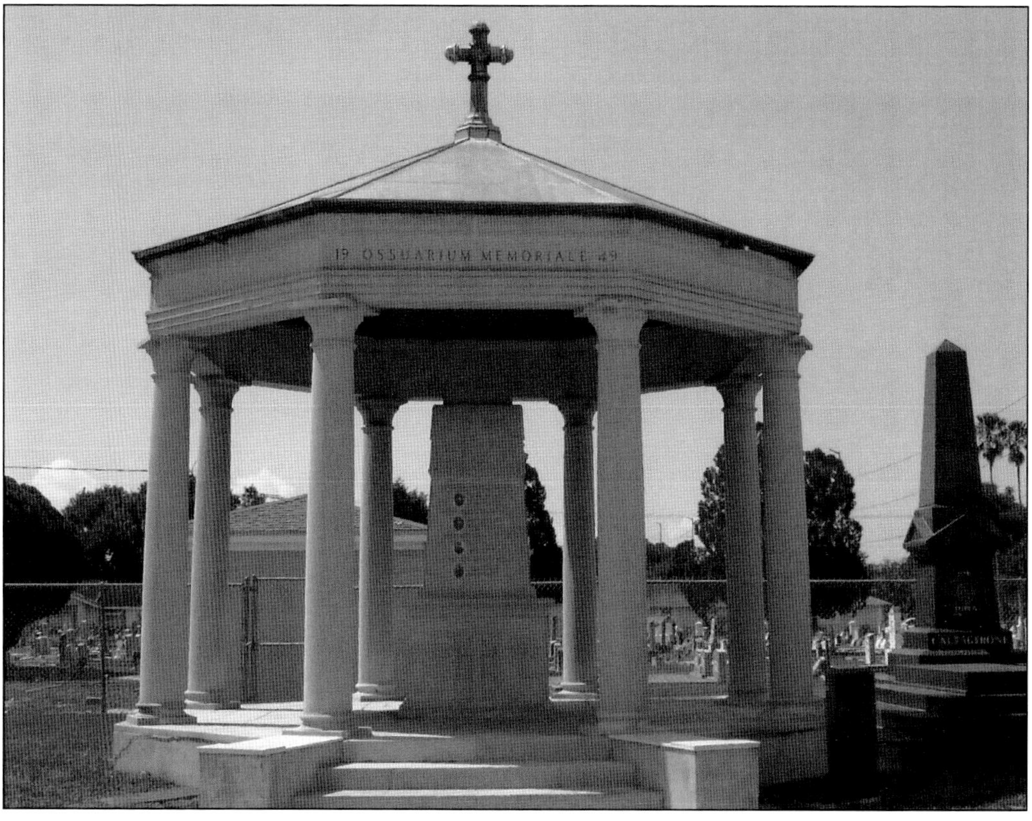

1st Lt. Cilio S. Guerriere was born on November 22, 1919, and died on January 2, 1942. (USFSPC.)

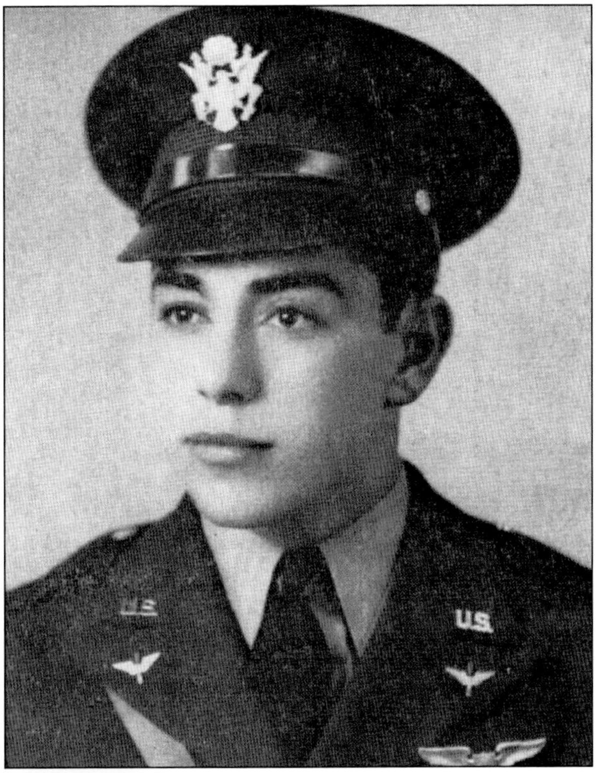

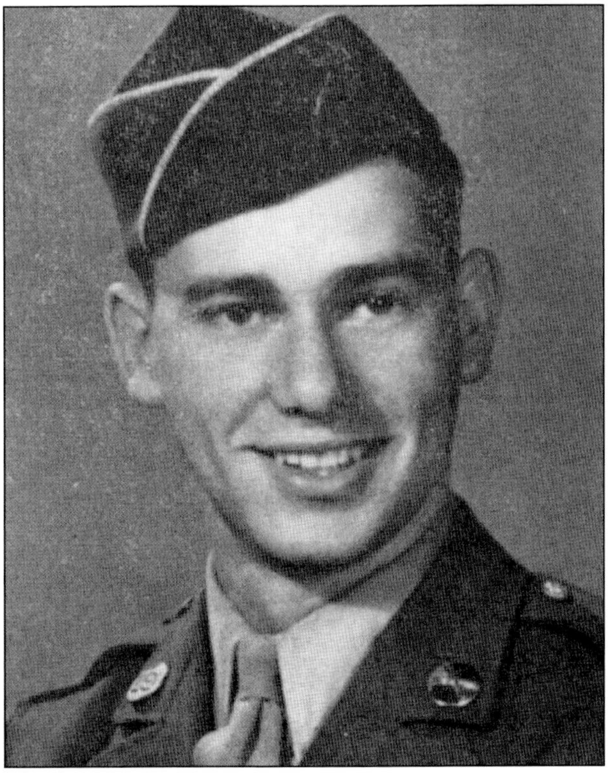

Pfc. John W. Boatwright Jr. was born on August 20, 1925, and died on November 4, 1944. (USFSPC.)

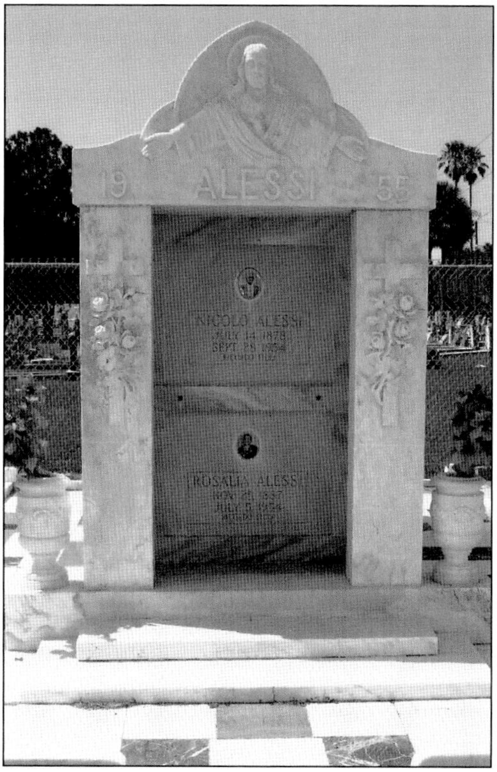

The private mausoleum for the Alessi family shows the heavenly Father watching over Nocolo and Rosalia Massaro. The latter is the daughter of Carmelo and Guiseppa Massaro. The roses upon the cross on the columns of the structure symbolize the brevity of their lives and that Christ was their salvation. According to the 1910 US Census, the Italian immigrant family lived in the West Tampa neighborhood. Alessi was a cigar maker.

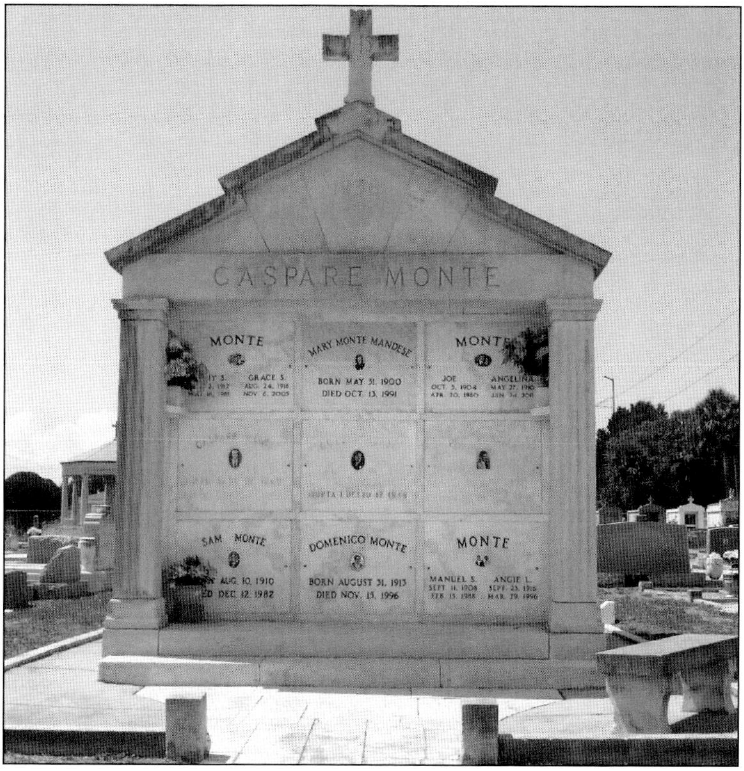

According to the 1920 US Census, Gaspare Monte immigrated to the United States in 1903. His wife, Grace, and their three oldest children—Frances, Maria, and Joseph—stayed behind and came in 1907. Children Henry, Manuel, Sam, Antonio, and Dominick were born in Tampa. Monte, along with sons Joseph and Manuel, were barbers, while other members of the family worked at the cigar factories. The 1930 USFC has a different immigration date.

The Ferlita family mausoleum is made of the finest marble stone available. The marble benches flanking the entry court were made by the Turner Marble & Granite Company at 2601 Seventh Avenue (East Broadway) in Ybor City. The Ferlita family in Tampa immigrated from the Sicilian communities in the early 1900s, and members have contributed greatly to the community.

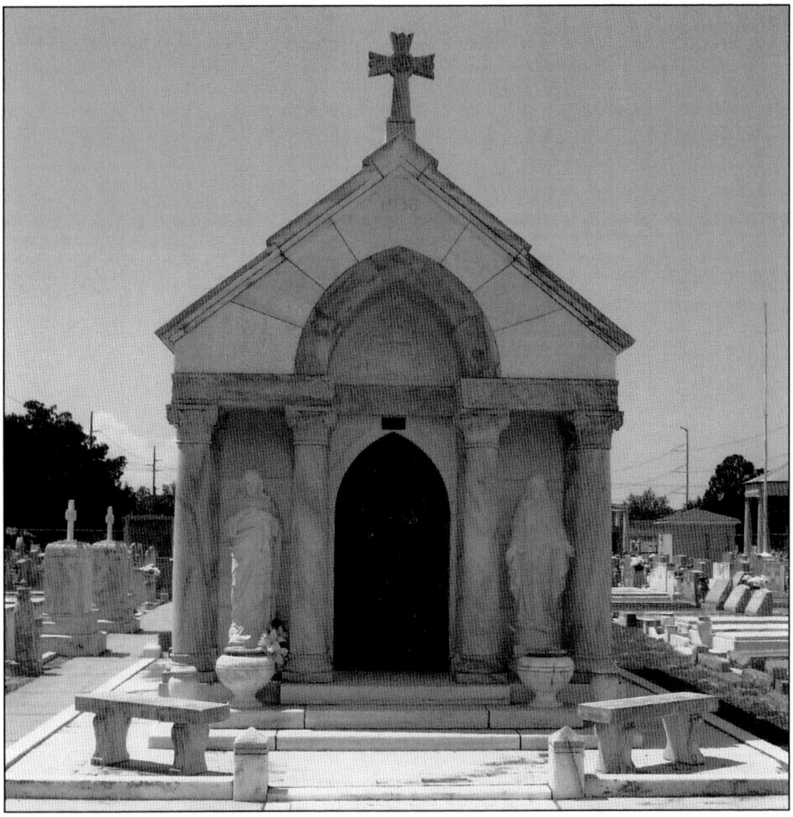

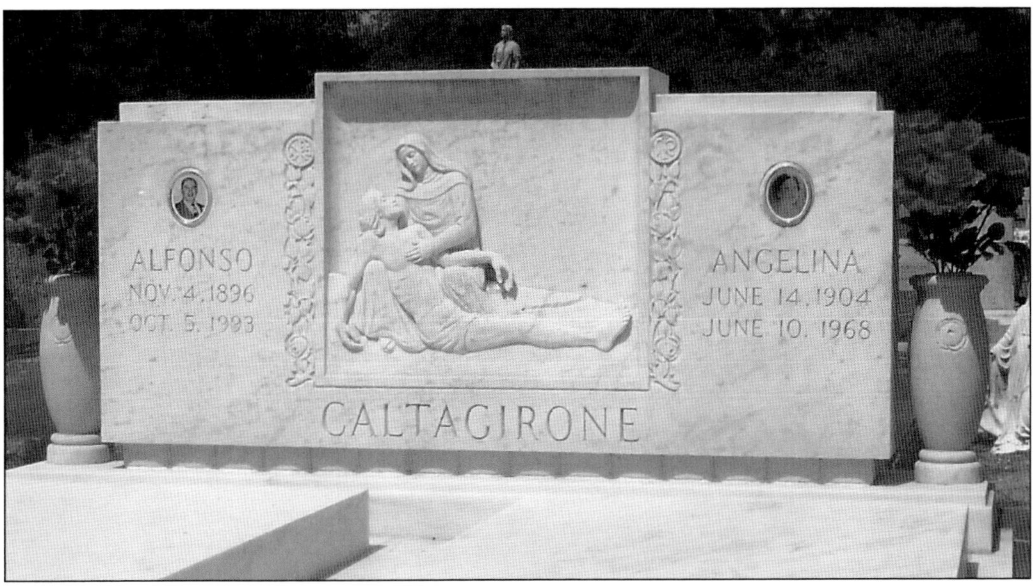

Alfonso and Angelina Caltagirone's large marble gravestone is a testament of love for their family and their faith. Their son Joe has served as the unofficial caretaker of the Italian Club Cemetery since the early 1980s. He knows the history of the cemetery and of all the families buried within. He even can identify the unmarked graves. Annual tours and fundraisers take place to support the upkeep and maintenance of the cemetery.

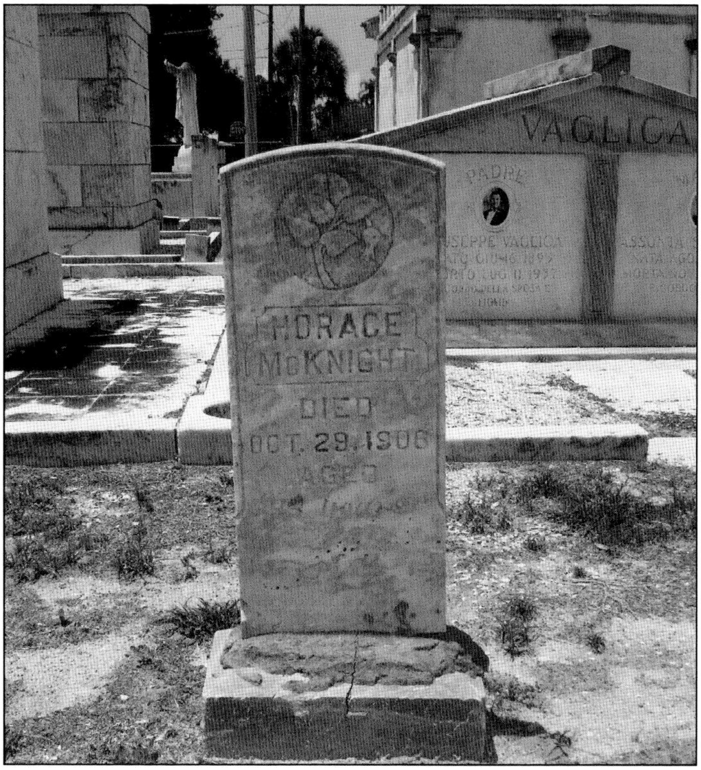

The grave of Horace McKnight is located in one of the older sections of the cemetery. The stone, which has been repaired, is carved with a drooping rosebud, a symbol of sorrow and brevity of life. The Italian Club Cemetery is well managed and maintained by a dedicated group of volunteer members of the Italian Club.

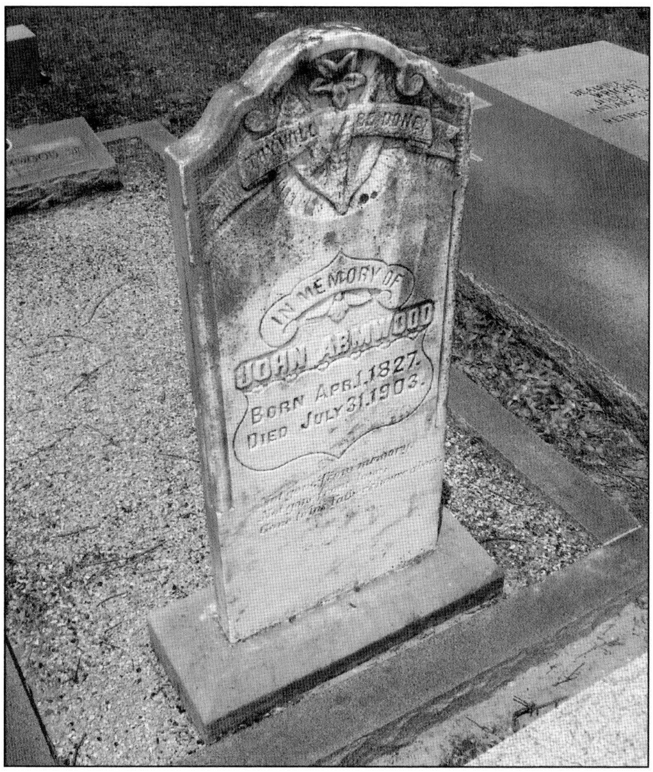

The land upon which this cemetery is located was purchased from the Armwoods, Tampa's pioneer African American family, in the 1890s. John Armwood's stone reads, "Not gone from memory. Not gone from love. Gone to his Father's house above."

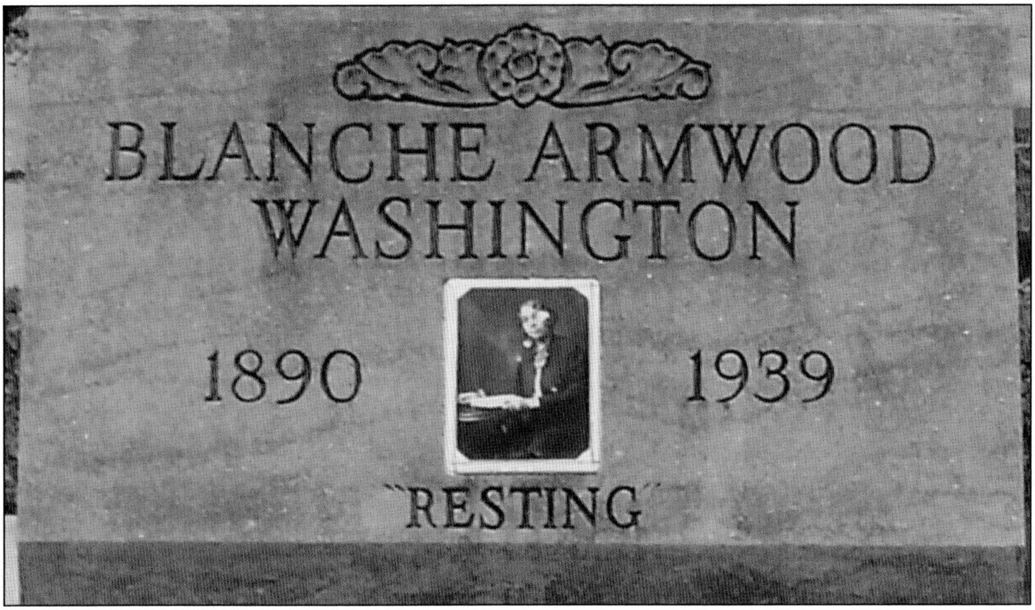

Blanche Armwood was born on January 23, 1890, a third-generation member of the pioneering Armwood family. She graduated with honors from the first class of St. Peter Claver Catholic School in Ybor City. After graduating summa cum laude from Spelman Seminary (now Spelman College), she returned to Tampa to teach in the area's segregated schools. Later, she began a second career as the US Department of Agriculture's state supervisor of home economics. In 1922, she helped organize the Tampa Urban League, becoming the first executive secretary. Enrolling at Howard University Law School in 1931, Blanche began the practice of law six years later. Pictured below is the May 9, 1925, gathering of the women of the Tampa Urban League, with Blanche Armwood (second from left, in striped shirt) and Clara Alston (center, in white dress). Seffner's Armwood High School is named in her honor. (THCPL.)

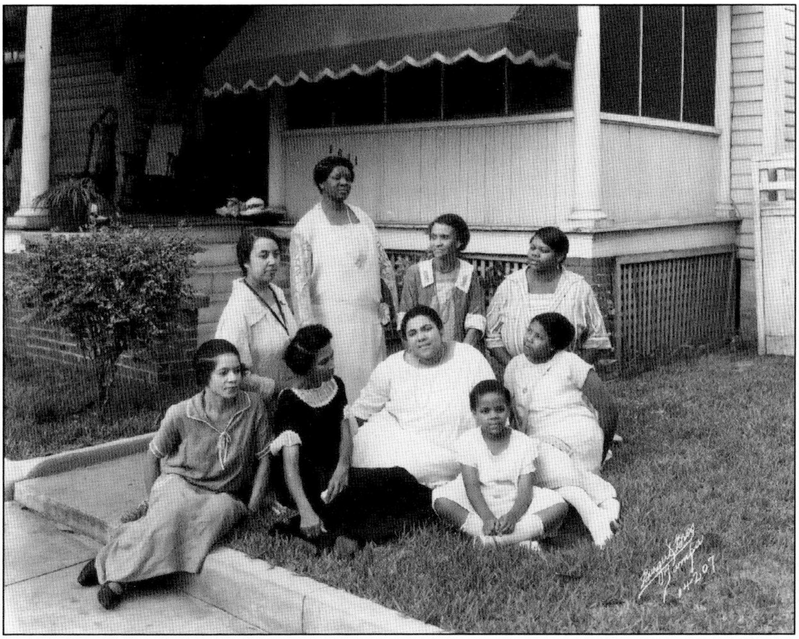

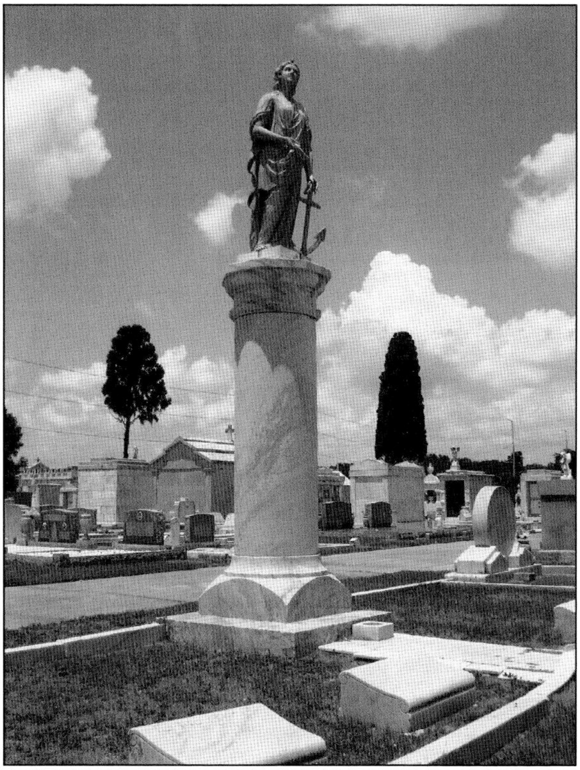

All ships must have an anchor, and this tall marble statue of a seafarer with his anchor in one hand, a wreath in the other, and a star upon his head could symbolize that he is on his path to heaven and is celebrating the victory of his life. The Ferrara family members who are buried within this plot are Antonio, Icnazio, Jennie, and Rosina.

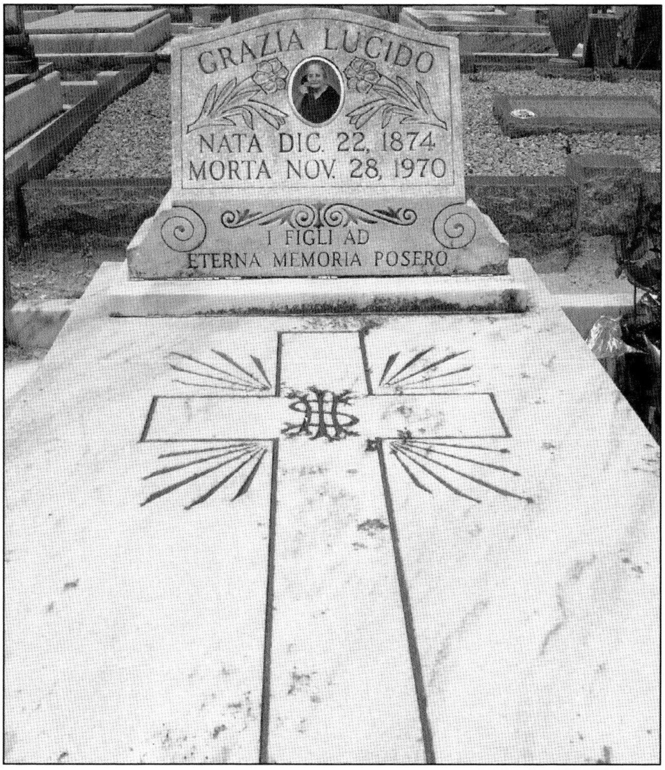

Grazia Lucido was born in Italy on December 22, 1874. The gravestone portrait of her talking on the telephone might make one wonder if she was a telephone operator or if she just liked to talk on the telephone. She died on November 28, 1970. Her stone is engraved, *I figli ad eternal memoria posero* ("the children put to eternal memory").

Seven

Mary Help of Christians School

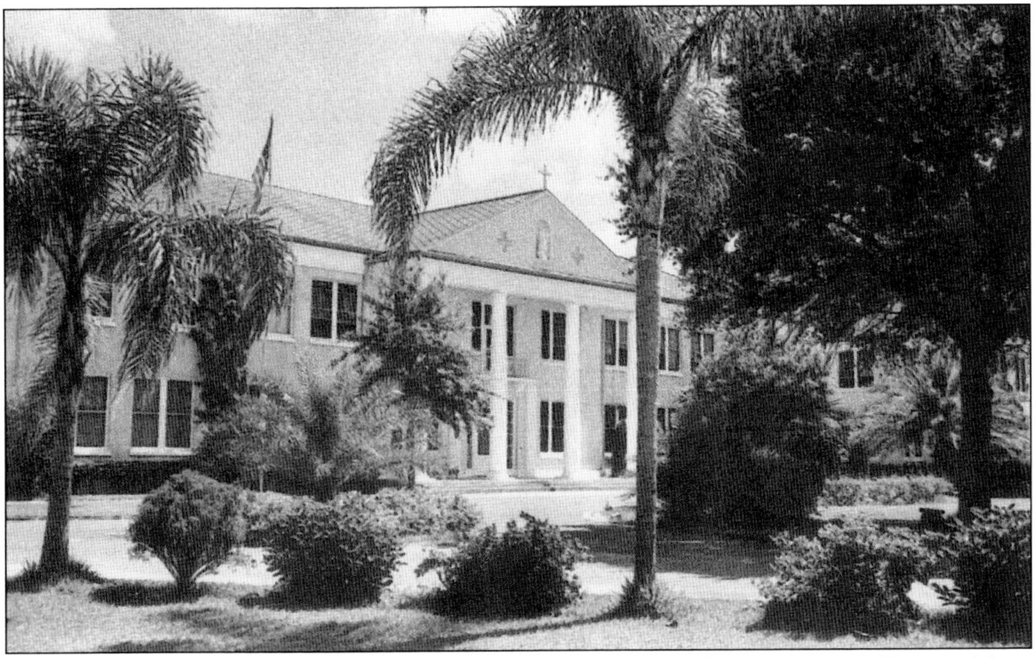

Mary Help of Christians School is situated in a beautiful, quiet location in east Tampa. Alicia Neve and her husband are buried in the school cemetery. They donated 40 acres and funds to build a school for homeless boys. It was dedicated in October 1928 by The Salesians of St. John Bosco, who "would provide an environment conducive to the spiritual, physical and mental well-being of countless homeless boys."

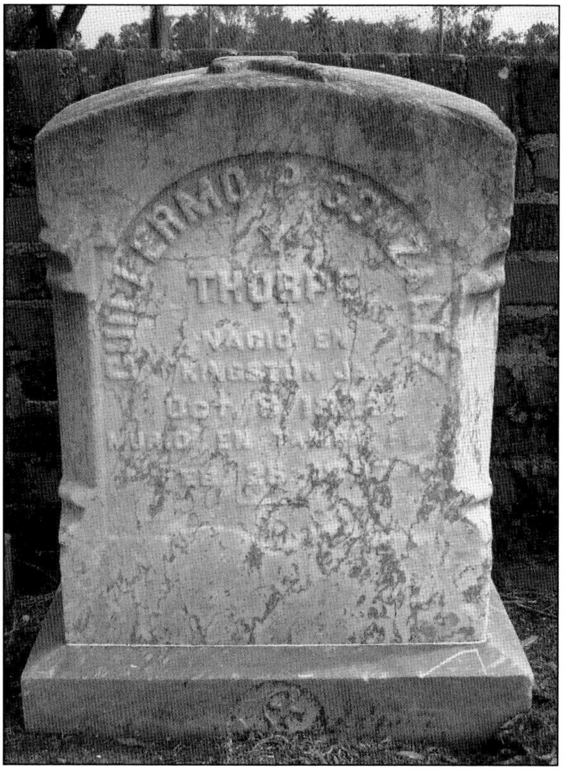

These next four graves were moved from the St. Louis Catholic Cemetery (Oaklawn) in April 1941. The information is taken from the *Tampa Morning Tribune* of Saturday, February 27, 1897. Guillermo P. Gonzalez Jr. (October 8, 1872–February 25, 1897), a purser on the H.B. Plant System steamship *Mascotte*, was a native of Kingston, Jamaica.

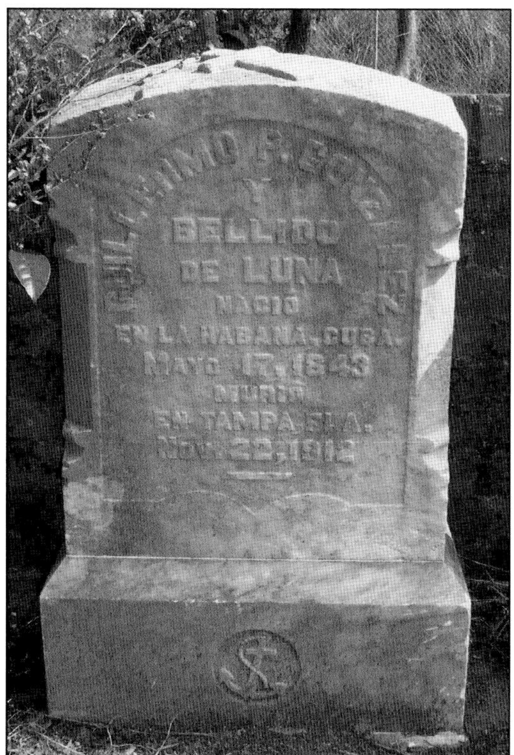

Guillermo P. Gonzalez y Bellido (May 17, 1843–November 22, 1912) was born in Havana, Cuba, was a school "professor," and was the father-in-law of E. Neve. He left a widow.

Susan W. Thorpe Gonzalez (July 24, 1838–September 17, 1915) was born in Bridgeport, Connecticut. She was the mother of Alicia Gonzalez Neve and was survived by a daughter.

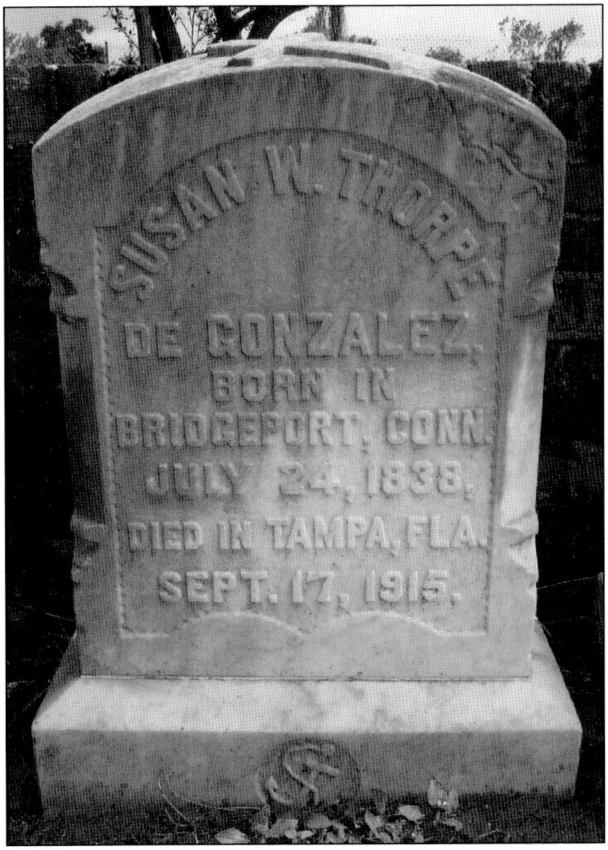

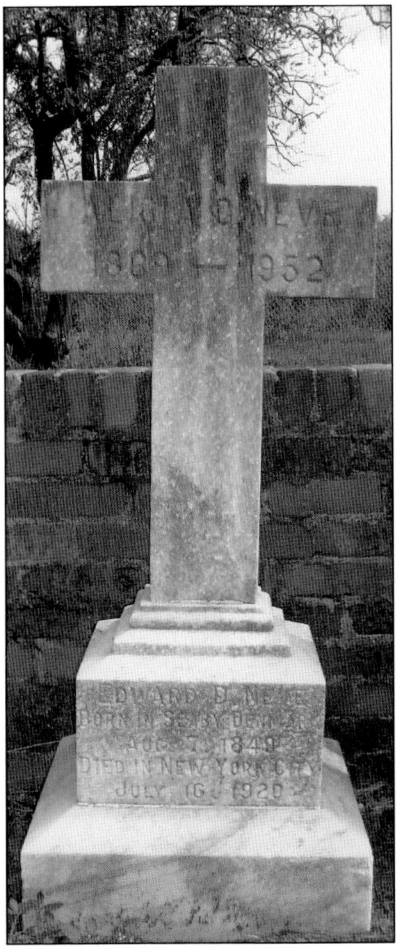

Edward Neve (August 8, 1849–July 16, 1920) was born in Denmark and was a dentist and jeweler in Tampa for over 40 years. He was also the owner of large citrus groves in the area of Myrtle Hill Cemetery and was the husband of Alicia Gonzalez Neve.

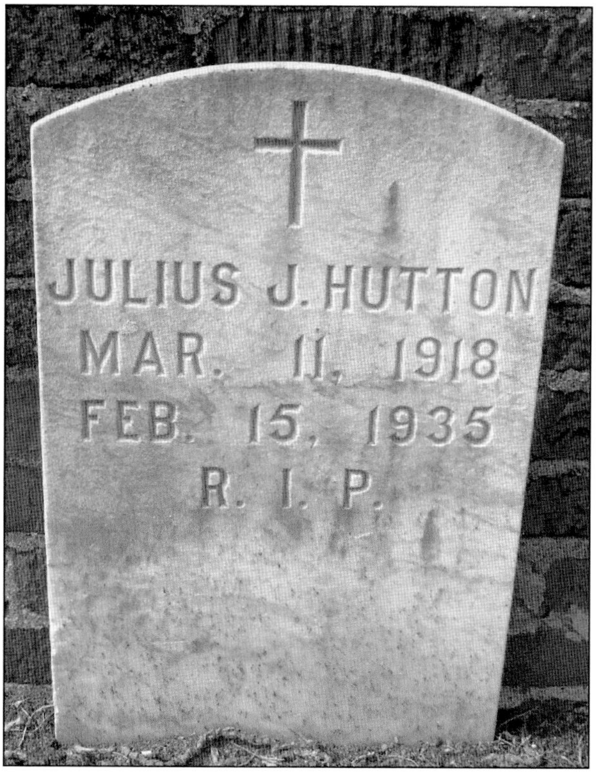

Julius Joseph Hutton (March 11, 1918–February 15, 1935) was born in Key West, Florida, to unknown parents. He was a student at the Catholic school. J.L. Reed, director of a Tampa funeral home, paid for this young man's funeral and burial.

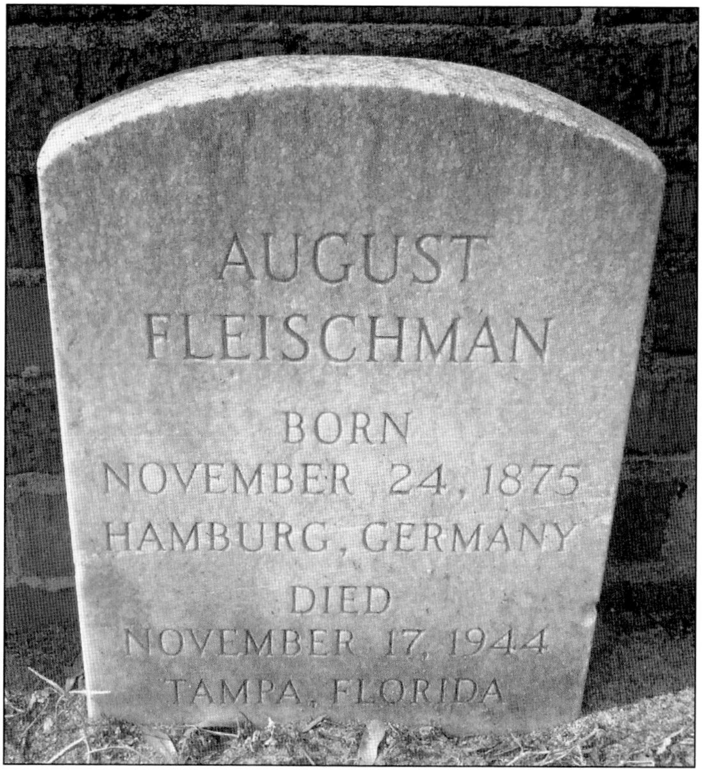

August Gustave Fleischman (November 24, 1875–November 17, 1944) was a member of Mary Help of Christians Orphanage. He died of pneumonia and was survived by a son, Gus Fleishman, of Houston, Texas, and three daughters: Mrs. Carl Geisenger and Mrs. Edward Simonech of Mineola, Texas, and Sister Mary Ola, SVD, of Oklahoma.

John Mayerhofer (March 10, 1877–June 26, 1949) was born in Moosburg, Germany. He was a member of Mary Help of Christians School and was survived by two brothers.

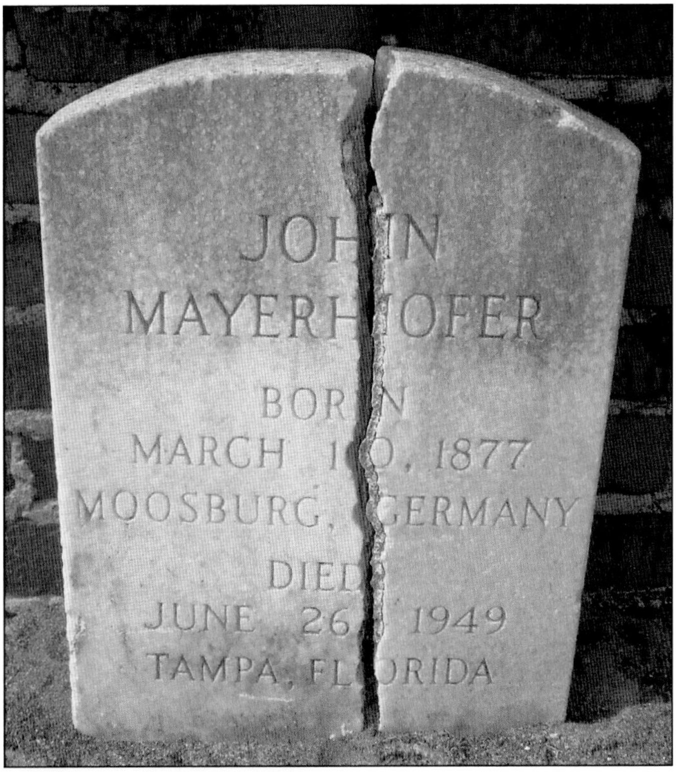

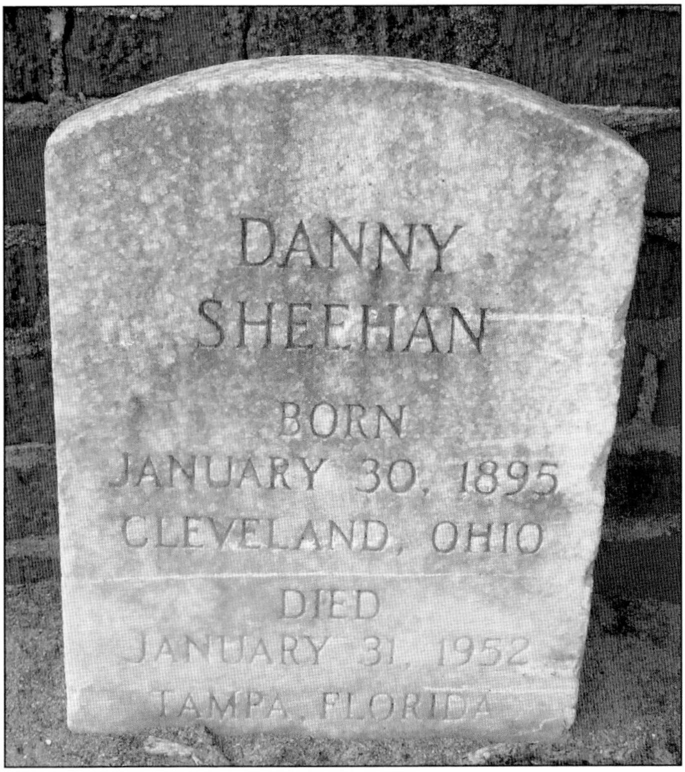

Daniel J. "Danny" Sheehan (January 30, 1895–January 31, 1952) was born in Cleveland, Ohio. A World War I veteran and member of Sacred Heart Church in Tampa and the Knights of Columbus, he conducted dancing schools in Tampa and St. Petersburg and played vaudeville.

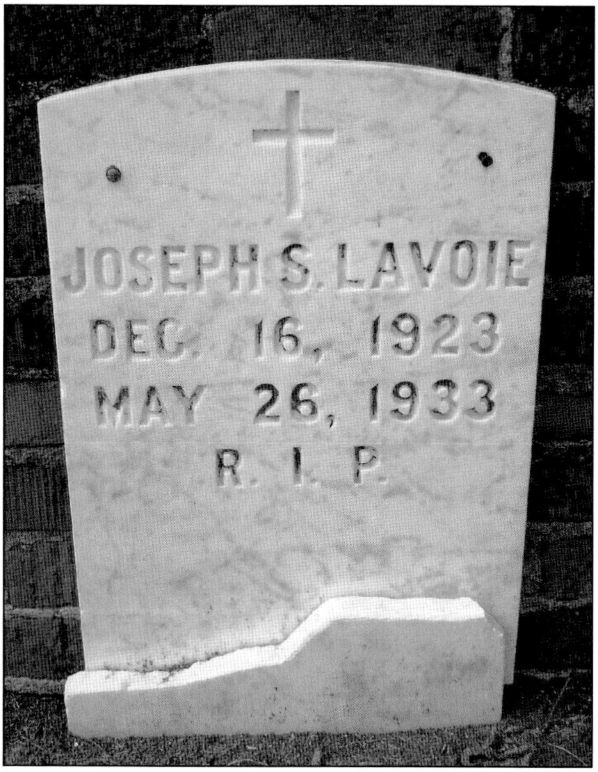

Joseph Samuel Lavoie (December 16, 1923–May 26, 1933), a nine-year-old resident of Mary Help of Christians Orphanage, drowned in San Antonio, Florida.

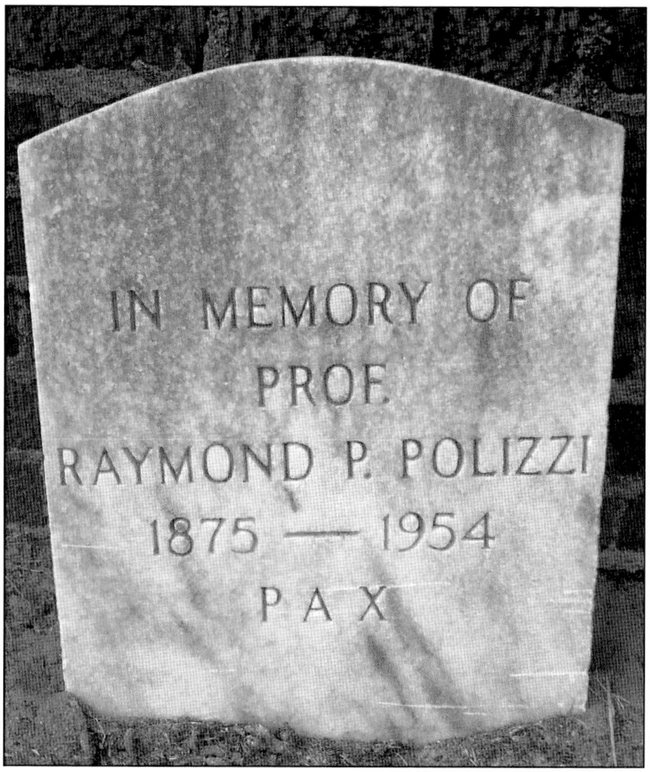

Raymond P. Polizzi (1875–January 24, 1954) was a resident for nine years and was survived by three sons—Mario, Hector and August—and his widow, Alfonsian Polizzi, all of New York.

Mason Dominic A. Wines (April 22, 1947–August 12, 1961), a 14-year-old Lutz boy, was struck by lightning as he was feeding ducks on a dock at Lake Lee near Mary Help of Christians School, where he was a student. He was the son of Elaine Wines and, according to the sheriff, had been missing from school. He was survived by his mother and three brothers—Donald, Gene, and Howard—and his maternal grandmother, Mrs. Lee Willard of Frederick, Maryland.

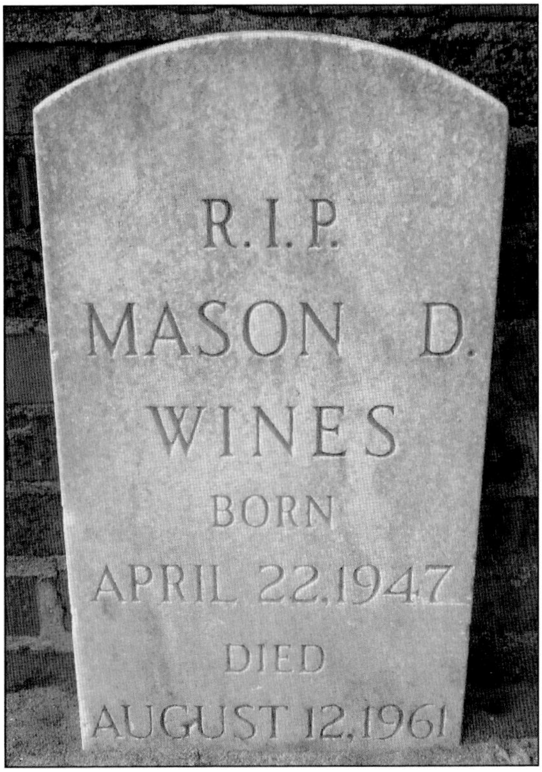

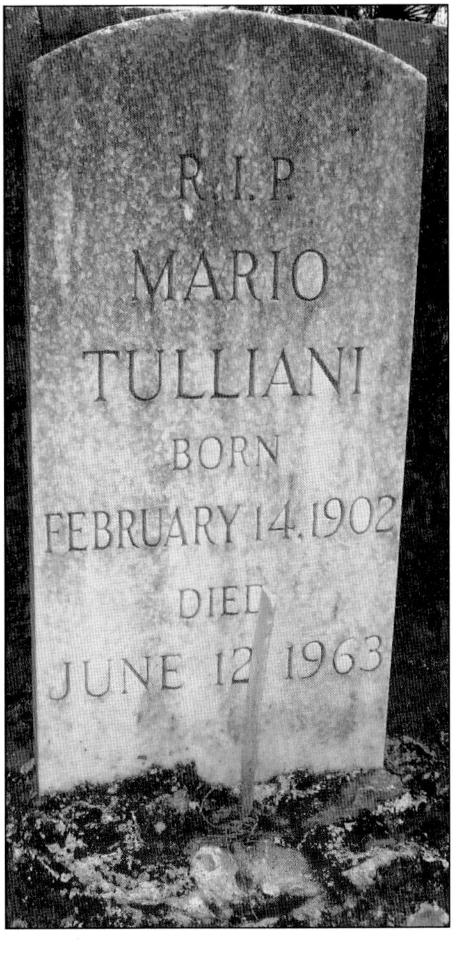

Mario Tulliani (February 14, 1902–June 12, 1963) was a native of Italy. He may have worked at the school or orphanage. He died in a local hospital.

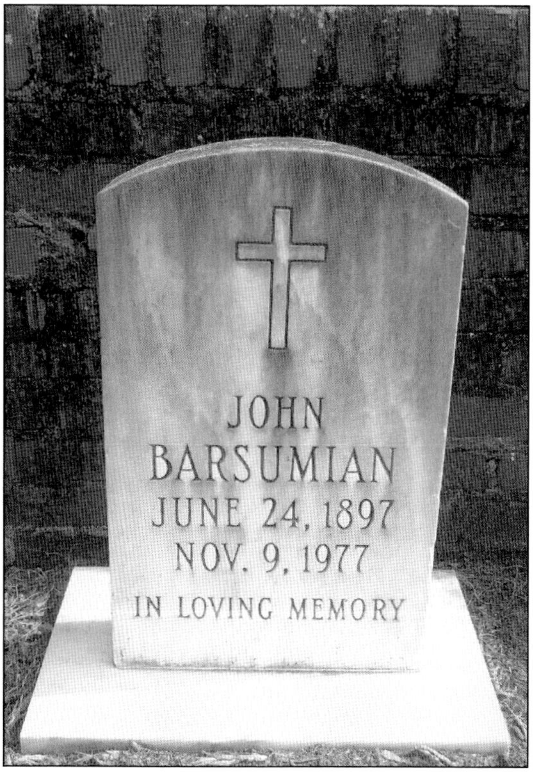

For John Barsumian (June 24, 1897–November 9, 1977), a "con-celebrated" funeral mass was held at Mary Help of Christians Chapel. He was survived by his widow, Angelina, a son and daughter-in-law Gregory and Cheryo Barsumian, step-granddaughters Sari and Robin Steller, and two nephews.

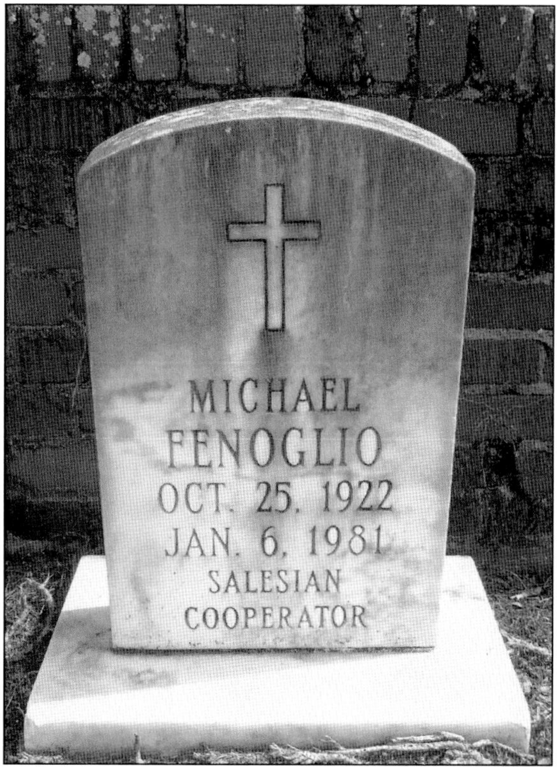

Michael Fenoglio (October 25, 1922–January 6, 1981) was born in Italy. A one-year resident of Tampa, he was a printer. He was survived by his mother and two sisters.

Edward "Edouard" Boisvert (around 1898–March 22, 1990) was a native of Three Rivers, Canada, and had lived in Tampa since 1948. He was a retired accountant. He and Elizabeth Boisvert (May 18, 1914–June 12, 1974) got married in 1933. No obituary was located in local newspapers for Elizabeth.

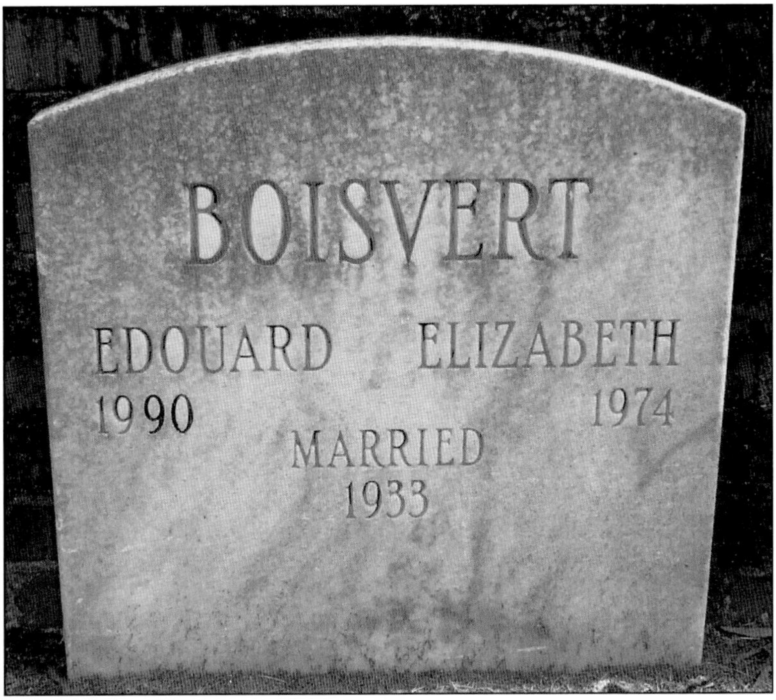

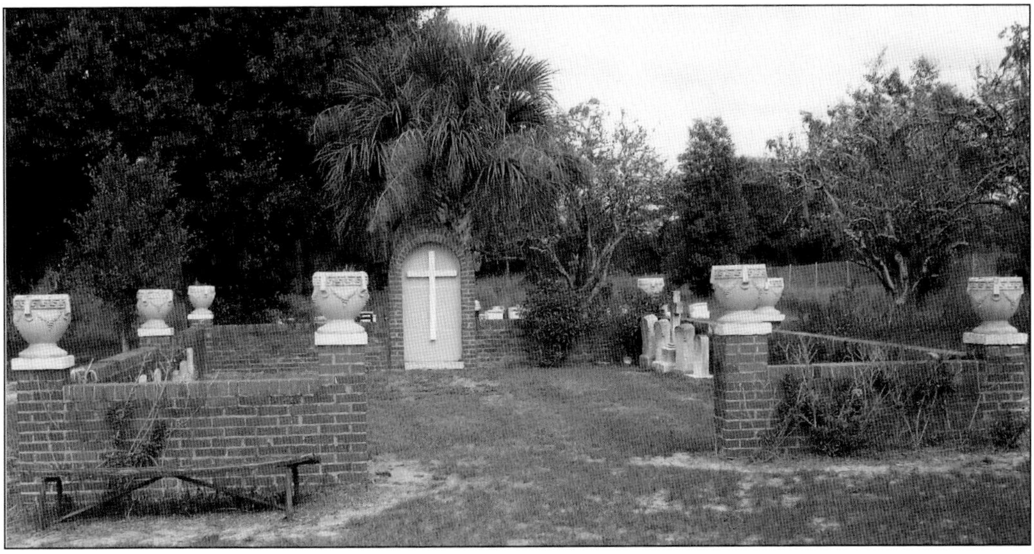

Due to a tragic drowning of one of the resident boys of the school, it became necessary to start a cemetery in 1933. When Interstate 4 was being planned, the targeted land included the cemetery. Officials were adamant about the need of this particular piece of property, but when made aware of the existence of this distinctive cemetery officials chose another tract of land. Totaling 17 graves, the last internment was in 1990. There are no plans for future burials.

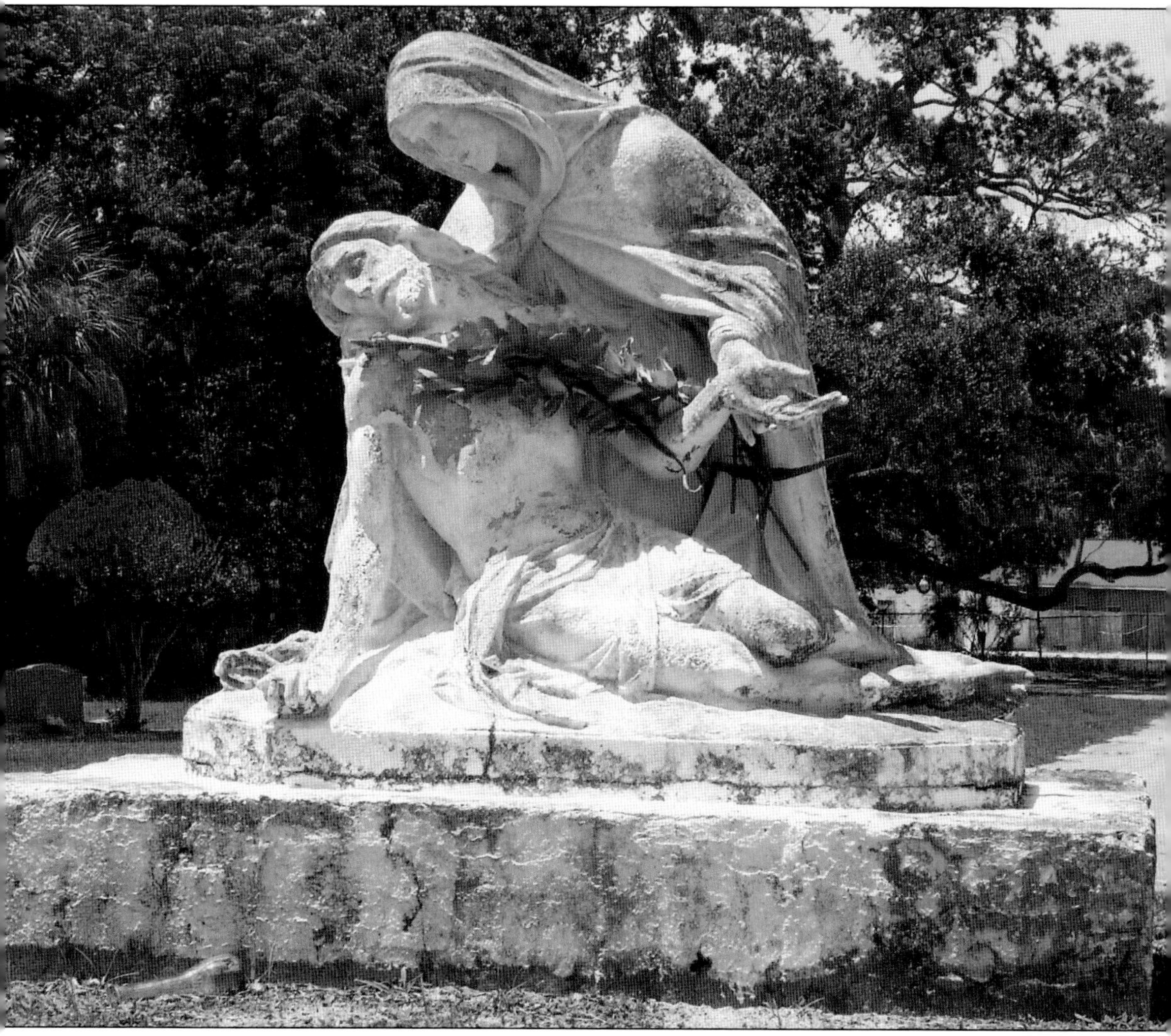

This statue of Mary and Jesus is located at Myrtle Hill Cemetery.

Do not stand at my grave and weep,
I am not there, I do not sleep.
I am a thousand winds that blow,
I am the diamond glints on snow,
I am the sun on ripened grain,
I am the gentle autumn rain.
When you awaken in the morning's hush
I am the swift uplifting rush
Of quiet birds in circling flight.
I am the soft star-shine at night.
Do not stand at my grave and cry,
I am not there, I did not die.

—"Do Not Stand at My Grave and Weep," 1932
Mary Elizabeth Frye (1905–2004)

BIBLIOGRAPHY

Baxley, John H., Julius J. Gordon, and Diane Moore Rodriguez. *Oaklawn Cemetery and St. Louis Catholic Cemetery. Volume I & Volume II*, 1999.

Brown, Canter Jr. *The Founding of the Children's Home of Tampa, 1892–1899*. Tampa: Tampa Bay History Center Reference Series, No. 6, 1997.

Burroughs, Lana, Tim Lancaster, Grant Rimbey, and The Temple Terrace Preservation Society. *Temple Terrace*. Charleston, SC: Arcadia Publishing, 2010.

Dunn, Hampton. *Yesterday's Tampa*. Miami, FL: E.A. Seemann Publishing, Inc., 1972.

Grismer, Karl H. *Tampa: A History of the City of Tampa and the Tampa Bay Region of Florida*. St. Petersburg, FL. The St. Petersburg Printing Co., Inc., 1950.

McKay, D.B., ed. *Pioneer Florida*. Tampa: The Southern Publishing Company, 1959.

Mormino, Gary, and Anthony Pizzo. *The Treasure City: Tampa*. Tulsa, OK: Continental Heritage Press, Inc., 1983.

Snyder, Robert E., and Jack B. Moore. *Pioneer Commercial Photography: The Burgert Brothers, Tampa, Florida*. Gainesville, FL: University Press of Florida, 1992.

Tampa Bay History Journal. Fall/Winter. Tampa: University of South Florida–Tampa, 1989.

The Sunland Tribune. Volume IV, No. 1. Tampa: Tampa Historical Society, November 1978.

Weatherford, Doris, with the Athenia Society. *Real Women of Tampa & Hillsborough County from Prehistory to the Millennium*. Tampa: University of Tampa Press, 2004.

Westfall, Loy Glenn. *Tampa Bay: Cradle of Cuban Liberty*. Key West: Key West Cigar City, 2000.